Latino Politics

Latino Politics

LISA GARCÍA BEDOLLA

polity

First published in 2009 by Polity Press
Reprinted in 2010 (twice), 2011 (twice)

Polity Press
65 Bridge Street
Cambridge CB2 1UR, UK.

Polity Press
350 Main Street
Malden, MA 02148, USA

ISBN-13: 978-0-7456-3384-8
ISBN-13: 978-0-7456-3385-5(pb)

A catalogue record for this book is available from the British Library.

Typeset in 9.5 on 13 pt Swift Light
by Servis Filmsetting Ltd, Stockport, Cheshire
Printed and bound in the U.S. by Edwards Brothers, Inc.

The publisher has used its best endeavours to ensure that the URLs for external websites referred to in this book are correct and active at the time of going to press. However, the publisher has no responsibility for the websites and can make no guarantee that a site will remain live or that the content is or will remain appropriate.

Every effort has been made to trace all copyright holders, but if any have been inadvertently overlooked the publishers will be pleased to include any necessary credits in any subsequent reprint or edition.

For further information on Polity, visit our website:
www.politybooks.com

To Pepe:
Thank you for sharing your life with me

Contents

Acknowledgments   viii
List of Illustrations   x

1 Introduction: Latinos and US Politics   1
2 Latina/o Participation: Individual Activity and Institutional   14
   Context
3 Mexican Americans: Conquest, Migration, and Adaptation   36
4 Puerto Ricans: From Colonized People to Political Activists   93
5 Cuban Americans: Occupation, Revolution, and Exile Politics   119
6 Central Americans: Inequality, War, and Solidarity   150
7 Conclusion: The Context of Latino Migration and   179
   Mobilization

Notes   189
Bibliography   198
Index   203

Acknowledgments

This book represents the coming together of two sets of interests that have driven my intellectual work: the politics of the domestic and of the international. Also, as an academic, I have always been interested in questioning how things came to be rather than accepting the conventional answers. Unfortunately, much of the study of US politics begins at the US border, with little reference to the broader world outside or focus on internal communities that do not hold power.

Consequently, when I began studying US politics I found little that described my experience or my history. Surely, I should not have been invisible to those who study 'American' politics, given that Florida, Louisiana, and what is now the western United States were once Spanish-speaking polities and that the term 'America' encompasses not only North America but also Central and South America and the Caribbean. Thus, on the domestic side, as a Latina growing up in the United States, I have had an ongoing concern with the political experiences of those of Latino origin residing there.

From an international perspective, as the daughter of Cuban immigrants, I have been faced with the geopolitical, historical, and social aspects of our family's experience at every Thanksgiving dinner where we add black beans, rice, and pork to the traditional menu of turkey and stuffing. Those meals were always served alongside often heated political debate. As a result of those spirited discussions, I have continually felt a strong desire to know better the history of my parents' country of origin and how and why my family ended up in the United States.

With this volume, I am finally able to bring together these two foci of experience. It is my hope that it helps readers to contextualize the US Latino experience beyond US borders, in order for them to understand more fully the factors influencing this community's migration, politics, and politicization in the United States. And, importantly, I hope that, through a greater knowledge of the history of US relations with the Americas and its inhabitants, readers will understand better how these relationships have influenced the trajectory of American democracy since the nineteenth century.

Such an enterprise cannot be undertaken without amassing considerable debts. This book would not have been possible without the support of my husband, José Luis Bedolla, who not only provided important intellectual encouragement but also balances his demanding career and our home life in a way that provides me the time and space necessary to do my work. I am continually humbled by the personal and professional support that he gives me. In my professional life, I also have had the good fortune of benefiting from the support and guidance of a broad intellectual community, all of whom have contributed in important ways to my thinking and sanity during this book's creation. This community includes, but is not limited to: Marisa Abrajano, Tony Affigne, Michael Alvarez, Cristina Beltrán, John Bretting, Amy Bridges, Daniel Brunstetter, Leo Chávez, María Chávez, Arlene Dávila, Heather Elliott, Cynthia Feliciano, Raúl Fernández, Paul Fymer, Gilbert González, Don Green, Michael Jones-Correa, Jane Junn, Claire Kim, Taeku Lee, Jessica Lavariega Monforti, Paula Mcclain, Melissa Michelson, Michael Montoya, Naomi Murakawa, Kevin Olson, Hector Perla, Karthick Ramakrishnan, Ray Rocco, Vicki Ruiz, Rubén Rumbaut, Mark Sawyer, Kamal Sadiq, Ronald Schmidt, Sr., Andrea Simpson, Rogers Smith, Dara Strolovitch, Jessica Trounstine, Deborah Vargas, Dorian Warren, and Janelle Wong. I am indebted to them for their generous support and cogent insights. Any errors that remain are my own.

My experience with Polity has been wonderful. I would like to give special thanks to Louise Knight for having the confidence to entrust me with this project and for her unflagging support of it. Emma Hutchinson was remarkably patient and compassionate when faced with my delay in delivering the final manuscript. I will always appreciate the understanding she gave me during a very difficult period in my life. Manuela Tecusan meticulously and cheerfully edited the manuscript, significantly improving my prose and the final product.

List of Illustrations

Figures

Fig. 3.1 'Whites Only': Poster from the 1930s, Texas   55
Fig. 4.1 Political Cartoon from the Popular Press   95
Fig. 4.2 Jennifer López and Husband Marc Anthony at the 2006   115
          Puerto Rican Day Parade in New York City
Fig. 5.1 Fidel Castro with Vice-President Richard Nixon,   128
          April 1959

Tables

Table 2.1 Age, Birth, Income, Household, and Education for   16
           Latinos and Total US Population
Table 2.2 Age, Birth, Income, and Education by Country of Origin   17
Table 2.3 Reported Registration by Race and Birth, 1972–2004   19
Table 2.4 Reported Voting by Race and Birth, 1972–2004   20
Table 2.5 Reported Registration and Voting in the 2004   21
           Presidential Election by National Origin, among
           Citizens
Table 2.6 Political Engagement by National Origin among the   27
           Total Population
Table 3.1 Mexican Migration to the United States, 1900–1997   48
Table 3.2 The States with Greatest Growth in Mexican-Origin   91
           Population, 1990–2000
Table 4.1 Migration from Puerto Rico to the United States,   103
           1900–2000
Table 4.2 The Puerto Rican Population by Selected States, 1990   117
           and 2000
Table 6.1 The Central American-Origin Population in the   153
           United States

Textboxes

Textbox 3.1   Letter from Youth Committee for the Defense of   58
              Mexican American Youth
Textbox 3.2   Selection from Poem 'I Am Joaquín' by Rodolfo   79
              'Corky' Gonzáles
Textbox 5.1   The Platt Amendment, 1901   123

CHAPTER ONE

Introduction: Latinos and US Politics

Objectives

- Understand the definitions of agency and structure
- Understand what it means for race to be a social construction
- Understand the historical meaning and privileges that have been attached to whiteness in the United States
- Understand how Latinos fit (or not) into the US racial structure
- Understand the political, social, and economic implications of how Latinos were categorized racially
- Understand the effect US foreign and economic policy has on Latin American countries, on Latinos' decisions to migrate, and on their treatment upon arrival

Latinos, Immigration, and Politics

Scholars studying Latinos in the United States focus a great deal on issues of immigration and of political participation. Interestingly, both these issues most often are conceptualized as individual acts. Immigration is seen as a personal decision made by an individual or family, with little consideration of the macroeconomic context that influences that decision. Similarly, political engagement is most often discussed as (by and large) an individual choice. Individuals choose to vote, contact their elected officials, or run for political office. If they do not do so, it is because of a lack of interest rather than because of any sort of larger, structural constraint.

Yet the fact of the matter is that none of us, as individuals, can act with complete freedom, or with *agency* – defined as 'the capacity, condition, or state of acting or of exerting power'.[1] In other words, agency is about how much we, as individuals, can accomplish on our own; about our ability to determine, by ourselves, the direction of our lives. Yet there are also institutional structures that may impede our ability to exercise that agency – to do exactly what we want, when we want it, and the way we want it. On the most basic level there are rules and laws which limit our freedom of action. But, more importantly, there are also other kinds of institutional structures, social, political, or economic, which may constrain an individual's ability to act. Those structures include, but are not limited to, the employment and the housing markets, the legal system, including immigration rules, the political system, the educational system, and so on. How these structures operate within an individual's life varies over time and by geographic location. They are not static, yet they are not always easy to change either. Thus structures have an important impact on the individuals' ability to change their life for the better.

In this book I will explore the migration processes and political activity of the population of Latin American origin in the United States, placing an emphasis on the interaction between agency and structure. For example, during the Central American solidarity movement, the United States government refused to characterize Central American migrants as political refugees, despite the violence and political upheaval that existed in their home countries. These migrants were able to exercise agency in deciding to leave their homelands, yet were structurally constrained by the US government when they attempted to regularize their migration status in the United States. Yet, as we will see in Chapter 6, in coalition with other migrants and political organizations, they mobilized to change the US government's position and were partly successful, thus changing the institutional structure which future Central American migrants would face when arriving in the United States.

The Central American case is a good example of the interplay between agency and structure and of why it is important. When considering political activity and engagement, particularly that of minority groups, we must realize that there is a historical background and an institutional context which frame an individual's decision-making process. In order to decide to act politically, an individual must feel empowered to do so and must feel that her action can make a difference. If that person comes from a community or group which, historically, has not had much influence in the political system, it is less likely that she will feel that that is the best way to spend her time; or it is more likely that she will choose non-traditional forms of engagement (like protesting) in order to express her political views. Thus individuals do not make decisions in a vacuum.

The purpose of this book is to give the reader the historical and institutional context within which to situate US Latino politics. Understanding that context will help the reader also to understand why Latinos make the decisions they do and what structural factors influence these choices. Only to look at one or the other is to miss an important part of the story.

Defining Latino: What's in a Name?

This text examines the history, migration, and politics of different groups of Latin American origin living in the United States. To begin with, it is important to consider what these groups should be called. The title of my book uses the word 'Latino', which is meant to describe all individuals, foreign and US born, who have ancestry in any of the Spanish-speaking nations of Latin America.[2] The term 'Hispanic' was adopted by the United States government during the 1970s and has the same definition as 'Latino'. 'Chicano' is meant to describe, specifically, individuals of Mexican origin in the United States. This term came directly out of the political organizing within the Mexican American community in the US south-west during the 1960s; hence its usage often presumes a certain political consciousness, in addition to being a national-origin identifier. 'Boricua' is a term used to describe Puerto Ricans in the United States (it comes from the name of an indigenous group native to the island), and 'Nuyorican', more specifically, is sometimes used to denote individuals of Puerto Rican origin living in New York City. Thus there are many terms which are used to describe individuals of Latin American origin; some of them are national-origin specific, others spring directly from the political mobilization of the community or from the desire of group members to come up with new terms to describe themselves. For the sake of simplicity, this text uses the term 'Latino' to refer to groups of Latin American origin generally, and national-origin specific terms to describe the experiences of individuals from particular countries. But it is important to note that these labels can be politically or personally important. Many Latinos choose to use different words to describe their identities – terms that are grounded in their particular historical, personal, and political experiences.

Latinos' 'Ethnicity' and 'Race'

The fact that this book focuses on the experiences of Latinos in the United States also implies that Latinos constitute a social group, one that should be the focus of the present study. But what does it mean for something to be a social group? Political theorist Iris Young described a social group as 'a collective of persons differentiated from others by cultural forms, practices, special needs or capacities, structure of power, or privilege' (Young 2000: 153). According to Young, what makes a collection of people into a group is 'less some set of attributes its members share than the relation in which they stand to others'. In other words, defining Latinos as a social group does not mean that we need to assume that all Latinos are the same, share the same experiences, or have the same goals· or aspirations. We will see in the next chapters that this is not the case. Latino national-origin groups have had very different experiences in the United States. They arrived at different points in American history, migrated for very different reasons, settled in different geographic settings, and have been treated in disparate ways by the United States government. There are important experiential differences within Latino national-origin groups as well; these are due to geographic location, class status, gender, sexual orientation, and other factors. Despite this heterogeneity, what is similar about the experiences of all US Latinos, however, is where they were placed in the US racial hierarchy and how that placement has affected their social, political, and economic opportunities.

Yet, given their differences of experience and background, if Latinos are a social group, are they also a racial group or an ethnic one? The distinction between these two characterizations has been the source of ongoing debates among scholars – debates which will not be resolved here. The term 'race' presupposes a common biological or genealogical ancestry among people. 'Ethnicity' places more of an emphasis on culture than on common genetic traits. In an attempt to bring together both concepts, sociologists Michael Omi and Howard Winant (1994) define 'race' as 'a concept which signifies and symbolizes social conflicts and interests by referring to different types of human bodies'. They emphasize social conflicts in order to get us away from biological understandings of what race is. There is no biological foundation for separate 'races' of humans. As recent DNA tests have proven, many individuals whom we see as 'black' are in fact more European than African in terms of their DNA. For example, Henry Louis Gates, a prominent African American intellectual, found he has as much European DNA as West African DNA (most African Americans are about 20 per cent European). This kind of testing forces us to reconsider what 'race' means and to see how these categorizations have more to do with society than with biology.

Feminist philosopher Linda Alcoff suggests using the term 'ethnorace' to describe the Latino experience in the United States. For her, ethnorace is a concept which combines the experiences of both ethnicity and race. She argues that 'using only ethnicity belies the reality of most Latinos' everyday experiences, as well as obscures our own awareness about how ethnic identifications often do the work of race while seeming to be theoretically correct and politically advanced. Race dogs our steps; let us not run from it else we cause it to increase its determination' (Alcoff 2000: 246). Through this concept of ethnorace, Alcoff is attempting to make us recognize that racialized group members sometimes share common cultural practices, which is not part of how race is typically understood. In general, scholars like Omi, Winant, and Alcoff are attempting to find ways to define a social phenomenon which has historical roots and important material consequences but which is nevertheless artificial in that its underlying reality is fluid and changes over time.

In order to study race in a way that recognizes this fluidity, scholars describe racial processes as social constructions. Social construction means that the values attached to particular external attributes, such as skin color, are defined, or constructed, by society. Put another way, the problem is not that of the recognition of racial/ethnic differences among people, but rather that of the values, or hierarchies, attached to those differences. For the bulk of United States history, being defined as 'white' gave members of that group access to social, legal, economic, and political privileges which were closed to those not defined as 'white.' For example, one of the first laws passed by the United States Congress in 1790 was a citizenship law which stipulated that no non-white person could become a naturalized citizen of the United States. This restriction remained in force until 1948, when individuals of Chinese origin were allowed to be naturalized for the very first time. This racial restriction on naturalization was finally removed completely for all groups in 1952, with the McCarran Walter Act. In addition, many states made it illegal for a non-white to testify in court against a white; to serve on juries; to live where they wanted to live; or to work in the most skilled jobs. These restrictions limited both non-whites' access to the protection of the legal system and their possibilities for social, political, and economic mobility. Thus racial constructs have been directly related to access to fundamental items like resources, citizenship rights, and the protection of the state (that is, to having a criminal justice system which actually defends your person and/or your property). Therefore race may be constructed, but which category an individual belongs to has had, and continues to have, significant material and political implications for their life chances.

Because racial categorizations determined access to resources, US federal and state governments had to come up with schemes in order to determine to what 'race' individuals belonged. Often referred to as the 'one-drop rule', these schemes attempted to define who was white and who was not. The 'one drop' refers to the fact that, in much of the country and particularly in the south, having one drop of black blood made it impossible by law to claim 'whiteness'. For example in California, in 1849, having half or more of 'Indian' blood would lead to one's being considered not 'white', and half or more of black blood made a person 'mulatto'. In 1851, the law was changed so that only one fourth of Indian blood would make a person not 'white'. Yet many of these laws were challenged, leading the courts to have to determine what constituted being 'white'. An especially good example is that of the prerequisite cases. These were cases brought by individuals who wanted to contest the 1790 law barring non-whites from being naturalized in the United States. Looking at petitions by Asian Indians from 1909 to 1923, we see that in 1909 the court in *Balsara* ruled that Asian Indians were *probably* not white, because the people on the jury thought it unlikely that Congress intended for Asian Indians to be considered white under the 1790 law. Yet in 1910 the court ruled in two cases that Asian Indians were white, on the basis of the petitioner's skin color and of scientific evidence regarding the origins of the Caucasian race. This ruling was reaffirmed in 1913, with appeal to legal precedent. Yet in 1917 the court ruled that Asian Indians were *not* white, on the basis of common knowledge and congressional intent. The same court reversed this position in 1919 and 1920, deciding again that the Asian Indians involved in those cases were white. Then in 1923 the Supreme Court ruled again, on the basis of common knowledge, that Asian Indians were not white. From that point on, on the basis of the 1923 legal precedent, the court ruled that Asian Indians are not white and therefore ineligible for naturalization.[3] The Asian Indian case shows how difficult it was for the courts to maintain these kinds of racial categorizations in the face of any sort of systematic scrutiny. Yet that is exactly what the United States government did; and its action had important consequences for those US groups which were considered non-white. Latinos were one of those groups.

When Latinos became part of the United States, either through immigration or through conquest (as in the case of Puerto Ricans, or of Mexican Americans in the nineteenth-century southwest), they were inserted into this established racial order. Even though many Latinos are recent immigrants, it is important to realize that this historical racial hierarchy continues to influence the playing field upon which their community sits today. For example, one complication for Latinos was that one-drop rules presupposed a strict, biological understanding of what race is. Under those schemes a person was black, white, or Indian, and there was no legal representation for intermediate categories like mulattos (people of black and white ancestry). Latinos, on the other hand, come from a variety of racial backgrounds. When the Spaniards arrived in Latin America, that continent had an indigenous population which numbered millions of inhabitants. Although a large proportion of this native population perished through disease and wars of conquest, a significant part survived, particularly in Mexico, Central America, Colombia, Perú, and Bolívia. The Spanish mixed with these groups, as did the Africans, creating what is called *mestizos* – individuals of mixed European, African, and indigenous descent. In the Caribbean, little of the indigenous population remained, which made it necessary for Spaniards to import African slaves to use as the bulk of the labor force. Those Africans mixed with the Spaniards and with the indigenous groups who remained on the islands, creating a new racial admixture; this is often called *mulatto*. After the end of slavery, Caribbean plantation-owners imported hundreds of thousands of Chinese laborers to work in the fields. In the nineteenth and twentieth centuries, large numbers of Asians from other countries, including Japan, settled in other parts of Latin America, adding to its racial mixture. This is why, in the early twentieth century, José Vasconcelos called Latin Americans *la raza cósmica*, 'the cosmic race' – one made up of the blood of all the world's races.

During the colonial period the Spaniards developed a complex *casta* system which laid out the racial hierarchy according to how much European, black or indigenous blood a particular individual had. Like the American system, the Spanish system had placed the white Europeans on top; but the remainder included many more racial options than were available in the United States. Most Latin American countries abolished the Spanish system after independence. But they still maintained the racial hierarchies. The difference was that their understanding of race included mixed race as a possibility, which was not true in most parts of the United States after the late nineteenth century.[4]

Thus, when Latinos arrived in the United States, they had to fit into a relatively rigid racial hierarchy, where it was very important whether a person was defined as 'black' or 'white'. Yet many Latinos are of mixed race. Those of Mexican or Central American origin tend to be of mixed indigenous background and those from the Caribbean are more likely to have African origins. But are they 'Indian'? Or are they 'black'? Or something else? The problem with people of mixed race is that often there can be significant differences in skin color even within the same family. One sibling can be quite dark-skinned, another one quite light-skinned. Since the US racial structure did not allow for the possibility of admixture, what often happened was that the lighter-skinned sibling would be treated as 'white', the darker as 'black'. At the height of segregation, this meant that they would go to separate schools, get to use separate bathroom facilities, and in general would have a very different set of opportunities, simply because one was seen as white and the other was not. Latinos, then, complicated the US racial structure and did not fit neatly into any of its racial categories. This racial ambiguity meant that the place they chose to settle in, and the particular history of that place, had an important impact on the kinds of opportunities open to them. There was no one, uniform response to, or treatment of, Latinos as a 'race'.

For example, there were large numbers of Latinos, mostly of Mexican origin, living in the state of Texas during the nineteenth century. Many had been there originally when Texas was part of Mexico. Texas turned into a slave state once it became part of the United States, and after emancipation it developed and enforced strict Jim Crow laws, requiring racial segregation in neighborhoods, schools, and public facilities. Like the rest of the south, Texas also passed laws to keep the blacks from voting. Yet in Texas African Americans were not the only large minority group; there were Mexican Americans as well. Jim Crow Laws were applied to the Mexican population because they too were seen as non-white, despite their legal categorization as white under the Treaty of Guadalupe Hidalgo. This was not true in New Mexico, however, where Latinos of Mexican origin remained in the majority until the twentieth century: in New Mexico segregation was not as extreme as in Texas. Mexican Americans were allowed voting rights. Moreover, they held public office positions and much of the political power until the mid-twentieth century. Thus local context had an important impact on racial definitions and racial restrictions, even in the case of the same national-origin group. These differences were possible because of Latino racial ambiguity.

Thus race is not 'real' in a biological sense, but racial categories still have important implications for the opportunities which various groups have in our society. Without an understanding of the historical legacy of race, it is difficult to understand the current distribution of resources and opportunities within American society. Being white gave individuals access to citizenship; access to land under the homestead act in the nineteenth century (which was restricted to whites); access to legal protection and the right to organize unions, which significantly increased unionized workers' wages and benefits (many unions prohibited non-white membership, and many people of color worked in industries not covered under the National Labor Relations Act); access to subsidized federal home loans (the FHA program redlined and excluded African American, Mexican American, and mixed race neighborhoods); and access to public education of quality.[5] Recent studies have shown that whites and African Americans with similar levels of income and education still have very different levels of total wealth because whites are much more likely to inherit real estate and other funds from their parents.[6] That inheritance is the fruit of a highly exclusionary racial history. Because of this history, 'color-blindness' will not erase the inequality which has accumulated from racial categorizations. It is only by looking at race that we can begin to address its negative legacy.

Latino Political Incorporation

But how does racialization relate to Latino politics? Racialization is important in terms of having shaped the way Latinos are seen by non-Latinos, the opportunities they have been afforded, and the kinds of restrictions which have been placed on their incorporation into political life. Some Latinos living in the United States have been present in their communities since before they became part of the United States. We will see in the following chapters the significance of that long-term relationship. Yet a very large proportion of Latinos in the United States have arrived there since 1970. So, even though not all Latinos are immigrants or recent immigrants, the community contains enough immigrants that thinking about how immigrant politics varies from non-immigrant politics is an important part of learning about the Latino political experience in the United States. Immigrant political incorporation is different from non-immigrant political incorporation because of two factors:

1   Immigrants choose to be part of the United States, and therefore must overcome important structural hurdles before they can even consider engaging politically.

2 Immigrant inclusion is about defining the boundaries of the US polity, and therefore speaks in important ways to issues of race, inequality, and power within American society, in ways that are somewhat different from (but related to) what is happening with US born racialized groups.

Yet immigrants do not arrive in their new country as a clean slate. They bring a set of resources and a historical experience that shape their decision to migrate and their opportunity structure once they arrive. Thus the study of immigrant incorporation needs to begin with the international structural context which embeds the decision to migrate. Immigrants' decisions to migrate are embedded in macro-geopolitical processes over which their subjects have little control, such as economic recession or dislocation, war, or natural disaster. Once immigrants arrive in the United States, they must deal with an immigration bureaucracy which, as we will see in the following chapters, does not treat them all the same. The country an immigrant comes from, and the relationship the US government has with that country at the time of migration, strongly affect how easy or difficult the legal aspects of the migration process are going to be. Hence not only the immigrants' legal and economic status upon their arrival, but even their tendency to come from particular countries and their choice to go to particular countries are intimately related with US foreign and economic policy.

US Foreign Economic Policy and Latino Politics

The United States' relations with Latin America have been deeply affected by two important US principles: manifest destiny and the Monroe doctrine. The idea of manifest destiny – that the United States was 'destined' to be an Anglo-Saxon Protestant nation that stretched from coast to coast – had its roots in colonial political thought. In 1811, John Adams summed it up like this:

> The whole continent of North America appears to be destined by Divine Providence to be peopled by one nation, speaking one language, professing one general system of religious and political principles, and accustomed to one general tenor of social usages and customs. For the common happiness of them all, for their peace and prosperity, I believe it is indispensable that they should be associated in one federal Union.

Like Adams, many Americans believed that it was God's will that the United States should control the north American territory, and that the nation needed to be based on a common set of political ideals, religious beliefs, and cultural practices. This creed was one of the main justifications underlying US territorial expansion through the US–Mexican War. We will see that it also had important consequences on how the US dealt with the incorporation of the Mexican population present in those territories when they were annexed into the United States. Over time, this idea that it was the US' destiny to control a particular geographic sphere would expand beyond the North American continent and extend across the western hemisphere through the Monroe doctrine.

James Adams' son, John Quincy Adams, developed the Monroe doctrine in 1823, when he was President James Monroe's secretary of state. The main thrust of the doctrine was that, as countries in the Americas were becoming independent from the imperial European powers, the United States did not want Europe to re-colonize the western hemisphere. In his State of the Union message in December of that year, President Monroe declared that the United States would not interfere in European wars or internal affairs and expected Europe to stay out of the affairs of the new world. European attempts to influence the new world would be interpreted by the United States as threats to its 'peace and safety'.

President James Polk invoked the principle of manifest destiny and the Monroe doctrine in an 1845 address to Congress in support of westward expansion into Mexican territory. In 1904, President Theodore Roosevelt added the 'Roosevelt corollary' to the Monroe doctrine, which defined US intervention in Latin American domestic affairs as necessary for US national security:

> All that this country [the United States] desires is to see the neighboring countries stable, orderly, and prosperous. Any country whose people conduct themselves well can count upon our hearty friendship. If a nation shows that it knows how to act with reasonable efficiency and decency in social and political matters, if it keeps order and pays its obligations, it need fear no interference from the United States. Chronic wrongdoing, or an impotence which results in a general loosening of the ties of civilized society, may in America, as elsewhere, ultimately require intervention by some civilized nation, and in the Western Hemisphere the adherence of the United States to the Monroe Doctrine may force the United States, however reluctantly, in flagrant cases of such wrongdoing or impotence, to the exercise of an international police power.

This corollary was used to justify US intervention in Cuba, Haiti, Nicaragua, and the Dominican Republic. It was officially reversed in 1934 with the advent of Franklin D. Roosevelt's 'good neighbor' policy towards Latin America. Yet the principle that the United States' political and economic interests are intimately related to that of Latin America remained. Throughout the twentieth century, the United States' economic interests played a central role in the development of Latin American banking, infrastructure, and industry. Similarly, the US government, particularly after the start of the cold war, continually intervened in Latin American internal governmental and military affairs.

This US involvement is critically important for understanding Latino migration flows to the United States. Many Latin American migrants worked for US companies in their home countries. Many were directly recruited by those companies to come to the United States, and those companies often lobbied the US Congress to ensure that these migration flows would continue. The economic development policies pursued by Latin American governments, and therefore the economic opportunities available to their populations, particularly employment, often were strongly influenced by the US financial sector and by the US government. After the advent of the cold war, US strategic concerns and levels of military aid often affected the success or failure of social movements to redistribute wealth in these countries. Thus the way the United States expressed its political and economic interests in the region affected the Latin Americans' economic and political situation on the ground, the facility with which they were able to migrate to the United States, and the legal terms under which they were accepted under US immigration policy.

Conclusion

We will see in the following chapters that there were important domestic and international political reasons why the US government involved itself in the politics of Latin American countries and encouraged or discouraged migration from them. For different reasons, the US government has made immigrant settlement much easier for some national-origin groups than for others. This, in turn, has affected how quickly and under what terms Latino immigrants have been allowed to join the polity. These decisions also have affected the immigrants' choice of places to settle, the kinds of transnational and co-ethnic social networks available to them in those places, and what political and economic opportunity structures were present in those communities. It follows that that experience has had an important impact on these immigrants' trust in government, feelings of personal efficacy, and willingness to become engaged politically. These opportunity structures also affect their socio-economic mobility; immigrants of higher socioeconomic status are more likely to engage politically. This means that having more economic opportunities also affects political incorporation. This is a good example of how agency and structure interact. A particular immigrant brings a set of skills (education, funding, personal drive) which affect her ability to succeed in her new country. But that success is also affected by the institutions she must interact with on the ground. How open those institutions are, and how much they will enable her to take advantage of their resources, is outside of her control.

What this interaction looks like for immigrants from each national-origin group also varies over time. Each community has faced particular challenges, has organized so as to improve their position, and all have achieved important successes. That mobilization, in turn, has changed the structural context for new immigrants. Therefore nothing in these stories is 'static'; there is constant movement across historical time. It is only by looking at the historical trajectory of each national-origin group that we may understand fully the Latino political incorporation process today. This is what we will be doing in the following chapters.

CHAPTER TWO

Latina/o Participation: Individual Activity and Institutional Context

Objectives
- Understand Latino demographics, particularly national-origin differences in socioeconomic status, age, and nativity
- Understand Latino participation patterns, including national-origin differences and differences in the types of activities Latinos engage in
- Understand the political institutional context in the United States, its majoritarian nature, and what that means for the participation and representation of minority groups

Latino Political Engagement

In the 2000 presidential election, for the first time the Republican candidate, George W. Bush, outspent his Democratic rival, Al Gore, in the amount his campaign spent on Spanish-language advertising targeting Latino voters. The Bush campaign hired veteran political strategist Lionel Sosa to develop a sophisticated and well run Spanish-language outreach campaign. This effort is credited with significantly increasing Latino support for Bush by comparison with support for the 1996 Republican candidate, Bob Dole. In 2007, candidates competing for the Democratic presidential nomination participated, for the first time ever, in a bilingual presidential debate televised on the most popular Spanish-language channel, Univisión. Why are we seeing increased attention being paid to Latino voters by both political parties, at the national level? The answer is simple: demographics.

Demographics

According to the 2007 Current Population Survey, there are 45.5 million Latinos currently living in the United States, making Latinos 15 percent of the total US population and the nation's largest minority group. Between 1980 and 2000 the rate of growth among Latinos was nearly four times higher than that of the general population. Future estimates of population growth in the US posit that this trend will continue at least until 2030, ensuring that Latinos will continue to represent a growing and significant proportion of the US population. In terms of the national-origin distribution of the US Latino population, individuals of Mexican origin constitute by far the largest group, at 65.5 percent. They are followed by Puerto Ricans (8.6 percent), Central Americans (8.2 percent), South Americans (6 percent), and Cubans (3.7 percent). Thus, although there is substantial national-origin diversity within the Latino population in the United States, it is important to keep in mind that almost two-thirds of US Latinos are of Mexican origin.

The Latino community varies from the US population at large along a number of parameters which include age, income, and education and which, we will see below, are important when considering the factors driving their participation patterns. Table 2.1 compares Latinos to the American population along several dimensions. We can see that the Latino population is significantly younger than the US population overall; in particular, there are more Latinos under the age of 18 and fewer aged 65 and over than there are among Americans generally. Latinos earn significantly less than other Americans, although, interestingly, there is less of a gender gap in earnings among Latinos than there is among the total US population. The poverty rate among Latinos is almost twice that of the general population, and is particularly high among children (those under 18). Latino households also tend to be larger, which means that household income for the Latino population is expected to support a larger number of people than income for the rest of the population. Latino educational attainment is also lower on average: many more Latinos than other Americans have less than a 9th grade education, and the number of Latinos with a college degree is less than half of that found in the general population.

This demographic information is important not only in terms of getting a snapshot of the community, but also in terms of how it may affect Latino public policy preferences. Given the relative youth of the community, one can imagine educational attainment and educational quality being very important issues, along with policies aimed at decreasing poverty rates among children. On the other hand, given the small number of Latinos over the age of 65, issues such as social security and retirement may not be as immediate. Because of these demographic differences, it is unlikely that voters from the general US population

Table 2.1 Age, Birth, Income, Household, and Education for Latinos and Total US Population

		Latinos	Total US Population
Age			
	median age	27	36
	population under 18	34.3%	25.2%
	population aged 65 and over	5.4%	12.1%
Birth			
	foreign population	39.9%	12.1%
Income and poverty			
	median annual earnings for men	$26,769	$41,386
	median annual earnings for women	$24,214	$31,858
	percentage of overall population living in poverty	21.8%	12.6%
	population under 18 living in poverty	28.3%	17.6%
Household size			
	population living in household with 2 persons or fewer	37.7%	59.6%
	population living in household with 4 people or more	42.7%	23.8%
Educational attainment			
	population with less than a 9th grade education	24.4%	6.1%
	population with a high school diploma or more	59.3%	85.5%
	population with one college degree or more	12.4%	28%

Source: Current Population Survey, Annual Social and Economic Supplement 2006

will have the same political concerns and policy preferences as Latinos. That is why it is important that Latinos have a voice in the political process which is equal to their demographic numbers. As we will see below, there are a number of reasons why that has yet to be established.

Not only do Latinos differ from the general US population; they also differ on a number of important parameters across national-origin groups. Table 2.2 summarizes age, nativity, income, and educational attainment across the Latino national-origin groups we will be studying

Table 2.2 Age, Birth, Income, and Education by Country of Origin

		Mexican	Puerto Rican	Central American	Cuban
Age					
	population under 18	36.7%	33.6%	27.7%	23.3%
	population aged 65 and over	4.3%	6.7%	3.6%	18.1%
Birth					
	foreign population	38.6%	NAª	68.8%	61.8%
Income					
	households earning less than $25,000 a year	34.9%	38.7%	25.8%	30.4%
	households earning more than $75,000 a year	15.1%	17.4%	18.1%	24%
Educational attainment					
	population with a high school diploma or more	53.1%	72.3%	50.5%	74.9%
	population with one college degree or more	8.5%	15.1%	10.2%	24.4%

a Since Puerto Rico is a US territory, no Puerto Rican is 'foreign-born', although those born on the mainland have a different legal status from those born on the island (see ch. 4)

Source: Current Population Survey, Annual Social and Economic Supplement 2006

in this book. In terms of age, Cubans stand out as the oldest national-origin group, with the largest proportion falling into the over-65 category. Mexicans have the largest under-18 population and Central Americans the smallest over-65 group. Central Americans and Cubans are also much more likely to be of foreign origin than Mexicans. In terms of income, Mexicans and Puerto Ricans look quite similar, with over a third of their populations earning less than $25,000 a year. Almost a fourth of the Cubans make over $75,000 a year, which is probably related to the fact that the community is older overall; older individuals tend to have higher earnings. Thirty percent of the Cubans still make less than $25,000 a year, despite the fact that Cubans have the highest levels of educational attainment overall.

Understanding these differences is important because they highlight the fact that the Latino community is not monolithic, but rather is made up of disparate national-origin groups. As we will see in the following chapters, each of those groups has a unique history and a distinct set of social, political, and economic challenges. Those differences can and do affect the kinds of public policies each group supports, their partisan attachments, and their political engagement.

Understanding Political Participation

Since the 1960s, political scientists have been studying American political behavior – what factors explain why individuals turn out and vote, or why they engage in other kinds of political activity such as contacting elected officials, contributing to campaigns, engaging in political protest, and so on. This work, which has focused mainly on the general US population, has found that a person's socioeconomic status (SES) – their education, income, and occupation – is the best predictor of their likelihood to vote. In other words, those who are more educated, have higher incomes, and come from professional occupations (versus more blue-collar jobs) are more likely to vote than those who are less educated, poorer, or do manual labor. This is intuitively logical. Higher SES individuals have more resources in terms of personal capacity, time, and flexibility; they can use to help towards paying the 'cost' of engaging in politics.

Yet when this work has been extended to minority communities it seems not to be able to explain all the aspects of their engagement. Katherine Tate finds that education and income are only occasionally related to African American participation, and studies of Latinos have found that SES can explain only part of the gap between Latino and Anglo electoral and nonelectoral participation.[1] Scholars attempting to find other explanations have turned to psychological resources – feelings of efficacy, trust in government and civic duty – as the explanatory factors. Studies using these approaches have found that levels of political interest and efficacy have a significant effect on participation. These models center around the idea that feelings of 'linked fate', 'political alienation', 'group identity', and 'group conflict' have an impact on minority groups' political attitudes and behavior.[2] In other words, individuals feel (or do not feel) connections to particular groups, and their political attitudes and levels of participation are influenced in important ways by those feelings.

So what do we know about Latino participation levels in particular, and in relation to other groups within the US political system? Table 2.3 compares registration and voting rates among non-Latino whites, non-Latino blacks, and Latinos over the age of 18 from 1972 to 2004.

Table 2.3 Reported Registration by Race and Birth, 1972–2004

Year	White Total population[a]	Citizens	African American Total population	Citizens	Asian American Total population	Citizens	Latino Total population	Citizens
2004	67.9%	73.6%	64.4%	68.7%	34.9%	51.8%	34.3%	57.9%
2002	63.1%	67.9%	58.5%	62.4%	30.7%	49.2%	32.6%	52.5%
2000	65.7%	70.4%	63.6%	67.5%	30.7%	52.4%	34.9%	57.4%
1998	63.9%	68.2%	60.2%	63.6%	29.1%	48.9%	33.7%	55.2%
1996	67.7%	72.0%	63.5%	66.4%	32.6%	57.2%	35.7%	58.6%
1994	64.6%	68.4%	58.5%	61.3%	28.7%	51.9%	31.3%	52.9%
1992	70.1%	76.3%	63.9%	70.0%	31.2%	61.6%	35.0%	62.5%
1990	63.8%	69.1%	58.8%	63.5%	28.4%	56.0%	32.3%	55.2%
1988	67.9%	72.8%	64.5%	68.8%	NA	NA	35.5%	59.1%
1986	65.3%	69.5%	64.0%	67.3%	NA	NA	35.9%	56.4%
1984	69.6%	74.5%	66.3%	72.0%	NA	NA	40.1%	61.4%
1982	65.6%	69.4%	59.1%	62.6%	NA	NA	35.3%	53.7%
1980	68.4%	73.4%	60.0%	64.1%	NA	NA	36.4%	56.0%
1978	63.8%	67.5%	57.1%	60.6%	NA	NA	32.9%	50.1%
1976	68.3%	NA[b]	58.5%	NA	NA	NA	37.8%	NA
1974	64.6%	NA	54.2%	NA	NA	NA	34.9%	NA
1972	73.4%	NA	65.5%	NA	NA	NA	44.4%	NA

a 'Total population' refers to the population over 18. 'Citizens' refers to the citizen population over 18.
b Data not available
Source: Current Population Survey, November 2004 and earlier reports

As is clear from Tables 2.3 and 2.4, nativity is a big issue for the two largest immigrant groups in the United States: Latinos and Asian Americans. If one looks only at the citizen population, their registration and voting rates are somewhat similar to those of whites and blacks, albeit still lower. Yet when these rates are compared to those of the general population, we see that the proportion of individuals over 18 who are registered and voting within these groups represents a significantly lower percentage than for the US population as a whole. This is due to the fact that Latinos have lower registration rates than whites or blacks, combined with the fact that about forty percent of the community consists of non-citizens, which means that they are ineligible to vote. Mexican immigrants, in particular, have some of the lowest

Table 2.4 Reported Voting by Race and Birth, 1972–2004

Year	White Total population	Citizens	African American Total population	Citizens	Asian American Total population	Citizens	Latino Total population	Citizens
2004	63.8%	65.4%	56.3%	60.0%	29.8%	44.1%	28.0%	47.2%
2002	44.1%	47.5%	39.7%	42.3%	19.4%	31.2%	18.9%	30.4%
2000	56.4%	60.5%	53.5%	56.8%	25.4%	43.4%	27.5%	45.1%
1998	43.3%	46.3%	39.6%	41.8%	19.3%	32.4%	20.0%	32.8%
1996	56.0%	59.6%	50.6%	53.0%	25.7%	45.0%	26.8%	44.0%
1994	47.3%	50.0%	37.1%	38.9%	21.8%	39.4%	20.2%	34.0%
1992	63.6%	69.2%	54.1%	59.2%	27.3%	53.9%	28.9%	51.6%
1990	46.7%	50.5%	39.2%	42.4%	20.3%	40.0%	21.0%	36.0%
1988	59.1%	63.4%	51.5%	55.0%	NA	NA	28.8%	48.0%
1986	47.0%	50.1%	43.2%	45.5%	NA	NA	24.2%	38.0%
1984	61.4%	65.7%	55.8%	60.6%	NA	NA	32.7%	50.0%
1982	49.9%	52.8%	43.0%	45.5%	NA	NA	25.3%	38.5%
1980	60.9%	65.4%	50.5%	53.9%	NA	NA	29.9%	46.1%
1978	47.3%	50.1%	37.2%	39.5%	NA	NA	23.5%	35.7%
1976	60.9%	NA	48.7%	NA	NA	NA	31.8%	NA
1974	46.3%	NA	33.8%	NA	NA	NA	22.9%	NA
1972	64.5%	NA	52.1%	NA	NA	NA	37.5%	NA

Source: Current Population Survey, November 2004 and earlier reports

rates of naturalization in any immigrant group of the United States.[3] Thus a smaller proportion of the population is eligible to vote than in other populations, and then a smaller proportion of that group chooses to register and vote than is true among whites or blacks. The result is that Latino voters do not come close to representing the demographic power of the Latino population as a whole. In the rest of this book, we will explore the historical and institutional reasons why this is the case, focusing specifically on the five largest Latino national-origin groups: Mexicans, Puerto Ricans, Cubans, Salvadorans, and Guatemalans.

Those national-origin groups vary in terms of their group histories and of the kinds of political activity they have chosen to engage in. Table 2.5 summarizes voting levels in the 2004 presidential election among the citizen population – registration reported by national origin.[4] Mexicans and Salvadorans report the lowest levels of registration and the lowest

Table 2.5 Reported Registration and Voting in the 2004 Presidential Election by National Origin, among Citizens

	Registered	Voted	Total Number
Mexicans	78.1%	62.2%	2881
Puerto Ricans	85.2%	72.0%	819
Cubans	91.3%	83.5%	321
Salvadorans	72.1%	53.9%	154

Source: 2006 Latino National Survey

levels of overall voting. Puerto Ricans fall in the middle, and Cubans are the most likely group to report being registered and voting. In fact, studies have found that Cubans turn out to vote at higher rates than the general US population. Although some of these differences are attributable to differences in socioeconomic status among the groups, they also highlight important differences in the kinds of activities each chooses to engage in. These differences are due to history, geography, and the US institutional context.

Institutional Context

When Latinos decide to incorporate themselves into the US political system, they must do so within the context of a specific set of electoral and legislative rules which affect how much power a minority group will be able to muster within that system. These rules fall into two broad categories: *electoral rules* and *legislative rules*. We will explore each in turn.

Electoral Rules

Electoral rules are the rules which underlie the American electoral system. The most important rules with regard to Latinos are: majority rule; rules surrounding voting rights; and citizenship requirements for voting.

Majority rule The most basic electoral rule underlying the American political system is the idea of *majority rule*: If you can get more than 50 percent of the vote, you win the election. That is why scholars describe the American political system as *majoritarian* – you must have a majority in order to win. Other democracies around the world are not organized this way. Some have proportional, representational rules which guarantee a certain number of parliamentary seats, for example, to a particular minority group or party. Others have quota systems to ensure the representation of women or minority groups. The fact that the United States' electoral rules are majoritarian places important structural constraints on the electoral participation of minority groups like Latinos.

Since Latinos constitute a minority community within the United States, majority rule significantly affects their ability to express their interests through voting. Nationally, Latinos make up about 15 percent of the total US population. Yet, because of the demographic issues discussed above – namely the community's significant non-citizen population, large under-18 population, and low registration and voting rates – exit polls estimated that Latinos made up only about 9 percent of the voters in the 2008 presidential election. The story is similar at the state level. In California, for example, Latinos make up over one third of the state's population, yet only about 15 percent of likely voters. Similarly, in New Mexico – the state with the largest Latino population: 42 percent of the state total – Latinos make up less than 30 percent of voters. Of course, at the municipal level, in cities with over 75 percent Latino population, Latinos can and often do make up the majority of voters. But that is rare. In most places and in most electoral races, for Latino voters to meet the 50 percent threshold they must build coalitions with like-minded groups in order to ensure the success of their chosen candidate or of their preferred policy proposal. This means that, in the electoral arena, Latinos are not in complete control of their destiny. As a minority group within a majoritarian system, they can win elections only if they join coalitions large enough to surpass the 50 percent threshold. This, of course, means that they must compromise with those groups regarding their policy preferences and their choice of candidate. Thus majority rule makes it difficult for US minority groups like Latinos to win elections.

The Voting Rights Act　Voting rights are important because, within a Republican democracy, voting is the main way citizens may express their political preferences. Voting is also substantively important because it has *instrumental* value; it is an instrument that citizens use in order to determine who gets to make the laws and what kinds of public policies are put into place. For most of American history, the majority of the country's population – women and people of color – was denied the right to vote. This is why achieving the ability to exercise that right was a centerpiece of the civil rights movement. One of the greatest successes of the civil rights movement was the passing of the Voting Rights Act (VRA) in 1965. This act was designed to outlaw the mechanisms – direct intimidation, poll taxes, literacy tests – which had been used to suppress African American voting in the south (we will see in Chapter 3 that these methods were also used to disenfranchise Mexican Americans). The VRA, although originally conceived to address the African American case, positively affected the Latino community's ability to exercise the right to vote and to elect Latino candidates to public office.

In addition to outlawing the voting restrictions listed above, the VRA also made a number of counties with histories of minority voting exclusion subject to federal electoral supervision. That supervision included 'preclearance' of county districting rules and other electoral logistics. Initially, these rules targeted largely African American jurisdictions. Yet when Congress renewed the VRA in 1970 the rules ensured that the number of counties subject to federal supervision expanded. As a result, for the first time counties with significant Latino populations were included under the preclearance rules, which provided important protections to Latino voting rights. In 1975 the VRA was renewed again, and this marked the first time when Latinos were included directly under its provisions. From 1975 forward, the VRA was expanded so as to cover the protection of 'language minorities', which included Latinos, Asian Americans, Alaska natives, and native Americans. Under the 1975 rules, jurisdictions with a language minority population of 5 percent or more were eligible to request federal election observers. The law also required that jurisdictions meeting this population threshold provide bilingual ballots to language minority voters. Latinos were not included under the law by accident; these changes were the direct result of political organizing on the part of Mexican Americans and Puerto Ricans in the late 1960s and early 1970s, which is discussed in chapters 3 and 4.

The VRA has had an important impact on Latino political activity and representation. First, it removed the most overt structural barriers to voting. It outlawed things like overt intimidation of voters, capricious changes in voting rules and/or polling places, English language requirements for registration and voting, lengthy residential requirements for voter registration, the manipulation or control over the Latino vote by economic elites, and the drawing of district lines so that they diluted the minority vote – a practice known as racial gerrymandering. Requirements of long-time residence for voter registration were especially detrimental to migrant workers, many of whom are Latino, because of their need to move regularly as part of their job. Most of these barriers existed for Mexican Americans in Texas, but variants of them were used also to exclude Puerto Ricans from voting in New York City.

Second, the VRA significantly increased the number of Latino elected officials across the country. Although Latinos, unlike African Americans, were never excluded from public office entirely, because of racial gerrymandering Latino officeholders were relatively rare before 1975. In 1973 there were 1,280 Latino elected officials serving in the six most heavily Latino states: Arizona, California, Florida, New Mexico, New York, and Texas. By 2007, there were 4,539 Latino elected officials serving in those states – more than three and a half times the number in 1973.[5] This was largely due to legal changes in districting practices that occurred under the VRA. By 1982, the federal courts and Congress had established that states and localities with large and con-centrated minority populations had an affirmative responsibility to create districts from which minority groups could elect the candidates of their choice. The VRA urged the creation, when possible, of major-ity–minority districts, which in practice guaranteed the election of minority representatives from a particular area. The downside to this move, however, was that it only allowed for minority representation from areas with high levels of racial segregation. That being said, even though African American candidates still find it difficult to be elected in majority white districts, Latino candidates generally need a Latino registration rate of over 35 percent of the majority party in order to have a strong chance of taking that seat. This is a big change, which is due in large measure to the VRA.

Thus legal changes under the VRA constitute an important structural change, which has had a positive impact on Latinos' ability to exercise the right to vote and to be represented by Latino elected officials.

Citizenship and voting rights   Over forty percent of the Latino population in the United States is of foreign origin. This means that the Latino com-munity continually has a large percentage of non-citizens. Since citizen-ship is, in most places in the United States, a requirement for voting, this means in turn that a large proportion of the population has no formal say in the US political system. Yet for much of US history citizenship was not a requirement for voting; this is a fairly recent phenomenon. During the nineteenth century over twenty states and territories had alien voting rights. During the colonial era, non-citizens voted and held public office throughout the colonies. These policies were maintained after independence. Instead of citizenship, the key criteria for granting voting rights were race, gender, property, and residence. As the country expanded westward, states used non-citizen voting rights to encourage immigrants to settle in their areas. For example, Congress approved non-citizen voting in Illinois, Indiana, Kansas, Kentucky, Michigan, Minnesota, Missouri, Nebraska, Nevada, North Dakota, Ohio, Oklahoma, Oregon, South Dakota, Washington, Wisconsin, and Wyoming. The year 1875 marked the height of non-citizen suffrage in the United States, with twenty-two states and territories granting immigrants the right to vote. Most of these states only required that voters be white, male, and express an intent to naturalize. States saw the provision of non-citizens voting rights as a way to teach civic ideals to future citizens.

Around the end of the nineteenth century, concerns arose regarding the power and influence exercised by immigrant groups. As anti-immigrant sentiment grew, states began to retract their support of non-citizen suffrage. Many states passed constitutional amendments limiting the franchise to United States citizens. By the late 1920s most states required that individuals must be citizens in order to vote. But non-citizen voting is not illegal. Currently a number of municipalities allow non-citizen voting. One of the most liberal statutes exists in Takoma Park, Maryland, where, since 1992, non-citizens have been allowed to vote in local elections and hold municipal office regardless of their migration status.

For the Latino community, the issue of non-citizen voting is not simply an academic one. Because non-citizens tend to be concentrated in particular geographic areas, their formal exclusion from the political process raises questions about democracy and representation in the United States. For example, the state of California has twelve municipalities where the foreign population makes up more than 50 percent of the adults living there.[6] These individuals work, pay taxes, have children in school, and yet have no formal say in who represents them in government. This is why many scholars and activists have called for non-citizen voting to be allowed at the local level, particularly in school-board and municipal elections. They argue that this helps to teach non-citizens about participation and democracy and ensures that their voices are heard in matters which affect them or their children directly. Given that Latinos make up such a large share of the non-citizen population in the United States, any changes in this direction would have an important impact on their participation rates and ability to influence the political process.

Nonelectoral participation Yet political participation is not solely about voting. There are many other ways in which individuals and groups can engage in the political process. These form what is called *non-electoral participation*, which can include activities such as engaging in political protest, working for a community-based organization, contacting elected officials, signing petitions, boycotting a particular company or product, and so on. Any sort of collective activity aimed at addressing a political problem can be defined as nonelectoral activity. Other than giving contributions to elected officials (which may only be done by US citizens or permanent residents), non-citizens can engage in any of these types of activities. Thus nonelectoral participation is an important way through which non-citizen Latinos can express their political views. Nevertheless, the factors which determine who engages in nonelectoral participation have been found to be the same as for electoral participation: those who have higher incomes, higher levels of education, and are older are more likely to participate in these kinds of activities than those who are young, less educated, and have lower income levels. Since the Latino community in the United States is younger and less affluent than non-Latino whites, Latinos are less likely than whites to engage in these kinds of political activities, even though there are no legal barriers (such as citizenship status) to their participation.

Table 2.6 summarizes Latino political interest and engagement in some nonelectoral activities. As we have seen with electoral participation, there are differences among Latino national-origin groups in terms of their preferred forms of engagement. Salvadorans are the least likely to report interest in politics in general, while about two-thirds of the Mexicans and Puerto Ricans say they find politics interesting. Cubans seem to be the group most interested in politics. Puerto Ricans are the most likely to report contacting an elected official and Salvadorans are the least likely. Just under a third of the respondents from all the groups prefer to use existing organizations to solve problems. All the group members seem slightly more likely to prefer to resolve problems informally, except for Salvadorans. Other studies have shown that Mexicans and Puerto Ricans are more likely than Cubans to engage in political protest. Thus, not all Latinos are the same in terms of their attitudes towards politics and the kinds of activities they choose to engage in. These differences reflect individual-level preferences combined with structural factors such as organizational density, local electoral rules, and the group's political history.

Table 2.6 Political Engagement by National Origin among the Total Population

	Mexicans	Puerto Ricans	Cubans	Salvadorans
somewhat interested to very interested in politics	66.2%	68.6%	73.3%	47.7%
have contacted public official to express concerns	30.3%	45.1%	38.8%	22.9%
prefer to resolve problems through existing organizations	27.5%	28.6%	24.0%	30.2%
prefer to resolve problems informally	31.1%	29.4%	30.0%	26.3%
Total Number	5704	822	420	407

Source: 2006 Latino National Survey

Therefore the US political system operates under a set of electoral rules which either limit or facilitate minority participation and representation. When considering the political incorporation of a minority group like Latinos, it is important to keep these rules in mind and to understand the consequences they may have on the strategies which groups choose to employ in order to express their political interests and on the chances that these tactics may enjoy success.

Legislative Rules

Legislative rules are the rules which govern decision-making within legislative institutions such as the United States Congress or the state legislatures. As with electoral participation, the emphasis on majority rule is very important within legislatures and dictates how decisions are made at the committee and floor levels. Party agendas and leadership are much more important within legislatures than they are within American politics at large, and they affect elected officials' abilities to serve their constituents' interests.

Committee rules   Most legislative bodies rule through committees. This means that the responsibilities of a body in terms of policy-making are divided up across a number of standing committees. Each legislator serves on a few committees which are in charge of issues which are of importance to the committees in question. For example, at the federal level, the Education and Workforce Committee is responsible for all legislation related to educational and workplace issues. Those legislators who serve on that committee have more of an impact on drafting legislation related to such issues than legislative members who do not serve on that committee have. The committee system is meant to streamline the law-making process. If all the members were able to have a say on every piece of legislation, the law-making process would be unmanageable. Instead, the proposed law is brought before the relevant committee, amended as the committee members see fit, and then voted on by the committee, which has to determine whether or not the revised legislation should be subject to a vote by the entire legislative body.

The committee system is an important part of the legislative process and is what makes law-making possible. However, for representatives of minority communities, it does have some important negative effects on their ability to pursue their political agenda. As we have seen with the electoral system in general, majority rule makes it difficult for minority communities to cross the 50 percent threshold necessary to win elections. This limitation is only compounded when majority rule is applied within the legislature itself. For example, from 2006–8 there were twenty-four Latinos serving in the US House of Representatives, which contains a total of 435 members. In order to get any legislation passed, a Latino member first has to obtain the support of the majority of the relevant committee. Then they have to persuade 217 other representatives to support their proposal for the floor vote. We saw above how majority rule in the electoral system often makes coalition-building necessary for being elected. Once representatives are elected, coalitions become an absolute requirement in order for legislation to be passed. Thus crossing the majority threshold in an election is only the very first step in the multiple levels of majority rule which affect the policy-making abilities of Latino elected officials.

Party influence and agendas　Majority rule is important not only within legislative bodies, but also within the two major political parties. For most Americans, political parties and their platforms have little relevance to their day-to-day lives. Within legislatures, however, parties are very important. In the United States, the political party system was created within Congress during the eighteenth century in order to help politicians to muster the number of votes necessary to pass legislation. This imperative remains valid today. To be successful, parties need their members to stick together and support the bills which the party leadership wants passed. Thus party loyalty is very important within legislatures, and this is something that party leaders spend a great deal of time working to develop. They do it through carrots and sticks – incentives and disincentives to following the party line.

On the side of incentives, the strongest incentive which party leaders have at their disposal is committee assignments. Who gets to sit on what committee is determined by the leaders of each party. And some committee assignments are much more popular than others. For example, within the US House of Representatives, the Appropriations Committee is responsible for all the appropriations (that is, spending) that go through the House. For obvious reasons, this is a very powerful committee and one that members want to join. If a member does what the leadership asks and votes with the party, the party leaders can reward him or her with a seat on a coveted committee. Conversely, if a member does not vote with the party on an important issue, their leadership can punish them by removing them from a particular committee or by denying them the committee assignment they want. Another incentive the parties can muster is support for a particular member when the time comes for reelection. Both political parties have national and statewide committees whose job is to raise money for the party's candidates. A loyal party member is more likely to receive this kind of financial support than a disloyal member. This is another way parties can encourage their members' support in legislative voting.

The question then arises: What are the members actually supporting? Individual representatives are focused on responding to the needs of their particular district or constituency. Party leaders, on the other hand, represent their districts but also have to consider the needs of the party in general. Because of the majoritarian electoral requirements both in electing representatives and in the legislatures themselves, party leaders need to develop policy proposals which appeal to the broadest possible number of people. Remember, any proposal must get over 50 percent of the vote. This makes parties often reluctant to take positions which can be seen as targeting the needs of a specific group. They would rather be seen as being as broad and inclusive as possible. The kinds of proposals which have this sort of broad appeal tend to represent the ideological center – to be not too extreme either in the liberal or in the conservative direction. Yet from a political ideology standpoint Latinos in general, and Latino elected officials in particular, tend to hold policy positions which are more liberal than those of Americans generally. For example, Latinos are more likely than other Americans to say they support increased government programs, particularly for education and health-related services. Thus, from a policy standpoint, the kinds of proposals Latino representatives are likely to advocate often fall to the left of the political center in the United States. Since party leaders want to put forward proposals which will be successful, the kinds of policy proposals advocated by Latino representatives will often not be included in the final legislation, or will be watered down so as to appeal to a broader number of people. In other words, the ability of Latino representatives to influence the party's agenda depends on the degree to which their policy preferences coincide with what will appeal to the party leadership and to a majority of the legislative members as a whole. Again, we see how having political influence can be difficult for minority group members within legislative bodies.

Representation

The issue of party leaders, elected officials, and their policy agendas raises the question of representation in general. When the founders were writing the US Constitution, the only democracies they had as models were those of ancient Greece and Rome. Both of those systems allowed all citizens to engage in decision-making.[7] Yet in a country the size of the United States this approach was not feasible. Instead, our founders developed a Republican system of government – one in which citizens choose representatives to uphold their interests in the decision-making process. If the citizens do not agree with their elected representatives, they can remove them in the next election. Yet the founders never truly answered the question of what representation means within a majoritarian context. James Madison argued that the 'tyranny of the majority' – the tendency of the majority to impose their will on the minority – could be avoided if the majority shifted continually. In other words, a particular individual may be in the majority on religious issues, but in the minority on economics; and, as long as the majority is made to shift across issues, this form of tyranny can be avoided.

Yet this formulation does not address the question of what a democratic system might do in a situation where a particular population, like Latinos, could potentially have different economic or educational preferences from the majority population. How can such a minority make its interests represented? And, more importantly, what happens if those interests can never be represented? Does that affect the legitimacy of the system? The VRA is meant to address this question by ensuring a minimal level of *descriptive representation* for minority groups – representation by an individual who shares the same race, gender, class, or national origin as the voter. But is this all that matters? Can we assume that a poor female representative can represent the interests of all poor females? The fact of the matter is that, at the state and federal levels, our elected representatives are predominantly male and much richer than the general population. Does that mean that they cannot represent the majority's interests?

This remains an open question – which is why some scholars argue for the idea of *substantive representation*: representation by someone who agrees with the voter ideologically and in terms of their public policy interests. The idea is that the voters have a representative with congruent policy views acting as their advocate. Yet how do we know what a voter's policy views are? And which voters should have their policy views represented? Any representative at any level of government will have constituents with opposing views. How should that representative decide which views 'matter'? Also, is an elected official's job simply to echo her constituents' opinions, or should she vote according to her own judgment? These are important, and to a large extent unanswerable, questions. Yet they go to the heart of the problem of defining and measuring 'representation'. It is likely that most voters want their representative to represent their substantive interest, and they use descriptive representation as shorthand, on the basis of the assumption that, if an individual has had similar life experiences, they probably have similar policy preferences. But it is important to point out that this is not always the case and that continually questioning representation and what it means is crucial within the context of a republican democracy.

For minority groups, the issue of representation also raises a number of other questions, in particular about authenticity and accountability. In terms of authenticity, the pertinent question is: how often do minority voters get represented by the people they want (that is, how often does the candidate they support win?). If the minority group votes as a bloc and continually loses, this threatens democratic legitimacy. As Madison pointed out, avoiding the tyranny of the majority requires that everyone should win every once in a while. This is why one of the factors taken into consideration in VRA litigation is the presence of racial bloc voting in a particular jurisdiction. This reflects authenticity; but accountability is equally important. If a politician has a very 'safe' seat, how driven will he be to protect his constituents' interests? This is a growing problem in American politics in general, as the political parties regularly draw district lines which insure very little party competition within legislative districts. For example, of the 435 seats up for election every two years in the US House of Representatives, only about forty are truly competitive. This issue is only exacerbated in majority–minority seats. Since most of the minority groups subject to VRA scrutiny (African Americans, Latinos, Asian Americans, and native Americans) vote overwhelmingly for the Democratic Party, creating a majority–minority seat often means creating a safe Democratic Party seat. This means, further, that those representatives are elected easily and have little competition for reelection. In addition, many of their constituents, for important historical reasons, are not as engaged politically as the general population. Within this context, who ensures that those representatives truly are accountable to the people that they represent? This remains one of the major challenges within American democracy and a particular problem for members of minority groups.

Minority representation also raises the problem of institutional compromise. To get their issues on their party agenda, minority representatives often need to make compromises in order to build coalitions. Yet many Americans, in the majority and in the minority alike, complain that their representatives forget them, or forget their promises, when they achieve political office. How much should minority representatives be willing to compromise? Democracy is built on the principle of compromise; yet is there a point, if they compromise too much, at which elected leaders cease to be 'representative'? This too is an open question, and one which applies to all US representatives. But in the case of individuals who represent groups which have continually been the 'losers' in terms of their public policy agendas, these questions take on additional salience.

Levels of Government and Regional Differences

The previous discussion was not meant to imply that all government is created equal. The scale required for election, funding, and success at the national level is exponentially greater than at the local level. This is one of the reasons why the majority of Latino elected officials is found at the local level. In general, it is easier for minority groups to be represented at the local level because it takes a smaller number of people to surpass the 50 percent threshold. From a districting standpoint, the creation of majority–minority districts at the local level still encourages segregation, but the size of overall community can be smaller and the community may still have representation. Thus it is much easier for minority groups to be represented, and to have political influence, at the local

level. Local governments, in turn, through their provision of basic services like putting up stop signs, fixing sidewalks, picking up trash, and
establishing zoning rules, can have huge direct effects on individuals'
lives. For minority groups, the municipal level is the level where they are
most likely to have a direct influence on political decision-making. Yet,
ironically, most Americans do not vote in their municipal elections.

But not all governments across the United States are organized the
same way. The structure of state and local governments in the United
States vary significantly by region. Almost 27 percent of Latinos in the
United States live in the west, 14.5 percent live in the south, 11.3 percent
in the north-east, and 5.3 percent in the mid-west. Most of the western
Latinos live in the southwest, which by and large is made up of 'post-
reform' cities – cities whose government structures were reorganized
after the progressive movement in the early twentieth century. The progressive movement arose out of concerns with the corruption that characterized many of the party machines which ran cities in the northeast,
such as Tammany Hall in New York City. Progressives wanted to reduce
the power of those machines and of the immigrants who ran them. To
do so, they advocated the bureaucratization of city government; this
included the use of civil servants instead of political appointees, the
enlargement of city council districts, and the weakening of city mayors
(so they could not use the office to appoint their friends, or use city
resources to support their pet projects).

The progressives were highly successful, and most local governments
in the south-west remain organized according to their ideals. Their
reforms did diminish political corruption. But they had other consequences as well. Having larger districts means that candidates need to
raise more money to run for public office and to have larger numbers of
people supporting them. This situation has some negative effects. First,
it makes it very difficult for a candidate to be successful without personal
wealth, party backing, or corporate support. Second, voters are more distant from their representatives because they represent a larger number
of people, which makes it nearly impossible for elected officials to have
personal contact with a significant proportion of their constituents. For
example, each Los Angeles County Supervisor represents about 2 million
people, and it costs more than $5 million to run for a seat on the board.
This clearly makes it difficult for constituents to feel connected to their
government or to have any personal contact with their supervisor. It also
puts the cost of running for a supervisorial seat outside of the realm of
most people. The need to raise large amounts of money to run for office

and to have large-scale name recognition also privileges incumbents. Few challengers other than the independently wealthy are up to the task of raising the funds necessary to compete with a well-funded incumbent within this context. This makes turnover for elected officials very low, which decreases representational accountability.

Another local-level factor of importance is whether or not a locality has at-large or single-member districts. At-large districts mean that a city is defined as one large district, and a certain number of individuals are elected 'at large' to serve on the city council. A single-member district system means that the city is broken up into a set number of districts, with non-overlapping geographic boundaries, and each district receives one representative. Studies have shown that cities with single-member districts are much more likely to elect minority representatives, because it is easier for the latter to surpass the 50 percent threshold within a small district than to do it within the city at large. As a result, under the VRA, courts have often ordered cities to adopt single-member district-ing when there is a geographically concentrated minority community which consistently supports candidates who lose under an at-large dis-tricting system. That being said, this remedy again requires residential segregation in order to ensure minority representation.

Conclusion

Voting is important because this is how we choose our representatives. Electoral rules have a significant effect on which groups are able to win elections and hence on which groups are able to have the representa-tives of their choice. Once in office, legislative rules affect those repre-sentatives' ability to represent their constituents' interests. But how do we know if these representatives are doing a good job? 'Representation' is one of the most difficult ideas to define or to measure. What exactly does it mean to be represented? It is likely that all members of the polity feel that their elected representatives reflect their interests on some issues but not on others. Looking from the outside, how can elected officials know what a particular constituency favors in terms of public policy? We cannot have ongoing surveys of every community in the United States. And, even if we did, the ranking of issues in order of importance would probably vary from month to month. In any case, even if representatives have perfect information about their constitu-ents' preferences, they may choose to vote in a different way, according to their conscience. Are these representatives supposed simply to echo the beliefs of their constituency or to take principled positions based on their own political preferences? Is a representative still 'representing' her community if she supports a minority position on the basis of a moral principle? These are very difficult questions to answer. Given that fact, many analysts use descriptive representation as a proxy for substantive representation, on the basis of the assumption that individuals with similar life experiences are better able to represent one another. On the descriptive side, Latinos remain significantly underrepresented at all levels of government, in relation to their population. This is due to the fact that US institutional structures, with their majoritarian rules and historical exclusion of people of color and women, make it difficult for minorities to get elected. It is unlikely that the situation will change in the future. The question is: To what extent does the US political system represent Latino substantive interests? We will see in the following chapters that the answer to this question varies across time, national-origin group, and geographic context.

CHAPTER THREE

Mexican Americans: Conquest, Migration, and Adaptation

Objectives

- Understand the unique relationship Mexico has had with the United States
- Understand how that relationship affected Mexican politics, including the US' annexation of half of Mexico's territory
- Understand how development policies in Mexico and the United States encourage Mexican migration to the United States
- Understand how the Mexican population was integrated into the US racial hierarchy and how this affected its economic and political opportunities
- Understand the many ways in which the Mexican-origin population in the United States has engaged in politics

Introduction

On 2 February 1848, the United States and Mexico signed the Treaty of Guadalupe Hidalgo, which is the oldest treaty still in force between Mexico and the United States. As a result of that treaty, the Mexican–American War was officially ended and Mexico ceded over half of its territory (California, Nevada, Utah, and parts of Arizona, New Mexico, and Wyoming) to the United States for a sum of 15 million dollars. At that time, about 100,000 citizens of Mexico lived in the ceded territories. They were given a choice between returning to Mexico, becoming US citizens, or remaining Mexican citizens living on the lands which had become part of the United States. From this point forward, Mexican Americans have had to be incorporated into American society. This process of incorporation has been strongly influenced by the justifications underlying the Mexican War, the proximity of Mexico to the United States, and US economic and political interests in Mexico and in the United States.

Mexico and the United States are unique insofar as they share a 2,000-mile border. It is one of the largest contiguous land borders in the world, and the only place in the world where a developing country exists directly next to an advanced industrialized nation. The asymmetry in power between the two countries, economically as well as politically and, since the United States' defeat of Mexico in 1848, militarily, has had important effects on Mexican migration patterns and on their political incorporation in the United States.

Mexican Independence and the Early Republic

Like all of Latin America except Brazil, Mexico was a colony of Spain. Mexico achieved independence from Spain in 1821. The Mexican war for independence lasted eleven years, from 1810 to 1821. It began on the morning of 16 September 1810, when Father Miguel Hidalgo, a parish priest in the town of Dolores, rang the church bell calling all who heard it to fight for their independence. The initial insurgency was made up mostly of peasants fighting for ideals of political and economic equality. They quickly took control of Zacatecas, San Luis Potosí, and Valladolid. Their frontward momentum stopped when they attempted to march on Mexico City. In March 1811, the insurgents were ambushed in Monclova, and many, including Hidalgo, were taken prisoner. Hidalgo was executed in Chihuahua in July of that year. After his death, the war remained at a stalemate for some time. Small guerilla bands organized raids around the countryside but neither they nor the Spaniards could claim victory. Independence was not secured until many powerful *criollos* (members of the Mexican elite), concerned about political instability in Spain, joined the fight. The newly created Mexican state was based on three guarantees: (1) the establishment of one national religion, Roman Catholicism; (2) the proclamation of Mexico as an independent nation; and (3) social equality for all groups within the new nation. Mexico was organized as a constitutional monarchy, modeled after those in Europe. In August 1821, Spain signed the Treaty of Córdoba, making Mexico an independent nation.

The length of the war, however, left the Mexican economy in disarray, and the new Mexican state was very weak. Elites were split between liberals and conservatives, and they staged numerous political *coups* in order to achieve their political and economic goals. Between 1821 and 1860 Mexico had fifty separate presidencies, thirty-five of which were held by army officers after *coups*. The other powerful force in Mexican politics was the Catholic church. Because the church missions held all indigenous lands in trust for the native peoples, at the time of independence it is estimated that the church owned one-third of all the land in Mexico.

The newly independent government in Mexico, in the midst of all this turmoil, realized that it needed to shore up its control over its northern territories. It began to grant tracts of land to individuals who were willing to live in these areas. Grantees did not have to be Mexican citizens when they received these grants. They simply had to be committed to living in the territories, learning Spanish, converting to Catholicism, and abiding by the laws of Mexico. Many American citizens took advantage of this opportunity and settled lands in northern Mexico, particularly in Texas. At the beginning, most of these settlers integrated themselves into Mexican society, often marrying into Mexican families. Yet by the 1820s the number of American settlers had grown, and many of these new arrivals wanted to engage in slavery. The 1824 Mexican Constitution had abolished slavery, which meant that the new slaveholders were violating Mexican law. When Mexican authorities attempted to enforce the law, American settlers and some native Tejanos revolted. This was the start of the Texas revolution of 1835.

At that time Andrew Jackson was president of the United States. A southern slaveholder, Jackson agreed with many of the pro-slavery Americans in Texas, who thought that the territory should be annexed to the United States. During his first term of office, Jackson offered to purchase Texas from Mexico, but Mexico refused. The Texans won independence during Jackson's second term, but he did not push for Texas' annexation because of northern resistance to the addition of another slave state into the Union. Instead, he showed his support by recognizing Texas' independence and by establishing diplomatic relations with the Republic of Texas. In 1845 James Polk became president of the United States. He ran for office on a platform of expansionism, saying he supported the annexation of Texas and Oregon. Carrying through on his platform, soon after Polk's election the US Congress offered Texas annexation. This led Mexico to sever diplomatic relations with the United States. Polk also supported the acquisition of California, and to that end he sent an envoy to Mexico empowered to offer up to $20 million, plus the forgiveness of US damage claims from the Texas war, in exchange for California and New Mexico. Mexican President José Joaquín de Herrera decided to meet with Polk's envoy to discuss the Texas situation. His act was so unpopular that he was accused of treason and deposed from office. Thus Mexico did not entertain Polk's offer.

Polk, however, remained committed to the idea of US expansion (based on the idea of manifest destiny), and in 1846 he sent a military force to occupy a disputed territory between the Nueces River and the Río Grande. Mexico saw this as military aggression on the part of the United States and attacked Taylor's forces. The US Congress then declared war on Mexico, officially commencing the Mexican–American War in 1846. The war lasted for two years and resulted in an overwhelming US victory over Mexico. It ended on 2 February 1848, with the signing of the Treaty of Guadalupe Hidalgo. The treaty was named after the city where the Mexican government had fled after the United States military captured Mexico City.

As I have already said, under the terms of the treaty, Mexico ceded over half of its territory, over 500,000 square miles, to the United States. This area included California, Nevada, and Utah, and parts of Arizona, Colorado, Wyoming, and New Mexico. In return, the United States paid Mexico $15 million. Initially there was a great deal of debate in the United States about how much of Mexico to annex. Some thought the entire country should be taken. Others, such as Senator John C. Calhoun, worried about incorporating a 'mongrel' race into the union. In a speech on the Senate floor, Calhoun laid out his concerns as follows:

> I know further, sir, that we have never dreamt of incorporating into our Union any but the Caucasian race – the free white race. To incorporate Mexico, would be the very first instance of the kind of incorporating an Indian race; for more than half of the Mexicans are Indians, and the other is composed chiefly of mixed tribes. I protest against such a union as that! Ours, sir, is the Government of a white race. The greatest misfortunes of Spanish America are to be traced to the fatal error of placing these colored races on an equality with the white race. That error destroyed the social arrangement which formed the basis of society . . . And yet it is professed and talked about to erect these Mexicans into a Territorial Government, and place them on an equality with the people of the United States. I protest utterly against such a project.
>
> Sir, it is a remarkable fact, that in the whole history of man, as far as my knowledge extends, there is no instance whatever of any civilized colored races being found equal to the establishment of free popular government, although by far the largest portion of the human family is composed of these races. And even in the savage state we scarcely find them anywhere with such government, except it be our noble savages – for noble I will call them. They, for the most part, had free institutions, but they are easily sustained among a savage people. Are we to overlook this fact? Are we to associate with ourselves as equals, companions, and fellow-citizens, the Indians and mixed race of Mexico? Sir, I should consider such a thing as fatal to our institutions . . .
>
> We make a great mistake, sir, when we suppose that all people are capable of self-government. We are anxious to force free government on all; and I see that it has been urged in a very respectable quarter, that it is the mission of this country to spread civil and religious liberty over all the world, and especially over this continent. It is a great mistake. None but people advanced to a very high state of moral

and intellectual improvement are capable, in a civilized state, of maintaining free government; and amongst those who are so purified, very few, indeed, have had the good fortune of forming a constitution capable of endurance. It is a remarkable fact in the history of man, that scarcely ever have free popular institutions been formed by wisdom alone that have endured.[1]

Calhoun's concerns were shared by many. In the end, the United States decided to annex the least populated of the Mexican territories, in the hope that the individuals living there would either choose to return to Mexico or would, because of their small numbers, be more easily incorporated into American society.

The treaty itself was meant to lay out the terms of that incorporation. One of the stipulations that the Mexican negotiators insisted upon was that Mexican citizens remaining in the ceded territories be given all the rights and privileges of United States' citizens. The treaty explicitly stated that Mexicans who lived within the newly annexed territories would be 'incorporated into the Union of the United States' with the 'enjoyment of all the rights of citizens'. We need to remember that slavery was legal at that point in the United States. In most states an individual had to be proven 'white' in order to vote. And the 1790 naturalization law still made it illegal for a non-white person to become a naturalized citizen of the United States. Therefore, to enjoy the rights of a United States citizen, an individual needed to be classified as 'white'. As a result, the terms of the treaty made it necessary for all former Mexican citizens in the annexed territories to be legally defined as white. However, this classification was not applied to Mexicans of indigenous backgrounds. Even though native Americans were full citizens of Mexico, the United States refused to grant citizenship to Mexicans of native American descent until the 1930s.

Another key aspect of the treaty was its treatment of property rights in the conquered territories. In Article VIII, the treaty gave individuals in the annexed territories the right to keep their land, whether remaining in the United States or returning to Mexico, or to sell their land if they so chose, without having to pay any tax or contribution to the United States' government. Article X, as signed, stated explicitly that the United States would recognize all Mexican land grants. But the United States Senate, when ratifying the treaty, refused to ratify that article. This did not mean that land grants would not be honored, but rather that all grant claims would have to be proven in US court before they would be recognized by American authorities. Thus the only land-related provision that remained in force after treaty ratification was that written in

Article VIII, which only provided a very general right for individuals to remain on the land they owned and to dispose of that land in whatever manner they chose, without penalty.

These two provisions of the treaty – the classification of Mexicans as racially white and the need to prove Mexican and Spanish land grants in court – would have far-reaching effects on the social, political, and economic status of individuals of Mexican origin in the conquered territories.

Mexican Citizenship Status after Annexation

Mexicans, then, became part of the United States as a result of territorial conquest. As we saw in the Calhoun quotation above, they were commonly considered to be non-white and therefore incapable of self-government. Yet they were brought into the Union at the height of slavery in the United States, a period when whiteness was key to exercising the rights of US citizenship. The degree to which Mexicans were able to exercise those citizenship rights depended on where they were located (each state dealt with the Mexican population a bit differently); on their class status (wealthier Mexicans often were accorded greater rights); and on their phenotype (darker-skinned Mexicans often were categorized as 'Indian', which severely limited their rights). Three important areas of citizenship are the exercise of formal voting rights, access to the protection of the criminal justice system, and the protection of private property. We will examine each in turn.

Formal Voting Rights

The Treaty of Guadalupe Hidalgo specifically stated that the Mexicans in the annexed territories should enjoy all the rights of citizens; but it also stated that that should occur 'at the proper time', according to the wishes of the United States Congress. Within a year of the treaty's ratification, Congress gave the legislators of the ceded territories and states the right to determine the Mexicans' citizenship status. This right, which is provided to states by Article II of the US Constitution, gives states the right to determine who is eligible for citizenship and on what grounds. The courts at this point also recognized that there were two levels of citizenship in the United States – state citizenship and federal citizenship. Thus, even though by ratifying the treaty the federal government implicitly recognized the Mexicans as 'whites' and therefore subject to the full exercise of federal citizenship, the state governments did not need to recognize them as such. In practice, and often depending on their class status, Mexicans were treated very differently by state and territorial governments throughout the southwest. For example, the 1849 California Constitution gave the right of suffrage only to white males of Mexican descent. In New Mexico, the 1850 constitution gave the vote to all whites and to the Pueblo Indians, but in 1853 the US Congress rescinded the Pueblos' voting rights. Arizona was originally under the laws of New Mexico and later, in 1863, adopted a constitution similar to that of California, which only granted voting rights to white Mexicans. Texas limited citizenship status to whites and to Mexicans who were not black or Indian.

Thus the state and territorial governments, in their granting of voting rights in the annexed territories, did not assume that all Mexicans were 'white'. In addition, these laws did not lay out any clear criteria for what constituted a 'white'. Many Mexicans in the annexed territories did not look 'white'. Most were what is called *mestizos*, 'mixtures' of European, indigenous, and African ancestry – the kind of compound which Vasconcelos described as '*la raza cósmica*'. Again, thinking about race as a social construction, the interpretation of an individual's physical characteristics was often in the eye of the beholder, and, at least during the initial period after annexation, it was related in important ways with class. Those Mexican citizens who were *hacendados* (or landowners) and therefore dressed in European fashion, were educated, and considered of the upper class, were more likely to be granted their voting rights regardless of their physical appearance. One good example of this is Manuel Domínguez, a prominent California *hacendado* who, despite his dark complexion, was one of the signatories of the California State Constitution. His social status in Californian society was high enough to allow people to overlook his skin color, at least in some instances. But there were exceptions. For example, in April 1857, despite being a former Los Angeles county supervisor and signatory to the state constitution, he was not allowed to testify on behalf of a defendant in a San Francisco court because the Anglo lawyer for the plaintiff argued that his Indian blood legally barred him from testifying in a court case. The judge agreed and dismissed Domínguez from the stand. Another example is Pablo de la Guerra, a very prominent landholding *Californio* from Santa Barbara, who was prosecuted in 1870 for trying to exercise the rights of a white person.

The annexed territories were brought into the United States before the civil war, and most adopted voting rules similar to those of other states. Thus exercising the right to vote required that an individual be categorized as white and not as African, Indian, or Asian. This left many Mexicans without the ability to exercise this basic right of citizenship.

Protection of the Criminal Justice System

The protection both of individual liberties and of property rights relate to an essential function of government: maintaining social order. This goes down to the principle of reciprocity, which lies at the heart of the relationship between citizen and government – the citizen gives up certain freedoms, and in return the government provides that citizen with a basic level of protection. Yet for Mexicans in the conquered territories this reciprocity did not hold in the same way for all group members. The degree to which the government (either federal or of the state) could be expected to protect your life or property depended in large part on the way your citizenship (and therefore rights) were defined by those governments and by the court system.

Under any governmental system, individuals agree to give up certain freedoms (for example, the right to run a red light, to play music loudly at night, and the like) in return for protection from the government. If someone breaks into your house and causes you harm, you expect your local police or sheriff to come to your aid, and, in an ideal world, arrest and prosecute the perpetrators. This legal protection from the state requires that an individual be recognized by law enforcement in important ways. For Mexicans in the annexed territories, the rights of particular concern were the right to testify in court against whites and the right to serve on juries. The first right is important because, returning to the home robbery example, if a white person were to come into a Mexican home and the Mexican in question had the right to identify and bring charges against the white person, it would be very likely that their actions had legal consequences. On the other hand, if that white person were to know that the Mexican cannot bring evidence in court, that person could literally murder his entire family before his very eyes and the victim would have no legal recourse. The issue of jury service is similar. The American justice system is based upon the principle of being judged by an unbiased group of your peers. Since Mexican Americans were excluded from juries throughout the southwest until the 1960s, they were not being tried by their peers. This made it much less likely that they would receive a fair trial. In 1939, the Supreme

Court agreed, ruling in *Pierre* v. *the State of Louisiana*, that the exclusion of individuals from jury service on the basis of their race or color is a violation of the Fourteenth Amendment guarantee of equal protection. Despite this ruling, however, Mexican Americans and African Americans continued to be excluded from jury service throughout the south and southwestern United States until the 1960s. Both these exclusions, from testifying in court and from serving on juries, made it difficult for Mexicans to have the protection of, or a fair relationship with, the US criminal justice system.

Protection of Property

By 1890, almost all Mexicans in the annexed territories had lost their land. There were two main factors that led to this result. The first was the US system of taxation. Under the Mexican and Spanish systems, landowners paid taxes only on what was produced within a given year. Since the south west is subject to highly variable weather conditions, such as recurring periods of drought and flood, this taxation system made it easier for Mexicans in the south west to weather these changes. Under the American system, however, taxes are paid on the land owned, regardless of its production in any given year. A large portion of Mexican landholders were ranchers. They owned a great deal of land, but only earned money during those years when enough of their livestock survived so that they could slaughter some of it and bring it to market. The period after annexation brought a great deal of extreme weather. For example in 1861 California experienced extreme flooding, which waterlogged many crops and drowned livestock. It is estimated that one fourth of the state's taxable wealth was destroyed. The floods were followed by two years of extreme drought, high winds, and a locust infestation, all of which made it difficult for livestock to find pasturage. As a result, in 1865 the Sacramento Union estimated that at least half of the 800,000 cattle in southern California had died. This made it very difficult for *hacendados* to raise the money needed to pay the taxes on their land.

The second factor affecting Mexican land ownership was the need to prove their land claims in American court. Article X of the original Treaty of Guadalupe Hidalgo provided for the recognition of all Spanish and Mexican land grants in the annexed territories. The US Senate deleted that article when it approved the treaty. But Article VIII, as was approved, read:

> In the said territories, property of every kind, now belonging to Mexicans not established there, shall be inviolably respected. The present owners, the heirs of these, and all Mexicans who may hereafter acquire said property by contract, shall enjoy, with respect to it, guarantees equally ample as if the same belonged to citizens of the United States.[2]

Yet all Mexican landowners had to get their land deeds honored and recognized by an American court. Until those claims were approved, the land did not 'officially' belong to the *hacendado*. As a result, it was perfectly legal for squatters to take control of portions of the *hacendado*'s land while the claims were being resolved in court. The landowner could do nothing to make these individuals leave their property. Quite the opposite – in many cases the squatters committed violence against the landowner's family or livestock, and the owner had no recourse because the local law enforcement officials refused to bring charges against the squatters. Many state governments, in fact, actually encouraged squatting on Mexican-owned lands. For example, one of the early acts of California state legislature was to pass a 'Squatters' Law' which, among other things, made squatting legal; barred the landowner from taking action against the squatters so long as his or her land claim was not confirmed; and, in case the original landowner's claim was approved, required that they compensate the squatters for any 'improvements' (dwellings, fencing, and so on) they made to the land while occupying it.[3]

In addition to having to deal with squatters, the *hacendados* also had to negotiate a new legal system (the Mexican system is based on Roman law, and therefore has very different rules of evidence and procedure), in a new language, and to engage in protracted legal fights in order to prove their claims. Even though about seventy-five percent of the land claims were eventually upheld for the original owner, it took an average of seventeen years to resolve them. The Mexican landowners had to pay legal fees throughout that period; face squatters killing livestock and destroying crops; and also deal with the natural disasters mentioned above. In order to raise cash, many had to take out short-term mortgages, with interest rates as high as 4 to 7 percent a month. Some also had to resort to selling off portions of their land. Since there were few individuals in these territories with enough resources to purchase land, they often colluded to drive down the selling price. The end result was that, within forty years from annexation, very few of the large landholders from the Mexican period still owned their original tracts of land.

Thus, even though the Treaty of Guadalupe Hidalgo guaranteed Mexicans in the annexed territories the full rights of US citizens, in practice the situation was very different. The ability of Mexicans to exercise their citizenship rights depended on where they were located, and often on their class status. As Mexicans lost their land, their class status eroded. This led to a decrease in their political power. Even though Mexicans had held high political office in many states during the first two decades after annexation, by the turn of the twentieth century few of them held political office (except in New Mexico[4]), and voting rates were down across the board. At the turn of the twentieth century, the Mexican-origin community was left in a subordinate status to the Anglo population. As a result of racial segregation, Mexicans at the turn of the twentieth century lived and worked largely in separation from the Anglos. The population was relatively stable and there was little immigration from Mexico.

The Porfiriato and the Beginning of Mass Mexican Migration to the United States

Mexico's defeat in the Mexican–American War led to even greater political upheaval in Mexico: from 1850 to 1876, the country was in civil war. Political instability ended in 1876, when General Porfirio Díaz, a former associate of the Mexican hero Benito Juárez, seized power. He held office for thirty-five years and dramatically transformed the Mexican economy. Under Díaz, the United States began to play a dominant role in the Mexican economy, a role it maintains to the present day.

When Díaz took office, the United States and Britain were in the midst of the industrial revolution. Díaz's goal was to follow suit, bringing Mexico into the modern age. To do that, he fundamentally restructured the economy, particularly in agriculture and landowner-ship. During the colonial period, the Catholic church had held indigenous tribal lands in trust for the native American populations. Some of these corporate titles were broken up when the newly independent Mexican government secularized the mission system in 1844. At that time, the lands attached to the missions were put up for individual sale and formed the basis of much of the south western *hacienda* economy. In central Mexico, however, many of these corporate landholdings were not tied to a mission, but rather attached to native American villages which were held in trust for future generations. Díaz abolished these systems, opening up the lands for private use. The result was a significant increase in landlessness among the peasantry. Those who, until then, had been subsistence farmers now had to move to urban areas in order to find wage labor.

The availability of this labor force was an important part of Díaz's modernization plan; workers were needed to provide labor for new export industries. His government strongly encouraged foreign investment, the bulk of which came from the United States. Railroads were the cornerstone of this economic strategy. The United States invested in building railroads in northern Mexico that would link with growing rail lines across the south western United States. By 1902, US railroad investment in Mexico totaled $281 million; fully 80 percent of all railroad investment in Mexico came from the United States.[5] The railroads were used to develop three main industries in Mexico: mining, export agriculture, and oil production. Mexico used the new lines to export their raw materials and to import the tools, machinery, and other products they needed to develop these economic sectors. But these sectors were heavily dependent on foreign capital, and largely owned by foreign firms. It is estimated that by 1910 half of the national wealth was owned by foreigners. American interests, in particular, owned three quarters of all mining production and half of the oil fields, which gave them significant influence over the direction of the Mexican economy and its politics.[6]

Newly landless peasants, with the help of these new railroads, left their tribal lands to move north, in search of work. It is estimated that 300,000 Mexicans moved from southern to northern Mexico during the Porfiriato. This internal Mexican migration could be seen as the first step towards Mexican migration to the United States. The railroads and American companies investing in Mexico would serve as a conduit to the continued northward migration.

Many scholars argue that it was the social upheaval caused by the Mexican Revolution, a bloody conflict which occurred from 1910 to 1920, that led to the first major wave of Mexican migration to the United States. Table 3.1 summarizes Mexican migration to the United States from 1904 to 1997. A closer examination at the number of yearly arrivals from Mexico after the turn of the century reveals that significant increases in Mexican migration to the United States began in 1908 and grew dramatically in 1909 and 1910, before the revolution had taken root. Similarly, migration levels continued to grow throughout the 1920s, despite there being an end to political violence in Mexico.

Table 3.1 Mexican Migration to the United States, 1900–1997

Year	Number of immigrants
1904	1,009
1905	2,637
1906	1,997
1907	1,406
1908	6,067
1909	16,251
1910	18,691
1911	19,889
1912	23,238
1913	11,926
1914	14,614
1915	12,340
1916	18,425
1917	17,869
1918	18,524
1919	29,818
1920	52,361
1921	30,758
1922	19,551
1923	63,768
1924	89,336
1925	32,964
1926	43,316
1927	67,721
1928	59,016
1929	40,154
1930	12,703
1931	3,333
1932	2,171
1933	1,936
1934	1,801
1935	1,560
1936	1,716

Table 3.1 *continued*

Year	Number of immigrants
1937	2,347
1938	2,502
1939	2,640
1940	2,313
1941	2,824
1942	2,378
1943	4,172
1944	6,598
1945	6,702
1946	7,146
1947	7,558
1948	8,384
1949	8,083
1950	6,744
1951	6,153
1952	9,079
1953	17,183
1954	30,645
1955	43,702
1956	61,320
1957	49,321
1958	26,791
1959	22,909
1960	32,708
1961	41,476
1962	55,805
1963	55,986
1964	34,448
1965	40,686
1966	47,217
1967	43,034
1968	44,716
1969	45,748

Table 3.1 *continued*

Year	Number of immigrants
1970	44,821
1971	50,324
1972	64,209
1973	70,411
1974	71,863
1975	62,552
1976	74,449[a]
1977	44,646
1978	92,681
1979	52,479
1980	56,680
1981	101,268
1982	56,106
1983	59,079
1984	57,820
1985	61,290
1986	66,753
1987	72,511
1988	95,170
1989	405,660
1990	680,186
1991	947,923
1992	214,128
1993	126,642
1994	111,415
1995	90,045
1996	163,743
1997	146,680

a Includes 58,354 entrants, plus 16,095 added due to changes in recordkeeping (transitional quarter).

Source: Susan B. Carter, Scott Sigmund Gartner, Michael R. Haines, Alan L. Olmstead, Richard Sutch, and Gavin Wright, eds, *Historical Statistics of the United States. Millennial Edition Online.* New York: Cambridge University Press, 2006, Series Ad162–172, pp. 1–571–574.

Thus Mexican migration flows to the United States are better explained by economic restructuring and by US involvement in the Mexican economic development policy starting in the late nineteenth century. These factors initiated an internal migration process in Mexico that led to an increasing movement from Mexico into the United States. US business interests and the US government facilitated this movement. US companies regularly sent recruiters to Mexico to bring back workers, often paying for their transportation costs. The US government and Congress, in response to strong lobbying from these business interests, supported Mexican migration by setting no limitations on the numbers of migrants who could enter the United States from the western hemisphere. This happened in spite of the fact that the US Congress severely limited European-origin migration through the 1924 National Origins Act. The US–Mexico border, as we understand it today, did not exist until 1925, when the United States created the Border Patrol to enforce the 1924 National Origins Act. Many in Congress were concerned that southern Europeans would use the Mexican border to cross into the United States. The Border Patrol was not meant to impede Mexican migration. Many Mexicans had family or other connections on the other side of the border and regularly traveled back and forth. Mexican workers were encouraged by US companies to harvest in the fields of California or to work in the steel mills of Indiana. Their work in the US helped them to support their families in Mexico, taking pressure off the Mexican government and providing cheap labor to a variety of business interests in the United States.

Deportations and US Immigration Policy

There were no restrictions on migration from the western hemisphere to the United States until 1965. The exclusion of Mexicans from the quota system was the result of heavy lobbying from south western agribusiness. They argued that Mexican labor was needed because Mexicans were physically better suited than whites to working long hours under the hot sun and that Mexican labor was safe because Mexicans would behave like 'homing pigeons' and return home once the work was done. The Mexican government, on the other hand, supported Mexican migrants traveling to the United States to work throughout the harvest season because that gave them access to wages which would allow them to subsist even though their plots of land in Mexico were too small to sustain their families.

So even those who argued in favor of Mexican migration to the United States did it on the assumption that Mexicans would eventually go back home. The intention was not to create a permanent Mexican population in the United States. This position was supported by periodic deportation programs undertaken by the United States government. During the Great Depression in the 1930s, many in the media began to blame the country's economic problems on Mexican migration. The government started a deportation campaign, requiring that Mexicans about to receive any kind of government aid should 'volunteer' to return to Mexico before receiving that aid. The largest deportation campaign was in Los Angeles: it is estimated that 500,000 Mexicans living there were deported with the assistance of the Los Angeles Police Department, although most of them (an estimated 60 percent) were US citizens. Another economic recession occurred after the Korean War in the 1950s. Again, the US' economic problems were blamed on Mexican migrants. The US government began 'Operation Wetback', which resulted in 1.3 million Mexicans being removed from the United States.

Ironically, Operation Wetback occurred less than a decade after the start of the Bracero Program, a contract labor program begun in 1942 to provide temporary Mexican workers for US agriculture during the Second World War. It is estimated that over 500,000 Mexican contract workers were imported into the United States through this program.[7] The Bracero Program remained in effect until 1964 – which meant that, as the United States was paying to deport Mexicans under Operation Wetback, it was also paying to bring Mexicans into the United States to work as contract laborers. This obvious contradiction highlights the complexity, and the mixed sets of economic interests, that lie at the heart of US immigration policy and underlie many of our immigration problems in the present day.

Another US policy which would affect Mexican migration patterns was the United States government's support for the development of *maquiladora* assembly plants (border-zone assembly plants) along the US–Mexico border. One of the concerns the Mexican government had in 1964, when the Bracero Program came to an end, was how they could provide employment to this labor force. Working in concert with the US government, the Mexican government developed the Maquiladora Program in order to create jobs for workers in Mexico. Companies were allowed to import unfinished components into Mexico without paying tariffs, so long as the finished products were re-exported into the United

States. Most of the companies taking advantage of this program were American companies. They were able to benefit from paying lower wages for final assembly. Mexico benefited too, because the plants created jobs and provided the government with a much needed source of foreign exchange.

The *maquila* assembly plants did create many problems, however. The first was that they failed to provide jobs for former *braceros* (contract laborers brought to the US under the Bracero Program). In practice, US companies preferred to hire women for these jobs because they were seen as more malleable and less likely to form unions. This preference caused friction within Mexican households, because men had fewer economic opportunities in the *maquila* areas than the women, and some argue that this change in the gender dynamics within families has led to increases in violence against women in these border towns.[8] The plants also did little to help the Mexican economy. Since the parts were produced outside Mexico and the final products were immediately exported, the plants provided no linkages to the Mexican economy. They did not lead to the development of new industries or to any significant technology transfer between the production companies and their Mexican counterparts. They simply provided low-wage jobs. Those job opportunities afforded by the *maquiladoras* also led to even greater increases in northward internal migration within Mexico. Many Mexicans from the southern provinces traveled to the border areas in order to seek work in these plants. The result was an exponential increase in population across many border towns. This phenomenon put great stress on the area's infrastructure, leading to increases in disease, crime, and pollution in the border region. Nor would the northward movement of the Mexican workers stop at the border. Once *maquila* workers gained factory skills, many chose to continue their migration into the United States in order to seek opportunities there.

The problems surrounding the Maquiladora Program reflect deeper issues related to economic development in Mexico. Since the end of the Mexican Revolution, the Mexican government has pursued an industrialization strategy which has done little to equalize the country's distribution of wealth or to decrease poverty substantially within the Mexican population. The United States, in its capacity as Mexico's largest trading partner, has played an important role in maintaining these development policies, particularly in terms of allowing Mexican migration to the United States to serve as a 'safety valve' for the Mexican regime. Migration to the United States provides economic opportunities to

Mexicans which make it possible for their families and communities to survive in Mexico, in particular through the remittances Mexican workers send home. For example, in 2003 Mexico received nearly $13.3 billion in remittances, an amount equivalent to about 140 percent of what Mexico received in foreign direct investment, and 71 percent of what the Mexican government earned from oil exports. Also the Mexican elite has benefited greatly from these policies and from its relationship with the United States. Thus the economic links between the two countries, in terms of the movement of labor and capital, are important to both of them and help to explain why Mexicans constitute the largest immigrant group in the United States.

US policy toward Mexican migration changed significantly in 1965. The Immigration and Nationality Act of 1965 placed limits on Mexican immigration for the first time in US history. But it also emphasized family reunification as a key policy goal of American immigration policy. Since there was already a significant number of individuals of Mexican origin in the United States, these individuals made up a large proportion of the visas awarded for family reunification. There are no limits on these visas. In addition, after the end of the Bracero Program, US companies, particularly in agriculture, continued to lobby the US government to pass temporary guest-worker programs to provide them with needed labor. Many of these companies continued to recruit these guest workers from Mexico. Thus, as a result of US government policy, of the lack of income redistribution in Mexico, and of direct recruitment of Mexican workers by US companies, immigrants of Mexican origin continue to make up a large proportion of immigrants to the United States, even after the 1965 changes.

Understanding the relationship between Mexican migration and US and Mexican economic interests is important because it not only affects the magnitude of the migration flows, but also determines the areas of Mexico where migrants originate from, the skills they bring with them, the parts of the United States where they end up settling, and, to some extent, the way they are treated by US political and economic institutions upon their arrival. Thus the decisions of individual migrants to leave are not simply the product of their particular preferences, but rather the result of structural constraints on their economic opportunities – constraints which make them decide to leave their country of origin. These migrants' choices, therefore, are embedded within a set of very powerful interests, which have an impact on the opportunities and difficulties they face in the United States.

Mexican Settlement in the United States during the Twentieth Century

The Mexican community in the United States is quite diverse. It consists of the descendants of those who lived in the south west when it became part of the United States. The community also includes recent immigrants and second, third, fourth, or fifth generation descendants of immigrants who settled in the United States for – most commonly – economic reasons. Those Mexican immigrants who began arriving in the United States in larger numbers after the turn of the twentieth century tended to settle in the areas which had formerly been part of Mexico. This was the height of Jim Crow segregation in the United States, and Mexicans, consistent with the way they had been racially constructed

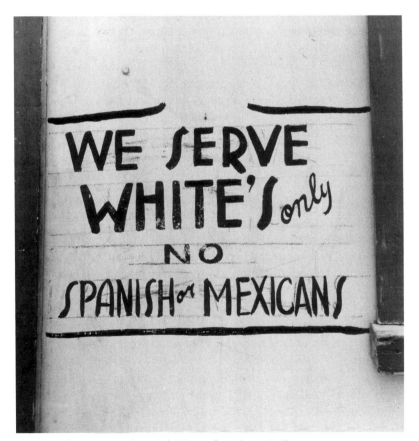

Figure 3.1 'Whites Only': Poster from the 1930s, Texas.
Source: © League of United Latin American Citizens

after annexation, were seen as non-white. So even in those areas which were not part of the 'south' (California, Arizona, New Mexico, Utah, Colorado), Mexicans were legally restricted in the choice of places they could live in, the kinds of jobs they could do, and the schools their children could attend.

During the first half of the twentieth century, Mexican residential segregation was carried out through the use of restrictive covenants. These were codicils added to home deeds which explicitly stated that the owner could not sell the home to anyone of African, Asian, or Mexican origin. These covenants were enforceable by law. In other words, if a landowner chose to ignore the restriction and sold their home to someone of the prohibited racial background, the neighbors could take that landowner to court and bar the sale. US courts upheld the legality of these restrictions until the US Supreme Court ruled that they were unconstitutional in 1948. In addition to housing, sports facilities, particularly pools and playgrounds, were often segregated across the south west. For example, in many places Mexicans had access to public swimming pools only on the day before the pools were cleaned, because Mexican swimmers were seen as 'dirty'. In terms of employment, many skilled trades were closed to non-whites, as were some labor unions, limiting Mexican Americans' access to well paying jobs. Schools throughout the south-west were also segregated. Mexican students were placed in one classroom and often tracked towards home economics (for the females) and vocational training (for the males). In most schools, Mexican students were strongly discouraged from attending high school.

The Jim Crow Laws, particularly in Texas, also had an important impact on Mexican Americans' ability to participate politically.[9] Throughout the south, a number of laws created to limit the black franchise also served effectively to disenfranchise Mexican Americans. The first one concerned poll taxes. These were taxes an individual had to pay in order to vote. Given the low socioeconomic status of many Mexicans, these taxes often put voting out of their economic reach. The second one consisted of literacy tests. These tests were ostensibly designed to ensure that voters were educated and therefore able to make informed electoral choices. In practice, there were no uniform standards for what constituted 'literacy' – it was up to the particular poll worker to determine it, and often Mexican Americans were found to be 'illiterate' just so as to be prevented from voting. The last law was the so-called 'white man's primary'. After the civil war, the south was universally Democratic. The Republican Party had little support in the south because Abraham

Lincoln had been a Republican. This meant that Republican candidates had little (if any) chance of actually winning an election. Thus the actual electoral competition occurred at the primary level, because whatever candidate was chosen to represent the Democratic Party would, in fact, win the general election. States throughout the south, including Texas, restricted voting in the primary election to whites only. The courts found these restrictions to be legal because parties were considered private organizations and the restriction did not apply to the general election. In practice, the result was that African Americans and Mexican Americans were prohibited from having any meaningful effect on the electoral outcomes of these states.

In Texas as well as across the south, the Jim Crow system was sustained by continual violence. Mexican Americans in Texas were often victims of lynchings, deportations, and other kinds of harassment. The Texas Rangers often were involved. The legendary Ranger King Fisher is said to have once been asked by a boy how many men he had killed. He answered: 'Seven.' The boy said: 'I thought it must be more than that,' and Fisher replied: 'I don't count Mexicans.'[10] Vigilante justice was also common. For example, Jesus Romo was being held in custody by officers in California when he was taken by a group of masked men and hanged. The majority of the Mexican Americans lynched between 1848 and 1870 were already in custody when they were taken and hanged.[11] This kind of violence was so customary that in 1921 the *New York Times* reported that in Texas 'the killing of Mexicans without provocation is so common as to pass unnoticed'.[12]

Although there was less overt violence against Mexican Americans outside of Texas, Mexican Americans did not have full access to, or the full protection of, the legal system. They often were victims of police harassment and differential treatment. One example is the 'zoot suit riots' in Los Angeles. 'Zoot suit' is a phrase which describes a popular style of dress employed by the youth of all races during the 1940s. For men, it entailed wearing wide-brimmed hats, broad-shouldered long coats, high-waisted peg-legged trousers and long dangling watch chains, often in bright colors. For women, the style included tight sweaters, short or long flared skirts and large earrings. In Los Angeles, the zoot suits became associated with Mexican Americans, who were called 'gangsters' or *pachucos* in the popular press and were seen as 'loafers' who were not contributing to the war effort. For this reason, in late 1942, clashes between white US servicemen stationed in Los Angeles and Mexican American youths became an almost daily occurrence. The sporadic

Textbox 3.1 Letter from Youth Committee for the Defense of Mexican American Youth

YOUTH COMMITTEE
for the
DEFENSE OF MEXICAN AMERICAN YOUTH
1700 East 22nd Street, Los Angeles (in care of Mrs. Telles)

Reginald Garcia, Chairman
Dora Baca, Vice Chairman
Frank Hermosillo, Secretary
Roger Cordona, Treasurer

Hon. Henry A. Wallace,
Vice President of the United States,
Washington, D.C.

Dear Mr. Wallace:

We are writing you this letter because we heard you speak on the 16th of September here in Los Angeles, and we feel you should know about the bad situation facing us Mexican boys and girls and our whole Spanish-speaking community.

What you said on that day was the truth, and you made us all think and wonder why everything around us was different than it should be.

On the very day you spoke there were 24 Mexican American boys accused of first degree murder. These 24 boys come from our neighborhood. In our neighborhood there are no recreation centers and the nearest movie is about a mile away, We have no place to play so the Police are always arresting us. That's why most of the boys on trial now have a record with the Police, from suspicion even up to robbery. A lot of the boys worked in Defense plants and have brothers in Australia fighting under Gen. MacArthur. Our folks work in some defense plants if they are citizens, but if they are not citizens they don't get jobs even though Mexico is in the war too. Our mothers and fathers would like to help in the Red Cross and Civilian Defense but they cannot because it's all in English. There is still a lot of discrimination in theaters and swimming pools and the Police are always arresting us and searching us by the hundreds when all we want to do is go into a dance or go swimming or just stand around and not bother anybody. They treat us like we are criminals just by being Mexicans or of Mexican descent. The newspapers have made us look like criminals too. They make fun of zoot suits and use the word "Mexicans" like it was a dirty word.

We have talked about all this in our club and we think it is very bad for the war because it is against unity and divides us from the rest of the people. Also some Mexican Nazi papers are saying that we are not satisfied and that we are sabotaging the war. Also there are some people around here that use these things to say that Uncle Sam is no good.

We know that is not true and we also know that us Mexican-American boys and girls can do a lot of things to win the war if someone will give us a chance.

We have got a Defense Club to help the 24 boys on trial and the way we are raising money for that is to collect scrap iron. That way we help the boys and also help the war and also prove that we are not any help to the Fifth Column.

Mr. Wallace, we know that you can help us. Please go and see Mr. Rockefeller and ask him to help us too. He can tell them to give us radio programs in Spanish to tell us how we can help. Also if the Government would print up the speeches of you and President Roosevelt and President Avila Camacho we would distribute them, if they are in Spanish so our folks could read them. There are a lot of things we could do and we will talk about them in our meetings.

Discrimination is what hurts the most, so help us with that particularly because discrimination is the thing that makes the other Americans divide from us. Maybe also you can ask the city to give us places to play. The other thing is to ask the Police to stop arresting us all the time and treat us like criminals because we are Mexican or of Mexican descent.

Mr. Wallace, you helped us very much with your speech on the 16th of September and we need your help more so we can grow up to be good American citizens and win the war.

We don't like Hitler or the Japanese either.

We thank you very much.

Respectfully
(signed)

Source: http://www.pbs.org/wgbh/amex/zoot/eng_filmmore/ps_youth.html (last accessed 14 December 2008)

violence intensified in June of that year, when fifty navy soldiers with concealed weapons left the Naval Reserve Armory to seek out *pachuco* youths. They attacked anyone they saw as a zoot suiter, beating them, stripping them of their clothes, and sometimes lighting the suits on fire. The Los Angeles police was unwilling to step in and protect civilians from the marauding soldiers. One policeman was quoted as saying, after the riots: 'You can say that the cops had a "hands-off" policy during the riots. Well, we represented public opinion. Many of us were in the First World War, and we're not going to pick on kids in the service.'

The rioting intensified over the next few days, with thousands of sailors, soldiers, and marines traveling from San Diego to participate. Taxi drivers offered free trips to soldiers wishing to travel to the riot areas. A Los Angeles newspaper published instructions on how to 'de-zoot' a zoot suiter. A mob of 5,000 people, soldiers and civilians alike, gathered downtown to engage in the violence. Finally, senior military officials brought the riot under control by declaring Los Angeles off-limits to all sailors, soldiers, and marines. The Los Angeles City Council then passed a resolution banning the wearing of zoot suits in public, which became an offence punishable by a 30-day jail term. After several days of rioting, more than 150 Mexican Americans had been injured and police had arrested and charged more than 500 Latino youths for 'rioting' or 'vagrancy', even though most had been victims rather than instigators. No white servicemen were charged. The zoot suit riots are a good example of the differential treatment the Mexican-origin community experienced through law enforcement.

School Segregation

While some school districts in the south west did not segregate Mexican youths, residential and educational segregation frequently went hand in hand. Restrictive real estate covenants made school districts based on neighborhood composition unlikely to be racially integrated. In places like Fort Stockton, Texas, the street that divided the 'white' school from the 'Mexican' school was called Division Street. In the 1930s, Phoenix Arizona had the Washington Carver High School for black students, the Phoenix Indian School for native Americans, and a number of elementary schools, including the Tempe Eighth Street School, for 'Spanish American' youths. In California, the segregation of school children on the basis of race and nationality dated to an 1855 legislative decision which apportioned school funds on the basis of the number of white children, aged between four and eighteen, in each county. The state's largest minority group, Mexican Americans, was concentrated in southern California, making segregated classrooms, if not segregated schools, the norm.

It was often argued that segregated schools were necessary in order to 'Americanize' their Mexican American students. These programs were supported by educational theories of the time, which emphasized the exclusive use of English and the adoption of American values and work habits. Such programs were supported by laws such as Arizona's Title XIX. Passed in 1899, the law stipulated English as the language of instruction in Arizona public schools. In the 1920s and 1930s, this law would be used to justify the segregation of Spanish-speaking students. This separation of Mexican students from whites was also supported by social prejudices that viewed Mexicans as a threat to the health and morals of the rest of the community.

Yet even under these circumstances, Mexican parents across the southwest sought educational equity for their children. In Lemon Grove,

California, white and Mexican American students had always attended the same schools. But in January 1931 the local school board decided to build a separate facility for the Mexican American pupils. The new facility consisted of a two-room barn containing second-hand equipment, supplies, and books. For many of the students, the new school was much further away from their homes than the old one. The Mexican parents formed *el Comité de Vecinos de Lemon Grove* (the Committee of Lemon Grove Neighbors) and decided to boycott the school. Every family except one kept their children home. With the assistance of the Mexican consul, the *comité* hired attorneys on behalf of the eighty-five children affected and filed suit. During the trial, the Lemon Grove board members justified their actions on the grounds that a separate facility was necessary to meet the needs of non-English-speaking children. To counter this argument, the students took the stand in order to prove their knowledge of English. In *Alvarez* v. *Lemon Grove School District*, Judge Claude Chambers ruled in favor of the parents and ordered the 'immediate reinstatement' of the Mexican children to their old school. In bringing forward one of the first successful efforts supporting school desegregation in the United States, this case shows the ability of Mexican immigrants to challenge their second-class status. In this instance they used the Mexican consul's office to secure the resources to challenge a policy which, they believed, hurt their US-born children. This was possible despite the fact that the 1930s was a period of heightened animosity towards Mexican immigrants, as is shown by the ongoing deportation and repatriation campaigns.

In the 1940s, Southern California was the site of another significant school desegregation case: *Méndez* v. *Westminster*. The *Méndez* v. *Westminster* ruling led to the desegregation of schools in the State of California and is widely believed to have laid the groundwork for the historical 1954 Supreme Court ruling in *Brown* v. *Board of Education*. The case began in the fall of 1944, when Soledad Vidaurri took her children and those of her brother, Gonzalo Méndez, to enroll them at the 17th Street School in Westminster, California. Although they were cousins and shared a Mexican heritage, the Méndez and Vidaurri children looked quite different: Sylvia, Gonzalo Jr and Gerónimo Méndez had dark skin, hair and eyes, while Alice and Virginia Vidaurri had fair complexions and features. An administrator looked at the five children. He said that Alice and Virginia could stay. But their dark-skinned cousins would have to register at the Hoover School, the town's 'Mexican school', which was located a few blocks away. Furious at such blatant discrimination, Vidaurri returned home without registering any of the children in either school.

After their children were turned away, the Méndezes organized other Mexican parents and together they persuaded the school board to propose a bond issue for the construction of a new, integrated school. When voters failed to support the measure, the school board refused to take further action. In 1945, with the help of LULAC, the parents, acting on behalf of their own children and of 5,000 others, filed suit against the Westminster, Garden Grove, Santa Ana, and El Modena school districts in Orange County.

The plaintiffs sought desegregation of California's schools on the grounds that perpetuation of school admissions on the basis of race or nationality violated the Fifth and Fourteenth Amendments of the US Constitution. The school districts argued that the federal court did not have jurisdiction over school issues, and that in any case student segregation was necessary so that Mexican students could become 'Americanized', which they deemed necessary because the Mexican students could not speak English. Yet the racial bias underlying these 'Americanization' programs became apparent when Garden Grove School District Superintendent James L. Kent testified under oath that he believed people of Mexican descent to be intellectually, culturally, and morally inferior to Europeans and Americans. In his testimony, Kent also said he believed Mexicans were inferior in personal hygiene, in ability, and in their economic outlook, and he stated that even if a Mexican child had the same academic qualifications as a white child, he would never allow the Mexican child to enroll in an Anglo school.

Federal Judge Paul McCormick ruled in favor of Méndez and his co-plaintiffs on 18 February 1946. His opinion was stated as follows:

> The common segregation attitudes and practices of the school authorities in the defendant school districts in Orange County pertain solely to children of Mexican ancestry and parentage. They are singled out as a class for segregation . . . The equal protection of the laws pertaining to the public school system in California is not provided by furnishing in separate schools the same technical facilities, text books and courses of instruction to children of Mexican ancestry that are available to the other public school children regardless of their ancestry. A paramount requisite in the American system of public education is social equality. It must be open to all children by unified school association regardless of lineage.[13]

The school boards appealed against the decision, which attracted national attention. The American Civil Liberties Union, National Association for the Advancement of Colored People (NAACP), the American Jewish Congress, and the Japanese American Citizens League filed briefs in support of desegregation. The case is seen as a precursor to *Brown* v.

Board of Education because Judge McCormick based his ruling not only on legal precedent but also on social science research, as the Supreme Court would later do in the *Brown* case. The case also marked the first time when a federal court concluded that the segregation of Mexican Americans in public schools was a violation of state law and was unconstitutional under the Fourteenth Amendment. The case led directly to the passing of the Anderson Bill in 1947, which repealed all California school codes mandating segregation and was signed into law by then California Governor Earl Warren – who seven years later would preside as Chief Justice over the *Brown* case.

Méndez v. *Westminster* established precedent for important cases in other states as well. In Texas, again with the aid of LULAC, Mexican American parents, led by Minerva Franco, successfully overturned the segregationist policies of the local schools. In *Minerva Franco* v. *Bastrop Independent School District* (1947), federal district Judge Ben Rice cited the *Méndez* case in his own decision. Moving beyond the California ruling, Rice specifically declared unconstitutional even the segregation of Mexican Americans into separate classrooms within otherwise integrated schools. Another federal district court followed suit by striking down school segregation in Arizona in 1950.

These rulings, of course, only outlawed the legally based segregation of Mexican students. In practice, residential segregation resulted in continued *de facto* segregation of Mexicans across the south west, a phenomenon which led scholars to estimate that by 1973 a larger proportion of Mexican children attended segregated schools in Los Angeles than they had in 1947.

Mexican American Political Organizing

As the organizing around these school desegregation cases shows, Mexican Americans did not simply accept their second-class status; the community organized itself and worked to defend itself from the beginning. From the nineteenth century on, they organized groups called *mutualistas* – mutual aid societies – who helped these communities to deal with economic uncertainty. Many of these organizations emphasized economic protection, education, and community service. They provided sickness and burial insurance, loans, legal aid, social and cultural activities, libraries, classes, leadership opportunities, and locations to house *barrio* ('neighborhood') events. *Mutualista* membership tended to be restricted to men, but many had a separate 'ladies' auxiliary' which the women could join; this allowed the men and women to work together in parallel, if separate, organizations.[14]

In California, Mexican Americans also were very active in their workplaces. The turn of the century brought increases in labor activism across the board, and Mexican American workers were very much involved. In Oxnard in 1903, about 800 Mexican and Japanese sugar beet workers joined together to demand better wages and to end what they saw as an unfair contracting system. They created the Japanese–Mexican Labor Association (JMLA), the first multi-racial labor union in the United States. This was no easy task. At their meetings, all discussions were carried out in Spanish, Japanese, and English. Despite these difficulties, the JMLA was able to recruit 1,200 workers to join, which constituted over 90 percent of the sugar beet work force. The sugar beet farmers hired strike-breakers, which led to community tensions and, in March of that year, to violence. Shots broke out over an altercation; three workers (one Mexican and two Japanese) were wounded and a Mexican worker was killed. The resulting scandal brought the local farmers to the negotiating table, and ultimately won the JMLA a victory. Shortly afterwards the JMLA petitioned to join the American Federation of Labor (AFL). The AFL refused to allow the Japanese workers to join its union, but was willing to include the Mexican workers. But the Mexican JMLA members refused to create a union without their Japanese colleagues and declined the opportunity to join the AFL. Without the AFL's organizational and financial support, the JMLA disbanded after a few years.

Wheatland in California was another site of labor organizing which turned violent. In August 1913, a group of about 2,000 hop pickers working at the Durst Ranch, many of whom were of Mexican origin, gathered around a platform to hear speeches by representatives of the International Workers of the World (IWW). They were considering striking to protest their abominable working conditions. The pickers earned $1.90 for a 12-hour day of work, and 10 cents of each dollar was held back by the owners as a 'bonus' to be paid to them if they remained until the end of the harvest season. They had to sleep outside, many of them without blankets; had to share nine shallow and doorless privies; and their drinking water was contaminated. During the rally, local law enforcement authorities attempted to rush the platform to arrest one of the speakers, IWW organizer Richard Ford. Part of the platform collapsed and a fight broke out. The sheriffs began firing into the crowd, leaving four dead, including a young boy who had been walking by. Hundreds of IWW members were arrested; Ford, along with another

IWW organizer not present at the event, were also arrested and eventually convicted of second degree murder. Even though the strike never happened, the riot, subsequent trial, and ensuing publicity brought the plight of farm workers to the public's attention. This led to the passing of more than three dozen Californian state laws designed to improve the conditions of working people. These included an act creating a commission to investigate farms statewide and, as the commission found conditions generally not much better than those on the Durst Ranch, the state began enforcing regulations which set strict standards for farm-worker sanitation and living accommodations.[15]

Mexican Americans in Texas also organized themselves to protest against their second-class status. In 1915, a group of Texas Mexicans called on blacks, Asians and Indians in Texas to rise up against their 'Yankee oppressor' and to establish a new country. When sixty of the rebels raided King Ranch's Norias Division, a group of Texas Rangers was called in and they killed between 100 and 300 Texas Mexicans. Many Texas Mexicans, however, opposed the revolt and turned to more traditional forms of organization. A group of such reformers, many of whom were veterans from the First World War, gathered together in Corpus Christi in 1929, to found the League of United Latin American Citizens (LULAC). Their goal was to fight segregation and discrimination. Given the overall hostility towards Mexicans in Texas at the time, LULAC chose to emphasize their American roots. They adopted the American flag as their official flag, 'America the Beautiful' as their official song, and the 'George Washington Prayer' as their official prayer. They also used Robert Rules of Order[16] as the governing rules during meetings and conventions and conducted all their business in English.

Although LULAC is often described as a Texan organization, it had chapters in New Mexico, Arizona, Colorado, and California. Even though there was contact and coordination among the LULAC chapters, each state organization emphasized different issues and focused on different kinds of social problems. In Texas, because segregation was such a major issue, LULAC focused its energies on fighting discrimination through lawsuits and other kinds of political organizing. In New Mexico, since segregation was present but not as blatant, social issues were more important. The role of women also varied across the organizations. Even though officially women were allowed, after 1934, to organize separate women's chapters, most chose instead to form women's auxiliaries to the men's organizations. In Texas, these auxiliaries were most often relegated to 'women's work' – for instance providing food and the like – and were kept separate from the men. In New Mexico, women and men were involved in more joint endeavors, and women attained organizational positions at state and national level sooner than the Texas women.[17] Interestingly, in 1939 the Albuquerque LULAC worked to establish a Hispano/Latin American Studies Program at the University of New Mexico, marking the first efforts for this kind of program within a higher education setting. Thus the LULAC case is highly reflective of the diversity of experience among Mexican Americans along the lines of geography, gender, and class. Because the central issues facing the individuals who made up the organization varied in important ways, so did their organizational focus and collective efforts. Across the south west, the LULAC chapters organized voter registration drives and campaigns to pay Mexican American voters' poll taxes, but much of this work was done quietly; officially they were not a political organization. The organization was explicitly apolitical; their main goal was to fight the effects of racism, discrimination, and segregation in the Mexican American community.

Another group working to advance Latino civil rights was *El Congreso de Pueblos de Habla Española* (the Congress of Spanish-Speaking Peoples). This was the first national Latino civil rights group organized in the United States. The driving force behind this effort was Luisa Moreno, a Guatemalan immigrant labor activist who was Vice-President of the United Cannery, Agricultural, Packing, and Allied Workers of America (UCAPAWA–CIO).[18] In her work with the UCAPAWA, Moreno successfully organized Mexican American and Jewish female cannery workers, who were able to win important wage increases from their employers and, during the Second World War, child care for their children.

To organize the *El Congreso* meeting, Moreno worked together with Los Angeles activists Josefina Fierro, Eduardo Quevedo, and Bert Corona, all of whom would take on leadership roles within *El Congreso*. The meeting was held on 28–30 April 1939; between 1,000 and 1,500 delegates attended who represented over one hundred twenty organizations. Delegates drafted a comprehensive platform, calling for an end to segregation in public facilities, housing, education, and employment. They also endorsed the rights of immigrants to live and work in the United States without fear of deportation, and they advocated the preservation of Latino culture and the creation of Latino Studies departments in US universities. This organization was very different from LULAC. It was explicitly political and focused on economic, social, and political rights – for citizens and non-citizens alike. Even though it was meant to become a national organization, in the end the delegates were able to organize only a few chapters in southern California. It is important to remember that the 1930s were a period of strong anti-communism and of organized deportation campaigns, particularly in California and the south west. *El Congreso*'s advocacy of immigrant rights was politically very courageous within this larger context. The larger context also goes probably a long way towards explaining why *El Congreso* was not able to expand as widely as the original organizers had hoped. Many feared being seen as communists and deported, a fear which was well justified, given that many of the organization's founders were in fact deported for being radicals. *El Congreso*'s platform is important because many of the basic tenets laid out in 1939 would strongly influence the goals set out by activists in the Chicano Movement during the 1960s.

Thus up until the Second World War Mexican Americans had been engaging in organizing labor and in forming organizations to combat the segregation and discrimination which the community faced. But few of these organizations saw themselves as being explicitly 'political'. This situation changed with the creation of the American GI Forum (AGIF) after the Second World War. It is estimated that 750,000 Mexican Americans served in the Second World War, where, in proportion to their numbers, they earned the highest number of medals of honor among all minority groups. Yet, when these soldiers came home, they encountered difficulty in receiving the veterans' benefits they were eligible for, for instance medical services from the Veterans' Administration or access to educational benefits under the GI Bill. To address these concerns, Dr Hector García founded the AGIF in Corpus Christi, Texas in 1948. Although the members of the AGIF initially were concerned with veterans' issues, their work soon spread into non-veterans' issues such as voting rights, jury selection, and educational desegregation and they advocated for the civil rights of all Mexican Americans. Eventually the AGIF would become one of the most influential Mexican American political organizations in the United States.

The AGIF's first campaign was on behalf of Felix Longoria, a Mexican American private who had been killed in the Philippines in the line of duty. Longoria lived in a small town called Three Rivers. That town had only one funeral home, which was restricted to whites. When Private Longoria's body was returned home, the funeral home refused to allow his family to use the chapel for the wake. The case received national attention. Dr García sent telegrams to fifteen government officials, denouncing the funeral home's actions. Then Texas Senator Lyndon

Johnson was the only official to respond. He arranged to have Longoria buried in Arlington National Cemetery with full military honors. This success brought the AGIF to national attention, and chapters were opened throughout the country; the groups also formed a women's and youth auxiliary.

The AGIF, along with the League of United Latin American Citizens, was a plaintiff in the case of Pete Hernández, a farm worker accused of murder; this was a case brought to the Supreme Court of the United States. In its decision, *Hernandez* v. *Texas* (1954), the court ruled that Mexican Americans and all other racial groups in the United States had equal protection under the Fourteenth Amendment of the US Constitution. The court held that Hernández was denied equal protection because he was convicted by an all-white jury; that all-white juries existed because of the *de facto*, systematic exclusion of Mexican Americans from jury service in Jackson County, Texas, where Hernández was tried.[19] Until this decision, because Mexican Americans were legally defined as 'white', they were seen as not experiencing discrimination in jury selection, since an all-white jury was made up of individuals of the same 'race'. The *Hernandez* decision was the first one in which the Supreme Court held that 'nationality' merited protection under the Fourteenth Amendment as well.

The GI Forum was different from LULAC in a number of ways. It was made up of Second World War veterans, which made it unnecessary for them to 'prove' their 'Americanness' (as LULAC had to) and provided them with instant moral credibility. The Longoria experience is an excellent case in point. Funeral homes in Texas had long been segregated and had long denied Mexican Americans and African Americans the use of their services. This practice only became controversial because Longoria was a veteran who had died in service to his country. In the face of that sacrifice, it became difficult to justify such overt discrimination against him.

In California the post-Second World War period also brought new kinds of political organization among Mexican Americans. In 1947 Antonio Ríos, Edward Roybal, and Fred Ross, Sr, founded the Community Service Organization (CSO). The CSO initially concentrated on organizing citizenship drives, voter registration, and voter turnout drives in Mexican American communities, all across California. Within two years, more than 5,000 people had joined the CSO and the latter had established chapters in thirty-five cities throughout California. The organization achieved its first major success in 1949, when it was instrumental in electing Edward Roybal to the Los Angeles City Council. Roybal was the first Mexican American to serve on the council during the twentieth century. The CSO was successful at getting Mexican Americans elected to local political office across the state, and would remain a major force in California politics through the 1960s. The CSO was significant not only because of its many political successes, but also because it served as the training ground for subsequent Mexican American political activists such as César Chávez and Dolores Huerta, two of the key organizers of the United Farm Workers movement.

César Chávez became a CSO organizer in 1952 and quickly rose to the head of the organization. In that position he worked closely with Dolores Huerta, a veteran political and labor organizer.[20] After working with the CSO for a decade, Chávez urged Huerta to leave the CSO and to join him in order for the two to form the (predominantly Mexican American) National Farm Workers Association (NFWA). Despite improvements in work standards which had been implemented in California after the Wheatland strike, farm workers were not entitled to collective bargaining rights because they were not included under the 1935 National Labor Relations Act. In April 1965 the Agricultural Workers Organizing Committee (AWOC), a group consisting mostly of Filipino grape workers, went on strike in Delano, demanding the federal minimum wage. One week later, the National Farm Workers Association voted to join their fight. The two groups united to form the United Farm Workers Organizing Committee (UFWOC). In 1966, in addition to the strike, the UFWOC decided to organize a boycott of Schenley liquor, one of the largest grape producers in California. To raise awareness about their cause, the UFWOC organized a 300-mile march to Sacramento, which garnered national attention. Many Mexican American college students participated in the 1966 march and began supporting the boycott activities. The success of the initial boycott led the UFWOC to call for a national boycott of table grapes. In 1969 the grape growers conceded and signed a contract with the UFWOC. They agreed to provide higher wages, a medical plan, fresh water and toilets in the fields, and to decrease the farm-workers' exposure to dangerous pesticides. In 1972 the UFWOC was accepted into the AFL–CIO and changed its name to the United Farm Workers Union (UFW).

The UFW grape boycott is important because it taught an entire generation of Mexican American youths about the effectiveness of collective action. This generation of Mexican Americans, because of the educational opportunities afforded by the GI Bill and by the post-Second World War expansion of the American university system, was able to attend college at much higher rates than ever before. On campus, students were informed about the work of the UFW and introduced to other kinds of political organizing. Many joined the anti-war movement and began to protest against the unequal levels of educational opportunities available to Mexican American children in public schools. This work, which took place among youths both on college campuses and in the general Mexican American community, would serve as the foundation for the Chicano Movement. But the transition to a large-scale social movement only occurred after the many decades of political organizing which the Mexican American political and labor organizations across the south west had engaged in.

Mexican Americans and Electoral Politics

The Second World War was a watershed because of the changes it wrought in Mexican American political organizing, and also in the attitudes of the country at large. Given that the US enemy was fascism, including Hitler's ideology of white racial superiority, it became difficult to justify racial segregation in the United States, because those justifications were often similar to Hitler's arguments about the hierarchy of races. Thus there was a great deal of change in US racial politics after the Second World War. The year 1948 was especially groundbreaking. In that year, President Truman desegregated the US armed forces; the Supreme Court outlawed the use of racially based residential restrictive covenants; and the California Supreme court struck down the ban against racial intermarriage and racial segregation in the state's public schools. These changes did not simply happen; they were the result of decades of political and legal work on the part of organizations like the NAACP and LULAC. The new Mexican American organizations coming out of the Second World War, for instance the GI Forum and the CSO, moved to expand these gains and to increase Mexican American political influence at the local, state, and national levels. Throughout the 1950s, both organizations worked towards putting an end to segregation and getting Mexican Americans elected to political office.

They were joined by a new, explicitly political Mexican American organization which was formed in 1959: the Mexican American Political Association (MAPA). Bolstered by the CSO's electoral success, MAPA was formed by 150 political activists in California and in response to their perception that the California Democratic Party was not supporting Mexican American candidates. Two Mexican Americans had been nominated for statewide office in California during the 1950s: Edward

Roybal for lieutenant governor in 1954 and Henry López for secretary of state in 1958. The Democratic Party strongly discouraged both candidates from running and subsequently did not provide support to either campaign. During the López campaign, some Democratic Party officials even refused to join López on the campaign platform. López ended up being the only statewide candidate from the Democratic Party to lose during that year.[21] MAPA's goal was to address this problem, to increase Mexican American political power in California, and to fight for Mexican American civil rights. Edward Roybal, co-founder of the CSO, served as MAPA's first president. To accomplish its goals, MAPA expanded on the work of the CSO, continuing the registration and get-out-the-vote drives, but also lobbying elected officials and working with other civil rights organizations to end segregation.

With John F. Kennedy's candidacy for president in 1960, MAPA and the GI Forum decided to extend this electoral activity to the national level. Mexican Americans supported Kennedy because the 1960 Democratic National Convention endorsed civil rights, school desegregation, equal opportunity, fair housing, and voting rights. The platform included comprehensive legislation for migrant workers – the first such commitment made by the Democratic Party. Kennedy also promised to appoint a Mexican American to an ambassadorship in Latin America. Kennedy began courting the Hispanic vote in June 1959, when he sent a message of congratulations to the national convention of the American GI Forum in Los Angeles; he joined the Forum in June 1960. Together with Dr García, Carlos McCormick, one of Kennedy's senatorial staff members who was also a Forum member, came up with the idea of the 'Viva Kennedy' movement. The movement would be made up of a network of 'Viva Kennedy' clubs which would conduct voter registration and get-out-the-vote drives for the Kennedy campaign. McCormick served as the clubs' national coordinator. In California, MAPA leaders Henry López and Edward Roybal were the state co-chairpersons for 'Viva Kennedy'.

The 'Viva Kennedy' clubs were highly successful in achieving their goals. In Texas, Kennedy won 91 percent of the Mexican American vote. Many believe that the clubs gave Kennedy the margin of victory; Kennedy carried the state by just 30,000 votes. In New Mexico, a state where he won by only 2,000 votes, Kennedy received 70 percent of the Mexican American vote. Kennedy lost to Nixon in California, Arizona, and Colorado, but he won 75 percent of the Mexican American vote in these states. Nationally, Kennedy is estimated to have garnered 85 percent of the Mexican American vote.[22]

Building on this success, Mexican American leaders used these organizational networks on behalf of Mexican American candidates, and they were successful. In 1962, the 'Viva Kennedy' network helped to elect Henry B. González of Texas and Edward Roybal of California to the US Congress. Seeing the importance of national coordination, leaders from LULAC, MAPA, the GI Forum, and the CSO met in order to try to develop greater unity among Mexican American political organizations. The result was the creation of the Political Association of Spanish-Speaking Organizations (PASSO or PASO). Although designed to be a national organization, PASSO was especially strong in Texas, where it constituted the first overtly political statewide Mexican American political organization. Unlike LULAC and the GI Forum, PASSO openly endorsed candidates and engaged in electoral campaigning. It also formed coalitions with African American groups to push for the inclusion of minorities in US politics.

One of PASSO's greatest successes was the role it played in the 1963 Mexican American takeover of the city government in Crystal City, Texas. The majority of the population of this town consisted of rural migrants or workers at the Del Monte plant, the area's largest employer. The Teamsters organized the Del Monte workers and worked with PASSO to build a coalition so as to influence the city's politics. They encouraged Mexican American voters to pay their poll tax and to support Mexican American candidates. As a result, despite intimidation by the Texas Rangers, five Mexican Americans were elected to the city council, a situation which gave them the majority. This voter 'revolt' was covered in the press nationwide, including in the *New York Times* and in the *Wall Street Journal*. Although the coalition was short-lived (it lost control of Crystal City in 1965), it was seen as an important, historic victory.

Mexican American Concerns and the White House

Thus the 'Viva Kennedy' work led to important, growing electoral success for Mexican Americans. Those organizers also hoped that it would lead to political influence on Capitol Hill. Keeping his promise to Mexican American voters, Kennedy appointed Raymond Telles as ambassador to Costa Rica: he was the first Mexican American appointed to a US ambassadorship. Many of the Mexican American leaders who had campaigned for the new president through the 'Viva Kennedy' clubs were, however, disappointed when they did not receive any cabinet-level appointments in the new Administration. In addition, as the civil rights movement began to heat up in the south, there was a perception among the Mexican American leaders that President Kennedy and his successor Lyndon Johnson focused solely on African American racial issues and were ignoring those of the Mexican American community. For example, for its 1964 White House Civil Rights Conference, the Johnson Administration only invited African American leaders; Mexican Americans, Asian Americans, Puerto Ricans, and native Americans were excluded.

Mexican Americans benefited economically from Johnson's 'war on poverty' programs, yet Mexican American leaders wanted more overt support from the president. In particular, they began lobbying Johnson for a White House conference on Mexican American issues. The Johnson Administration had held two conferences on the problems facing African Americans. By 1966, a group of GI Forum members marched in front of the White House on Easter Sunday to express increasing frustration with the White House's unresponsiveness and to protest against the Equal Employment and Opportunity Commission's (EEOC) exclusion of Mexican Americans from a conference in Albuquerque. They called their demonstration a *huelga* ('strike'), to underscore their solidarity with the Californian UFWOC farm-workers, who were on strike. In an effort to ease tensions, Johnson met with leaders from the GI Forum, LULAC, and MAPA in the White House in May 1966. They reiterated their desire for a White House conference on Mexican affairs and requested the appointment of a Mexican American White House Aid. President Johnson rejected the provision of an aid (he is quoted as saying that otherwise every group would want one) but promised to begin planning a conference to be held in spring 1967.[23]

Yet the planning moved slowly. Johnson felt he needed the support of south western state governors, particularly of Texas Governor John Connally, before he could move forward with the conference. Connally refused to respond to White House requests, making Johnson less and less inclined to support a meeting. Mexican American leaders saw that planning was not moving forward and began to get frustrated. On 12 February 1967, the major Californian organizations, 'expressing unanimous frustration, disappointment, and impatience', announced 'their own White House conference on their community problems'.[24] In an attempt to address the growing strain, Johnson's domestic policy advisor Henry McPherson had breakfast with Mexican American leaders on 17 February to discuss the conference planning. In a memo to the president reporting on the meeting, McPherson assessed the leaders as 'pretty level-headed activists [who] told me that the Mexican community wants a conference, expects a conference, will be bitterly disappointed without a conference, and that their bitterness would have serious political consequences.'[25] McPherson concluded by telling the president that 'the Mexicans are a major political factor in five states and we should not risk losing them; that risk is greater if we deny them the conference . . . than if some hell is raised'. President Johnson responded to the memo with a terse 'Keep this trash out of the White House,' effectively vetoing the possibility of any conference on Mexican American issues being held there.[26]

Instead, the White House decided to organize a Mexican American conference to be held in El Paso, Texas, in October 1967 and timed to coincide with President Johnson's signing of the Chamizal Treaty with Mexico – a treaty which resolved the last border dispute between the two nations, returning about three hundred acres of land to Mexico. The meeting was to be organized as a cabinet hearing, with the 1,000 invited leaders being given the opportunity to meet and discuss their issues with a number of cabinet secretaries, including the secretaries of labor, agriculture, health, education, welfare, and housing and urban development. The director of the 'war on poverty' would attend, as would the first Mexican American EEOC commissioner, GI Forum member Vicente Ximenes, the conference organizer. Having waited for years for a conference at the White House, many Mexican American leaders saw this meeting as insufficient. MAPA decided to boycott the meeting as an organization, but to allow individual members to attend if they so chose. César Chávez declined the invitation on account of Johnson's refusal to support the farm workers. Other prominent leaders also refused to attend, citing the exclusion from the meeting of a number of important political figures such as Corky Gonzáles and Reies López Tijerina (who are discussed below, pp. 77–80). In the end, most invitees attended, and the conference included fifty panels on Mexican American issues (five of which addressed women's issues).

Those in opposition to the meeting organized protests outside the hearings. The protesters called their gathering '*La raza unida*', which means 'our people united'. The speakers argued for a new political movement, one which was more militant and radical than what had come before. They expressed their disillusionment with the fruits of two cycles of political activism within partisan presidential campaigns and argued that Mexican Americans needed their own political party – La Raza Unida Party – to achieve their goals. This event reflected the radicalization of many organizers who, up to that point, had believed that their political goals could be reached through traditional electoral politics. The lack of attention to Mexican American issues within the Kennedy and Johnson Administrations made them change their mind and join those members of the community who advocated a more radical approach to political activity. This meeting marked a move towards more radical politics among Mexican Americans and the coming together of three separate political movements which, together, are now commonly referred to as 'the Chicano Movement'.

The Chicano Movement

Even though the political organizing by Mexican American communities in the late 1960s and early 1970s is commonly referred to as 'the Chicano Movement', there was not one unified movement, but rather a number of distinct groups organizing activities in different geographic areas. There was contact among the groups and some attempts at coordination (which we saw above in El Paso in 1967 and will see more of below), but the consolidation was never successful. The 'heyday' of Chicano organizing is considered to go from 1963 (beginning with La Alianza) to 1972. Originally the word *Chicano* was a pejorative for 'Mexican American', but it was purposefully adopted by Mexican American activists in the 1960s as a way to transform a negative stereotype into something positive. The name was meant to denote not only a particular national origin but also a leftist political consciousness. For some members of the community, the use of the name remains controversial to the present day.

Reies López Tijerina and La Alianza

Reies López Tijerina arrived in New Mexico in 1956, 'with the checkered past of a fugitive from the law and the fire of a Bible Belt fundamentalist turned political insurgent'.[27] A former evangelist, he soon became fascinated by the history of land grants in the area. Over the next five years he investigated land grant law extensively and traveled to Mexico and Spain in order to conduct his research. He was convinced that the people of New Mexico had had their land grants stolen, or in any case taken away from them illegally. In order to ensure their rightful return, Tijerina drafted the first plan for *La Alianza Federal de Pueblos Libres* (the Federal Alliance of Free Peoples) in 1962; it called for an alliance of towns and settlers to join together to have their rightful lands returned to them. The group was incorporated officially on 2 February 1963, the 115th anniversary of the signing of the Treaty of Guadalupe Hidalgo, with Tijerina elected president. La Alianza had one goal: the return of historical lands to the 'Hispano' settlers of New Mexico.[28]

La Alianza published a weekly newspaper called *The News Chieftain*, and sent letters to the governments of the United States and Mexico reminding them of their responsibilities under the Treaty of Guadalupe Hidalgo. By 1964 La Alianza had 6,000 members, and that number increased to 14,000 within the following year. La Alianza's 1966 convention included 20,000 people of varied class backgrounds. In 1965 Tijerina began broadcasting a daily radio program, which he turned into a television program in 1966.

The group staged protests and set fires to the homes and barns of Anglo ranchers whom they believed not to have a right to their land. They organized a three-day march from Albuquerque to Santa Fe, at the end of which they met with the state governor and asked him to investigate the theft of communal landholdings. When the governor failed to act, La Alianza began to take more radical action. In 1966 it occupied a section of the Carson National Forest which had been part of the San Joaquín del Río de Chuma land grant. La Alianza proclaimed that area to be the 'Republic of San Joaquín del Río de Chuma'. When two US forest rangers tried to remove La Alianza, they were arrested by it at gunpoint. The rangers were tried, convicted of trespassing, given suspended sentences, and released along with their trucks. After five days of occupation, the members of La Alianza turned themselves in to authorities. Of the 300 people involved, only five, including Tijerina, were arrested. They were charged with assault on the rangers and with the conversion of government property for personal use; their bail was set at $5,000.

Tijerina's legal difficulties increased with an event that La Alianza is most famous for: the Río Arriba Courthouse raid. It is important to keep in mind that in New Mexico individuals of Mexican descent constituted a large proportion of the population and never lost political power completely. Thus the Tierra Amarilla District Attorney was a Mexican American, Alonso Sánchez. He, like many Mexican Americans in New Mexico, was strongly opposed to La Alianza's tactics, particularly their use of violence. On 3 June 1967, Sánchez ordered the police to raid an Alianza meeting and to arrest all those attending. The police conformed and took eleven members into custody; Tijerina managed to avoid arrest. On 5 June, Tijerina led an armed raid on the Río Arriba County Courthouse in Tierra Amarilla, New Mexico. His goal was to free the arrested Alianza members and to place a citizen's arrest on District Attorney Sánchez for violating La Alianza's constitutional right of assembly. When the raid occurred, however, Sánchez was not in the courthouse and two of the sheriff's deputies were shot during the confrontation. Tijerina escaped, but New Mexican authorities organized the largest manhunt in New Mexican history to capture him. Tijerina ended up surrendering to authorities in Albuquerque a few days later and was charged with fifty-four criminal offences, including kidnapping and armed assault. Tijerina was incarcerated for thirty-five days before trial. His case garnered national attention and he was visited in jail by Corky Gonzáles (discussed below, pp. 77–80). At his trial, Tijerina defended himself with the help of two court-appointed lawyers. He was acquitted of all charges stemming from the courthouse raid and was released. Legally, he did not fare as well with regard to the national park occupation. In that trial, he was convicted of destruction of federal property and assault on a federal officer, for which he was sentenced to two years in prison. In early 1970 he was brought to trial again, on charges related to the courthouse raid. The presiding judge rejected the defense's claims of double jeopardy (being tried twice for the same crime, which is barred under the constitution). He was sentenced to another two years in federal prison.

When Tijerina went to prison in 1969, the La Alianza movement lost much of its momentum. One of the terms of his release in 1971 was that he could no longer engage in activities for La Alianza. Even though La Alianza achieved a great deal in terms of raising awareness for land grant issues and some grants were returned, little substantive change resulted from this campaign. Tijerina is still alive and lives in Mexico, where he continues to speak out on issues of justice. With the help of José Angel Gutiérrez (discussed below, pp. 82–84), he published his memoir, *They Called me 'King Tiger': My Struggle for the Land and Our Rights*, in 2000.

Corky Gonzáles and the Crusade for Justice

Rodolfo 'Corky' Gonzáles started his career as a very successful boxer. He retired from boxing in 1953, but his success in the ring gave him celebrity and a name recognition that would help him with his political work. In the late 1950s he began his political career by engaging in traditional politics. A GI Forum member, he joined the Democratic Party and was one of the key organizers of 'Viva Kennedy' in Colorado. He was later made the head of Denver's National Youth Corps, a 'war on poverty' program. Dissatisfied with the degree of attention paid to Mexican American issues and of willingness to support Mexican American candidates which he saw in the Democratic Party in Colorado, he resigned from his post and from the Party in 1965 and began looking for alternatives to address the issues facing the Mexican American community. In a 1966 speech in front of Denver City Hall, Gonzáles stated: 'We are on a crusade for justice.' The name stuck. The crusade worked for better education for Mexican Americans, greater economic opportunities, better housing, an end to segregation in public facilities (including parks and swimming pools), and the return of all land grants stolen after the Mexican–American War.[29] The group ran its own school in Denver, Escuela Tlatelolco, and provided college scholarships to *barrio* youths.

The crusade organized and supported high school walkouts, demonstrations against police brutality, and legal cases seeking Mexican American civil rights. It also organized mass demonstrations against the Vietnam War. Gonzáles began to speak out against the war in 1966, saying: 'Would it not be more noble to portray our great country as a humanitarian nation with the honest intentions of aiding and advising the weak rather than to be recognized as a military power and hostile enforcer of our political aims?' If we, who are privileged to live in the United States, enjoy a prosperity built on the backs of poor nations, he asked, are we not living the good life 'at the expense of the blood and bones of our fellow human beings?'[30]

As a leader, Gonzáles is credited with capturing the attention of the urban Mexican American youth, a feat which he accomplished through the issues he focused on and through a poem he wrote, called 'I am Joaquín', which galvanized the nascent Chicano student movement. In this text he lays out what many see as the defining parameters of the new Chicano identity, emphasizing his indigenous roots and connecting their current struggles to Mexico's long history. The poem was an instant success, and was published in Mexican American newspapers across the country. Its success was attributed to the degree to which it addressed the identity issues facing many of these youths. As the scholar and movement participant Carlos Muñoz writes, 'this search for identity and the dilemmas that it posed are the key to understanding the Chicano Movement of the 1960s . . . the movement was a quest for identity, an effort to recapture what had been lost through the socialization process imposed by US schools, churches, and other institutions' (2007: 60).

Textbox 3.2 Selection from Poem 'I Am Joaquín' by Rodolfo 'Corky' Gonzáles

Yo soy Joaquín,

perdido en un mundo de confusión:

I am Joaquín, lost in a world of confusion,

caught up in the whirl of a gringo society,

confused by the rules, scorned by attitudes,

suppressed by manipulation, and destroyed by modern society.

My fathers have lost the economic battle

and won the struggle of cultural survival.

And now! I must choose between the paradox of

victory of the spirit, despite physical hunger,

or to exist in the grasp of American social neurosis,

sterilization of the soul and a full stomach.

Yes, I have come a long way to nowhere,

unwillingly dragged by that monstrous, technical,

industrial giant called Progress and Anglo success.. . .

I am Cuauhtémoc, proud and noble,

leader of men, king of an empire civilized

beyond the dreams of the gachupín Cortés,

who also is the blood, the image of myself.

Source: http://www.latinamericanstudies.org/latinos/joaquin.htm (last accessed 14 December 2008)

In May 1968, Gonzáles and Tijerina were elected to lead the Chicano contingent to the Washington DC march of Martin Luther King's 'poor people's campaign'. Despite significant setbacks such as the assassination of Dr King and the bombing of Tijerina's Albuquerque home, both of which occurred in April of that year, the march went forward. Gonzáles and Tijerina, with busloads of their followers, joined Mexican Americans from Los Angeles and Texas and a group of Puerto Ricans from New York, in order to take part in the campaign. While there, Gonzáles issued his 'Plan of the Barrio', which called for better housing, education, *barrio*-owned businesses, and restitution of *pueblo* lands. This plan would serve as the blueprint for the 'Plan de Aztlán' (see below). The poor people's campaign was supposed to bring attention to poverty and inequality in the United States and to create a broad-based multi-racial movement for economic justice. Without King's leadership, however, the campaign failed to have a significant impact on economic policies within the United States.

In March 1969, the Crusade for Justice hosted the Annual Chicano Youth Liberation Conference in Denver, which brought together two thousand Chicano youths from across the United States. The 1969 meeting resulted in the production of a document entitled *El Plan Espiritual de Aztlán* ('The Spiritual Plan of Aztlán'), which laid out a nationalist call for Mexican American self-determination and included a set of political, social, and economic demands for Chicanos in the United States. The second Chicano Youth Conference, in 1970, moved this call for self-determination further by leading to the formation of the Colorado Raza Unida Party. The crusade remained active until 1978, and Gonzáles remained involved in Denver politics until his death in 2005, at the age of 76.

Student Groups: UMAS, MAYO and Others

In the mid-1960s, Mexican American student groups began organizing in California, Texas, Arizona, New Mexico, and the mid-west. The students organized groups such as the United Mexican American Students (UMAS), the Mexican American Student Confederation, the Mexican American Student Organization, the Mexican American Youth Organization (MAYO), and others.[31] The first MAYO was co-founded by José Angel Gutiérrez in 1965 at St Mary's College in San Antonio, Texas. Echoing the 1939 platform laid out by the *Congreso de Pueblos de Habla Española*, the student organizations called for increased Mexican American educational opportunities and for programs dedicated to the study of the Mexican American experience. By 1967 there was a number of MAYO groups in existence in Texas and California. In California, student activists were involved in the UFW movement, participating in the 1966 march to Sacramento, delivering food to the strikers, and picketing grocery stores to support the grape boycott.

Their activism reached another level in 1968, when UMAS, in cooperation with other Chicano groups, organized the 'blow-outs' in Los Angeles. One thousand Mexican American students walked out of Lincoln High School in east Los Angeles to protest against the low quality of education they were receiving there. They called for freedom of speech in school, for the hiring of Mexican American teachers and administrators, and for the addition of classes on Mexican American history and culture. By afternoon, several thousands of other students had walked out of five *barrio* schools. When the 'blow-outs' ended one week later, over 10,000 students had walked out of school. The protest made the national news, and the *Los Angeles Times* called it 'the birth of Brown Power'.[32] The mastermind of the strike was not a student but rather a teacher, Sal Castro. He, like many of the activists we have seen, attended college on the GI Bill and had been active in the 'Viva Kennedy' campaign and Democratic Party politics. Disillusioned with the slow pace of change, he believed that Mexican Americans needed their own civil rights movement.[33] He was suspended from his teaching post when the school board learned of his role in the strike.

Three months after the strike, thirteen Mexican American activists were indicted by a Los Angeles County grand jury for their roles in organizing it. Called the 'Los Angeles Thirteen', they were accused of 'willfully destroying the peace and quiet of Los Angeles'.[34] Interestingly, all of the activists targeted by the police were men, despite the fact that Mexican American women played important roles in organizing and coordinating the walk-outs.[35] If convicted, the thirteen could have faced up to sixty-six years in prison. This indictment only increased Chicano student activity across college campuses in California. In Crystal City and Denver, activists organized high school strikes modeled after the Los Angeles actions. This student and youth activity culminated in the 1969 Youth Conference in Denver, which brought together Mexican American youths from across the country and included Puerto Rican youths from Chicago and New York. The conference called for community control over the schools, for the establishment of Chicano Studies programs, and for bilingual education programs designed to ensure Mexican American cultural maintenance.

In California, in 1969, the Chicano Coordinating Council on Higher Education (CCHE) held a conference at the University of California, Santa Barbara, in order to attempt to implement the 'Plan of Aztlán'. At the meeting, the CCHE adopted *El Plan de Santa Bárbara*: A Chicano Plan for Higher Education. The plan outlines a proposed curriculum for Chicano/Latino Studies, including laying out a role for the community in Chicano education. The plan also is the founding document for *El Movimiento Estudiantil Chicano de Aztlán* (the Chicano Student Movement of Aztlán or MEChA). The various Mexican American student organizations agreed to drop their names in favor of being called MEChA. The document laid out two goals for the new organization: (1) to remain tied to the social life of its communities and to continue to work for Chicano social, economic, and political development; and (2) to work on campus to get university attention and resources directed at Chicano students and Chicano communities. The organization saw the university as key to community development, both individually and institutionally, and as a source of political change.

The Chicano Moratorium

In addition to its campus organization, MEChA in California played a key role in organizing the Chicano Moratorium in 1970. The movement's central goal was a moratorium on the Vietnam War draft. Participants also called for an increase in social justice in the United States. They organized a large-scale march, called the Chicano Moratorium, to bring attention to their concerns. Approximately 25,000 people attended the march, coming from Chicano organizations across the south west. The crowd was non-violent and included many families with children. The Los Angeles police and county sheriff deputies attacked the crowd with clubs and tear gas, sparking a riot, with Chicano youth burning cars and businesses along Los Angeles' Whittier Boulevard. In the end, three Mexican Americans were dead, hundreds injured, and over two hundred protesters were arrested, including Corky Gonzáles. Among the dead was *Los Angeles Times* columnist Rubén Salazar, who was 'accidentally' shot in the head with a tear gas canister by a Los Angeles police officer while he was sitting in a local bar.

La Raza Unida Party

The preceding discussion contains a unifying thread: a general dissatisfaction among Mexican American political activists with the responsiveness of the Democratic Party and its leaders to the needs of their communities. In 1967 this frustration coalesced in El Paso into the formation of La Raza Unida Party. Not a great deal happened beyond this initial statement until 1970, when Corky Gonzáles in Colorado and José Angel Gutiérrez in Texas organized La Raza Unida, creating committees for their respective states. In 1971 the party spread to California, and in 1972 to Arizona and New Mexico. But by far the most successful organizing committee was Gutiérrez's party apparatus in Texas.

Gutiérrez was instrumental in organizing MAYO in South Texas in 1965. This group organized a program called the Winter Garden Project, which was funded by the Ford Foundation, VISTA, and by OEO (both being federal 'war on poverty' programs). The goal of the program was to direct social, political, and economic resources to a ten-county area of south Texas which had extremely high levels of poverty. The program was expanded through the creation of Raza Unida in 1970. Shortly after calling their first organizational meeting, the Texas La Raza committee filed preliminary papers to establish themselves as a party in all the counties of the Winter Garden region.[36] The new party was thrown off the ballot in all the partisan races, but its candidates were able to remain on the ballot for the non-partisan city council and school board contests. La Raza Unida filed candidates for all available offices in the three cities in the area. Of a total of sixteen races for which they fielded candidates, they won fifteen. In Crystal City they were able again to take control of the city council, Gutiérrez himself being one of the candidates elected. Between 1970 and 1972 the party grew in power and won additional city-level positions in Crystal City, Cotulla, and Carrizo Springs. In the 1971 party convention, La Raza Unida decided to field statewide candidates; they held the first statewide nominating convention in San Antonio in June 1972. The meeting was attended by 500 delegates from twenty-five counties.[37] The movement to statewide elections, however, was not successful. La Raza Unida did best in South Texas, because that was the region where Mexican Americans constituted a majority. Beyond that area, it was difficult for them to surpass the 50 percent threshold necessary to win election. That being said, they were quite successful at the local level in terms of winning elections, and they mobilized large numbers of Mexican Americans into electoral politics.

The national La Raza Unida Party never really got off the ground, because of internal factionalism and the lack of a clear program. In 1972, Corky Gonzáles called for a national convention of La Raza Unida. Three hundred delegates from eighteen states and from the district of Columbia attended the convention held in El Paso in September 1972. There were two main factions at the meeting: supporters of González and of the Crusade for Justice, and supporters of Gutiérrez and of La Raza Unida in Texas. The delegates from other states were caught in the middle. The convention also took place during an ideologically heated presidential campaign between George McGovern and Richard Nixon. Gonzáles went to the convention expecting to be elected as party president in time for the presidential campaign, in which he hoped that La Raza Unida might play a role. This was not to be. Instead, the convention refused to endorse any candidate for president; Gutierrez was elected party chairman over Gonzáles; and the fundamental split in the party between the two factions made it impossible for it to move forward as a coherent political organization.[38]

What is true is that La Raza Unida managed to mobilize large numbers of people and to get them to question the two-party system for the first time. La Raza's threat to exit helped those Mexican American political leaders working within the Democratic Party, like Henry B. González of Texas, to convince the party to take Mexican American issues seriously. Henry González and José Angel Gutiérrez had a notoriously conflictual relationship. González, like many centrist Mexican American leaders, strongly disagreed with La Raza Unida, its nationalism, and its tactics. Yet its more radical approach helped to make the demands of more mainstream Mexican American leaders more palatable. As we will also see in the case of Puerto Rican political activity, Mexican American political organizing in the 1960s followed two tracks: one was more radical, sometimes violent, and more demanding of a fundamental change in the system; the other was more traditional and middle-of-the-road, asking for substantive, if not fundamental, change in the opportunity structure available to Mexican Americans. The work of the more traditional groups, such as LULAC and the GI Forum, laid the groundwork for the activism of the late 1960s. That activism changed the rhetoric and the strategies exercised by the more traditional organizations and helped to move the Democratic Party and its elected officials to be more responsive to Mexican American social, economic, and political concerns in general.

Women and the Chicano Movement

One of the main tenets that brought together these disparate groups of Chicano activists was the idea of *chicanismo*: a cultural nationalist view which argued in favor of a uniform experience of discrimination and exclusion that united all Chicanos toward a common purpose. Even though this nationalist ideology worked well in bringing very disparate groups of activists together, many Chicana women within the movement became critical of the movement's inability to address the gender inequality that existed among Chicanos.[39] Although most of the movement leaders were male, as was also the case in the political and labor organizing discussed above, Chicana women were highly involved in all of this political activity. They helped to coordinate and organize events and worked to develop community social networks. Some of these activist women, for instance Anna Nieto Gomez, María Varela, and Elizabeth Martínez, complained that the assumption of a uniform 'Chicano' experience across region, class, sexuality, and gender made it impossible for the inequalities which did exist in the community to be eradicated. This created conflict and tension within the movement; many Chicanas and Chicanos called the feminists disloyal and *vendidas* – 'sellouts' to white feminism and not true supporters of the movement. Not surprisingly, no real attempts were made to address or incorporate the feminists' concerns, as is reflected in the official movement documents. Neither *El Plan de Santa Bárbara* nor *El Plan Espiritual de Aztlán* mentions women, or gays and lesbians. In both plans, women are only present as part of the Chicano *familia*, which is defined as heterosexual and is seen as the basis for Chicano organizing. This silence is especially telling with regard to the *Plan de Santa Bárbara*, which was meant to lay out the blueprint for research on the Chicano community. Its lack of any discussion of women makes it clear that the activists drafting the plans did not see Chicana women or their issues as a necessary point of focus for that research.[40]

These gender issues were never resolved within the movement and continued to play themselves out in Chicano Studies programs and organizations in academic settings. The conflict undermined the cohesion and effectiveness of movement organizations and often led to feminist Chicanas forming their own, separate organizations. It also led to the development of a new feminism of the Chicana – one which criticizes both Chicano cultural nationalism and white middle-class feminism. This movement has expressed itself through art, poetry, theatre, literature, and academic writings focused on the experience of the Chicana woman.[41]

The Movement's End and Consequences

Gender conflict was only one of the sources of factionalism that led to the end of the movement. Personality conflicts were also present, and they were exacerbated by the organizational infiltration of FBI agents as part of the COINTELPRO (Counter Intelligence) program. These agents were tasked to become part of the organization not only in order to keep watch over what members were doing, but also to foment conflict and mistrust within the groups as much as was possible. In the heated political environment of the late 1960s and early 1970s, the FBI agents were quite successful. As a result, many of the groups splintered into factions and most of the intensive mobilization within the movement had ended by 1973.

Nonetheless, the Chicano Movement has a significant long-term legacy. Most importantly, for the first time in US history, the movement caused Mexican American issues to be recognized and addressed at the state and national levels. It was only after the movement mobilization that Mexican Americans were included under the Voting Rights Act and under other civil rights legislation such as laws on equal employment and housing, and affirmative action programs. Those pieces of legislation opened up the US political process to Mexican Americans for the first time and gave thousands of them access to higher education, fair employment, and housing.

Another important part of the legacy of the movement is the institutionalization of a new Mexican American political identity, one that values Mexican history, culture, and language. As a result, older organizations like LULAC changed their platforms, allowing for greater support for the maintenance of Mexican culture. In addition, there was a movement among Mexican American organizations to include all members of the community – immigrants and US born alike. LULAC, for example, rescinded their requirement that all members should be US citizens. Thus the movement caused changes in the way older Mexican American organizations approached issues of cultural maintenance and membership. It also led to the creation of a new set of Mexican American organizations, for instance the Mexican American Legal Defense and Education Fund (MALDEF) and the National Council of La Raza (NCLR). Both are highly successful national organizations which work to ensure that Latino civil rights are protected and to promote the social, political, and economic well-being of Latinos living in the United States. Similarly, the Southwest Voter Registration Education Project (SVREP) was created in 1974, to register Mexican Americans for voting and to educate them in the political process. With offices in California and Texas, SVREP continues to register and conduct get-out-the-vote drives targeting hundreds of thousands of Latinos during every electoral cycle. They, like MALDEF, NCLR, LULAC, MAPA, and the National Association of Latino Elected and Appointed Officials (NALEO), now focus on issues facing Latinos generally, and not simply Mexican Americans. Yet it is important to remember that these national groups began from a Mexican American focus and that, because Mexican Americans make up the majority of immigrants of Latin American origin in the United States, they remain a key part of each group's constituency.

In addition to these national organizations, movement activists went on to work within thousands of smaller, locally based social service organizations within their respective communities. Many became labor organizers, social workers, or teachers, and allowed their experience in the movement to inform their professional careers. This legacy has contributed to the economic development and social well-being of Mexican American and Latino communities throughout the United States.

On university campuses, the movement led to the establishment of Chicano Studies programs, which housed scholars engaging in the systematic study of the Mexican American experience in the United States. These programs not only greatly expanded the amount of information available on the Mexican American experience, but also added to the university curriculum by offering courses on community history, literature, culture, and politics. On high school and university campuses across the country, MEChA chapters continue to exist, to engage in efforts towards improving the educational opportunities available to Mexican American and Latino students, and to ensure the latter's academic success. Many chapters also engage in cultural programming in order to educate their members and their campus communities about Mexican American culture and experience in the United States.

Mexican American Politics Today

The period from the end of the Chicano Movement until today can be seen as the institutionalization of Mexican American politics in the post-civil rights era. Legislation passed in response to these political movements opened up the political process, educational and economic opportunities, and improved the social well-being of all racial/ethnic groups in the United States. In order to promote these gains, politically minded Mexican Americans have engaged in a wide range of activities, including political office-holding, community activism, labor organization, philanthropy, and social work. The result has been a growth in collective organizational structures within Mexican American communities and the development of coalitions with other, similarly situated, groups in American politics.

From a political standpoint, this development has led to a greater representation of Mexican Americans at all levels of government, as elected and appointed officials. On the federal level, Colorado voters recently elected Ken Salazar as the first Mexican American US Senator from that state. At the time of this writing, President Obama had nominated Salazar to serve as Secretary of Interior. A number of Mexican Americans served in the 110th Congress (2006–2008), including: Joe Baca (D–CA), Xavier Becerra (D–CA), Henry Cuellar (D–TX), Charlie González (D–TX), Raúl Grijalva (D–AZ), Rubén Hinojosa (D–TX), Grace Napolitano (D–CA), Solomon Ortiz (D–TX), Ed Pastor (D–AZ), Silvestre Reyes (D–TX), Ciro Rodríguez (D–TX), Lucille Roybal-Allard (D–CA), John Salazar (D–CO), Linda Sánchez (D–CA), Loretta Sánchez (D–CA), and Hilda Solís (D–CA), who is half-Mexican. Congresswoman Roybal-Allard was the first Mexican American woman elected to the US Congress. At the state level, there have been a number of Mexican Americans elected governor, including Jerry Apodaca and Bill Richardson in New Mexico and Raúl Castro in Arizona. Cruz Bustamente served as California's lieutenant governor and in the state legislature. Los Angeles Mayor Antonio Villaraigosa also served as speaker of the Californian state assembly, as did Mexican American Fabián Nuñez. Mexican Americans have been elected as mayors of a number of major cities and serve on city councils and local school boards across the United States. They also serve in many state legislatures.

On the non-elected side, Alberto Gonzales, who served under George W. Bush, was the first Mexican American to serve as US attorney general. Rosario Marín was the forty-first US treasurer, the first Mexican American woman to hold this position – which made her at the time the highest ranking Mexican American woman in the Administration. She was succeeded in that position by another Mexican American woman, Anna Escobedo Cabral. Under Bill Clinton, Henry Cisneros served as secretary of housing and urban development, and Federico Peña, former Denver mayor, served as secretary of transportation and energy. Bill Richardson also served in the Clinton Administration as energy secretary and US ambassador to the United Nations. María Echaveste served as Clinton's deputy chief of staff, and Janet Murguía, currently NCLR president, was Clinton's deputy director of legislative affairs. Cecilia Muñoz, who was senior vice-president at NCLR, will be Barack Obama's director of intergovernmental affairs. Mexican Americans have served as judges at the state and federal levels, including on state supreme courts.

Thus Mexican American politics today is characterized by growing political representation and a well developed network of locally and nationally based political organizations. This institutional and organizational development has its roots in the political organizing which has been going on within the community since the nineteenth century. It was pushed forward by the civil rights movements of the 1960s and by the legal changes which came out of that era, all of which resulted in greater political, economic, and social opportunities for Mexican

Americans. Although Mexican Americans remain descriptively under-represented in relation to their population numbers and still experience high levels of poverty, labor market discrimination, poor access to quality public education, a lack of health care coverage, and other forms of inequality, their presence and voice in American politics has grown dramatically since the mid-twentieth century.

Mexican Migration and the Future of Mexican American Politics

Mexicans make up the largest proportion of Latino immigrants to the United States, a fact largely due to the country's geographic proximity, the unique relationship the two countries have had, and the economic dislocations caused by the economic policies implemented by the Mexican government: all these factors have led to significant increases in Mexican migration to the United States after 1970. As the Mexican government began to embrace trade liberalization in the 1980s – a trend which culminated in the passing of the North American Free Trade Agreement (NAFTA) – these flows only accelerated. Those hardest hit by the economic changes wrought by NAFTA were Mexico's rural poor, particularly in the southern part of the country. In 1980, 36 percent of Mexicans worked in agriculture. By 2002 that number had decreased to 17.5 percent. In 2001, 81.5 percent of rural Mexicans lived in poverty and 80 percent of rural families had at least one family member working outside the community. Many of these Mexicans are working in Mexico City, in the border area, or living abroad, so that they may send money home.[42] Northward migration has been Mexicans' response to economic difficulties since the early twentieth century. That process was facilitated by interests and networks in Mexico and the United States which encouraged migration. For example, migration requires resources and support for the journey, which often is outside the economic reach of the migrant. The migrant often turns to moneylenders and other social network members, who facilitate migration for a profit. Similarly, US agricultural interests continue to recruit workers from Mexico, encouraging their migration and inclusion in these networks. Mexican government actors are often complicit in these activities, as they benefit economically and politically from the migration flows.[43] Given these interests, barring some dramatic action on either side of the border, it is likely that Mexican migration flows will continue.

The migration flows and the long-term economic connections between the two countries have also led to the growth of transnational political organizing within Mexican immigrant communities. The last two dec-ades have seen the growth of Mexican Hometown Associations. These organizations developed from social networks made up of Mexican migrants from the same hometowns or villages. They host social and cultural events in the United States, and also work to raise money to fund public works in their hometowns in Mexico. Mexican immigrants had long sent remittances to support their families at home. It is estimated that Mexicans currently send over $13 billion in remittances to Mexico every year, which makes remittances one of Mexico's top three sources of foreign exchange. The hometown associations take an activity which used to be individual or family-focused and make it community-focused by pooling immigrants' money in order to address the economic develop-ment needs of their hometowns. Although these kinds of organizations have existed in Mexican communities since the 1950s, the numbers have expanded dramatically over the past two decades; there are now over 600 Mexican hometown clubs and associations registered in thirty different cities in the United States.[44] This transnational political engagement has grown because of decreases in transportation and communication costs, which make the clubs' work much more feasible. The clubs and associa-tions often coordinate their work with the Mexican government.

Because of the organizational and political infrastructure which had developed within Mexican American communities in the United States by the early 1970s, Mexican American organizations were better able to respond to these increases in Mexican migration, and the new migrants had access to resources and services which had not been available to previous generations of migrants. Thus the structural envi-ronment which Mexican Americans faced was very different, as were the opportunities available to them. These migrants are also creating a new structural environment across borders through their hometown associations. The economic development programs they are funding are likely to have important effects on the economic situation in Mexico, and most probably will affect migration patterns in the future.

By and large, Mexican immigrants have settled historically in the US south west, including in states like Arizona, California, New Mexico, Colorado, and Texas. There has always been a significant Mexican popu-lation in Illinois too, particularly in the Chicago area. Those areas, in turn, were the location of the bulk of Mexican American political activ-ism and mobilization. In recent times, because of increases in the cost of living in traditional immigrant-receiving states, coupled with growing economic opportunities in other parts of the United States, Mexican

Table 3.2 The States with Greatest Growth in Mexican-Origin Population, 1990–2000

State	Mexican-origin population, 1990	Mexican-origin population, 2000	Percentual increase, 1990–2000
Alabama	9,509	44,522	368%
Arkansas	12,496	61,204	390%
Georgia	49,182	275,288	460%
Kentucky	8,692	31,385	261%
Minnesota	34,691	95,613	176%
Nebraska	29,665	71,030	139%
Nevada	85,287	285,764	235%
North Carolina	32,670	246,545	655%
South Carolina	11,028	95,076	762%
Tennessee	13,879	77,372	457%

Source: US Department of the Census, 1990 and 2000; summary files compiled by the author

immigrants have begun to settle in non-traditional locations, outside of the south west. Table 3.2 lists the states with the greatest growth in Mexican migration since 1990.

In addition, there are states outside of the south west which have a growing and significant population of Mexican origin: Iowa, Kansas, Michigan, Missouri, Oregon, and Wisconsin. Such states are struggling to address the needs of this fast-growing population. Similarly, US born Mexicans and Mexican immigrants settling in the new states are adjusting to life in places which – in terms of services and community organizations – lack the kind of community infrastructure which exists in the more traditional immigrant-receiving areas. These differences will probably affect the opportunity structures immigrants face in the new communities, as well as their ability to engage effectively with the political system and make it address their concerns. The history of migration and settlement among Mexicans suggests that this change in geographic location and settlement patterns will continue into the future.

Conclusion

Upon arriving in the United States, each subsequent generation of Mexican Americans has faced different challenges and has been assisted by the ongoing social, economic, and political mobilization which took place within the community. Those arriving during the period when segregation was legal in the United States faced particular hardships, especially those living in Texas. Across Mexican American communities during this period, individuals experienced limitations in terms of their access to education, well paid employment, and quality housing. Through labor organizing, political activism, and legal challenges, the community was able to respond to these structural constraints and to improve the opportunity structure, which in turn has benefited subsequent generations of Mexican immigrants. Yet Mexican Americans in the United States still face many social, economic, and political challenges. As more Mexican Americans settle in non-traditional locations such as Georgia, North Carolina, and Iowa, they will face a different set of obstacles and a less developed organizational infrastructure. Only time will tell in what ways the settlement experiences of these new arrivals are similar to or different from those of the immigrants who chose to locate in areas with more established Mexican American communities. At any rate, the Mexican American experience in the United States will continue to vary according to area of settlement, generation, gender, and class status. All these factors will have an impact on the nature and depth of Mexican Americans' incorporation into the US political system.

Guide to Further Readings

González, Gilbert G. and Raúl A. Fernández. 2003. *A Century of Chicano History: Empire, Nations, and Migration*. New York: Routledge.

Mariscal, George. 2005. *Brown-Eyed Children of the Sun: Lessons from the Chicano Movement, 1965–1975*. Albuquerque: University of New Mexico Press.

Menchaca, Martha. 2001. *Recovering History, Constructing Race: The Indian, Black, and White Roots of Mexican Americans*. Austin: University of Texas Press.

Pycior, Julie Leininger. 1997. *LBJ and Mexican Americans: The Paradox of Power*. Austin: University of Texas Press.

Ruiz de Burton, María Amparo. 1997. *The Squatter and the Don*, 2nd edn. Houston, TX: Arte Público Press.

Ruiz, Vicki. 1998. *From Out of the Shadows: Mexican Women in Twentieth Century America*. New York: Oxford University Press.

CHAPTER FOUR

Puerto Ricans: From Colonized People to Political Activists

Objectives

- Understand why the US entered into the Spanish–American War and the effects this had on Puerto Rico, including what it means for Puerto Rico to be a US commonwealth
- Understand the role US economic policy has played in Puerto Rican development and migration patterns
- Understand the obstacles faced by Puerto Rican migrants in the United States
- Understand in what ways the Puerto Rican movement reflected a shift in Puerto Rican identity within the United States

Introduction

Puerto Rico was one of Spain's last colonies in the new world. Its proximity to the United States meant that Puerto Rico had significant economic ties with the United States prior to the Spanish–American War. These ties, and the United States' subsequent occupation of Puerto Rico after the war, have had important effects on the presence of Puerto Ricans in the United States as well as on their politics.

The indigenous population of Puerto Rico was that of the Taínos. The Taínos are thought to have lived across much of the Caribbean. After the Spanish conquest, many of the Taínos died of disease and mistreatment, but their legacy remains an important part of Puerto Rican history and national identity. The Taínos in Puerto Rico called the island 'Boriquen'; hence, Puerto Ricans on the island and in the United States often refer to themselves as 'Boricua'. The demise of the Taínos also changed the demographic make-up of Puerto Rico, creating a need for the Spanish to import large numbers of African slaves to provide labor for the Puerto Rican economy. Thus Puerto Ricans are of European, indigenous, and African descent. Puerto Rican geneticist Juan Martínez Cruzado recently conducted an islandwide DNA survey and found that a majority of

Puerto Ricans have Indian blood: 61 percent have Amerindian mito-chondrial DNA, 27 percent African, and 12 percent Caucasian.[1] Thus it is not by accident that the island's Taíno heritage and indigenous practices remain important parts of Puerto Rican culture.

Until the mid-nineteenth century, the Puerto Rican economy was based on sugar production, which was centered in the coastal areas. Starting in the mid-nineteenth century, Puerto Rico also began to develop its coffee production, which was located inland. The largest market for these goods was the United States. Because of Spanish colonial restrictions, Puerto Rican producers were able to trade with the United States only on a limited basis until 1819, when Spain and the United States signed the Adams–Onis Treaty, formally renewing commercial ties between the two countries. From that point forward, US trade with Puerto Rico grew rapidly. As a result of this contact small numbers of Puerto Ricans began settling in the United States, mainly in the New York City area.

The Puerto Rican independence movement began in 1868, with the '*Grito de Lares*' (the Revolt of Lares). As other Spanish colonies gained their independence in the nineteenth century, Puerto Ricans began to demand greater autonomy from the Spanish government. There were also economic pressures building up against Spain in Puerto Rico. In 1868 sugar prices fell dramatically and Spain, in order to raise revenue and quell a rebellion in the Dominican Republic, increased the tariffs on Puerto Rican goods. Puerto Ricans felt even more strongly that they needed to have control over their economy and government. The autonomy movement culminated in 1868 with an uprising in the town of Lares. The rebel group, the *Comité Revolucionario de Puerto Rico* (the Puerto Rican Revolutionary Committee), took over the town church and city hall, demanding Puerto Rican independence. The Spanish militia quickly stopped the rebellion, imprisoning about 475 rebels. These were initially sentenced to death, but the new Spanish governor released them in 1869, in an attempt to ease tensions on the island. Even though this rebellion failed to achieve Puerto Rican independence, it did move Spain to grant Puerto Rico more autonomy. Puerto Rican representatives had long been urging Spain to abolish slavery on the island, which Spain did in 1873. In 1897, after much negotiation, Spain passed the *Carta Autonómica* (the Autonomy Charter), which, for the first time since the conquest, granted Puerto Rico political and administrative autonomy. The Autonomy Charter established an independent government for Puerto Rico, gave Puerto Rico representation in the Spanish parliament, and allowed Puerto Rico to negotiate trade agreements directly with the

Figure 4.1 *Political Cartoon from the Popular Press.*
Source: Wisconsin Historical Society, PH 2714

United States and other countries. The new Puerto Rican government was also granted the right to accept or reject any trade agreements negotiated for Puerto Rico by Spain. Elections were held and Puerto Rico's new autonomous government began to function in 1898.

The year 1898 was also a time of mounting tensions between the United States and Spain. In the United States there was increasing concern about the situation in Cuba and growing support for Cuban independence. In early 1898 it became clear that the United States was likely to intervene in Cuba. Puerto Rican leaders wrote letters to President

McKinley in March 1898, to ensure that Puerto Rico was included in any US invasion plans. They also provided the United States with intelligence about the Spanish military presence on the island. After the war began, little of the fighting occurred on Puerto Rican territory, and Spain ceded the island, along with its other holdings, under the Treaty of Paris, which was signed in December 1898. General John R. Brooke subsequently became the first US military governor of Puerto Rico.

The Status of Puerto Rico

The US occupation of Puerto Rico began the ongoing, and still unresolved, debate over the status of the island. The fact that Puerto Rico remains in a political 'limbo' – neither being a sovereign nation nor having the rights of a US state – has been a central issue in Puerto Rican politics, both among Puerto Ricans living in the United States and among those living on the island. All the political parties on the island are organized according to their position on the status question, and the status question has been a key part of all the forms of political organization which Puerto Ricans have undertaken in the United States.

Puerto Rico was under US military rule until 1900, when the US Congress passed the Foraker Act. This act established a civil government and free commerce between Puerto Rico and the United States. The Puerto Rican government would include a governor appointed by the US President, an appointed executive council (the equivalent of a senate), and an elected legislature with thirty-five members. The legislature could override a governor's veto with a two-thirds vote. President McKinley appointed the first Executive Council in June 1900; it included five Puerto Rican members and six US members. The first legislative elections took place in November. The act also allowed Puerto Rico to have a non-voting representative to the US Congress (this representative was called a Resident Commissioner). The act established a Puerto Rican Department of Education, which was headed by an American. Teaching in the new public school system was conducted entirely in English, Spanish being treated as a special subject. However, both Spanish and English were considered official languages on the island.

In addition to establishing the parameters of the Puerto Rican government, the Foraker Act also made Puerto Rico, officially, an unincorporated territory of the United States. In 1902 Puerto Rico became a US territory. With the passage of the Jones Act in 1917, Puerto Ricans officially became US citizens. The act was passed despite opposition from the Puerto Rican legislature. But this is a 'statutory' citizenship – a citizenship status granted by law rather than by right of birth, as in the case of citizens born in the mainland United States. Thus Congress may revoke the citizenship of Puerto Ricans if it can be shown that the revocation serves a legitimate federal purpose. Congress could also decide that Puerto Ricans born in the future will no longer be considered US citizens. This means that Puerto Ricans born on the US mainland have a citizenship status which is different from that of Puerto Ricans born on the island insofar as birth-right citizenship may be lost only as a result of a person's own actions (for instance through their renouncing it), rather than by an act of Congress.[2]

The Jones Act also altered the Puerto Rican governmental structure, establishing two legislative houses (a 19-member Senate and 39-member House of Representatives), which would be popularly elected. The governor of Puerto Rico was still to be appointed by the US president, and he (along with the president and the US Congress) retained the right to veto any act of the Puerto Rican legislature. The governor's cabinet appointments had to be approved by the US Senate. The Jones Act also made English the official language of Puerto Rico.

Despite the fact that the Jones Act gave Puerto Ricans more direct control over their government, it did not satisfy many Puerto Ricans' desire for self-determination. The Puerto Rican independence movement had continued after the US occupation and gained strength in the 1930s and 1940s. The movement was led by the Puerto Rican Nationalist Party, which was founded in 1922. In 1930, the Party elected Pedro Albizu Campos as its leader. Albizu Campos had attended Harvard University and had served in the US army (in a segregated African American unit) during the First World War. Shortly after his election as party president, the US-appointed governor of Puerto Rico, Blanton Winship, began cracking down on the party and its activities. Leaders were jailed and supporters were subject to harassment. For example, police and nationalist supporters clashed in 1934 on the campus of the University of Puerto Rico in Ríos Piedras. Four nationalists were left dead, and one police officer was wounded. The officers involved were never prosecuted. In 1936 Albizu Campos was arrested for sedition, along with other members of his party. In the initial trial, with a jury of seven Puerto Ricans and five Americans, Albizu Campos was found not guilty. The judge ordered a retrial and the new jury, made up of ten Americans and two Puerto Ricans, found Albizu Campos guilty. In 1937, a group of supporters appealed against the verdict, but the Boston Court of Appeals (which had jurisdiction over federal matters in Puerto Rico) upheld the ruling. Albizu Campos and the other nationalist leaders were sent to federal prison in Georgia. Shortly afterwards a group of nationalist supporters held a peaceful march in the city of Ponce to protest their imprisonment. The police opened fire on the marchers, killing nineteen people, including a seven-year-old girl who was passing by. Police used guns and clubs, wounding over one hundred marchers. This event is called the 'Ponce Massacre'.

In response to the uprisings and violence, some Puerto Rican leaders, such as Luis Muñoz Marín, moved away from advocating independence. They pushed instead for commonwealth status for Puerto Rico, which would entail more autonomy and a greater amount of self-determination in island affairs. Those favoring commonwealth status began negotiations with President Roosevelt; they were successful under the Truman Administration. In 1946, President Truman appointed the first Puerto Rican-born governor of the island, Jesus Piñero. The following year, the United States granted Puerto Rico the right to elect their governor. In the 1948 elections, Luis Muñoz Marín became the first democratically elected governor of Puerto Rico. He would serve in that capacity for sixteen years, until 1964.

Yet many nationalists did not consider these moves sufficient. They began to plan the Jayuya uprising, which took place in October 1950. Nationalist leaders took up arms in seven Puerto Rican cities, including San Juan, Ponce, and Jayuya. In Jayuya, the nationalists raised the Puerto Rican flag in the town square (between 1898 and 1952 it was illegal to carry the Puerto Rican flag on the island) and held the town for three days. The US government declared martial law on the island and called in the Puerto Rican National Guard. Jayuya was attacked by US bomber planes from the air and by US artillery on the ground; the city was destroyed. The top leaders of the nationalist party, including Albizu Campos, were arrested and sentenced to long prison terms. Two nationalists, Griselio Torresola and Oscar Collazo, were living in the United States at the time and made a plan to assassinate President Truman. They attempted it unsuccessfully at Blair House in November 1950. Torresola was killed and Collazo was arrested and sentenced to death. President Truman commuted his death sentence into life imprisonment.

In response to this violence, President Truman allowed for a democratic referendum to be held in Puerto Rico, to determine if Puerto Ricans wanted to draft their own constitution.[3] The referendum passed, and the new constitution was adopted in July 1952. That constitution established Puerto Rico as a US Commonwealth (on the island the status is called *Estado Libre Asociado*), which is the status the island holds today.

Puerto Rico is considered by the US government to be an unincorporated organized territory of the United States, subject to the powers of the US Congress and with the right to establish a constitution for the internal administration of government and on matters of purely local concern. In other words, Puerto Ricans on the island may directly elect their governor and their legislature, and those bodies may pass laws relating to local issues of the island. But this is subject to the discretion of the US Congress, which can rescind these rights at any time. Should the US Congress disagree with any of the island government's actions, it may reverse them. The head of state for Puerto Rico is the US president, not the island's governor. Yet Puerto Ricans do not have the right to vote for president.[4] Puerto Rico has an elected, non-voting representative to the US Congress. From a financial standpoint, Puerto Ricans on the island pay federal payroll taxes (Social Security, Medicare) but do not receive the level of Medicare benefits they would be entitled to if they were a state. They also pay taxes to support the Puerto Rican government.

The establishment of the Puerto Rican commonwealth did not end the independence movement; the nationalists wanted nothing short of independence for the island. In 1954, in order to bring attention to the Puerto Rican issue, a group of nationalists led by Lolita Lebrón attacked the US House of Representatives. Lebrón was a poor single mother who had migrated to New York City during the 1940s in order to help with supporting her daughter. There she experienced racial discrimination and became a follower of Albizu Campos. The nationalists chose 1 March as the day of the attack, in order to mark the anniversary of the passage of the Jones Act. Four nationalists, Lebrón, Rafael Cancel Miranda, Irving Flores, and Andrés Figueroa Cordero, unfurled a Puerto Rican flag from the balcony of one of the visitors' galleries and opened fire in the House of Representatives chamber. Lebrón is quoted as yelling: 'I did not come to kill anyone; I came to die for Puerto Rico! Viva Puerto Rico Libre!' According to Miranda, Lebrón shot her pistol towards the ceiling (so that she would not hurt anyone) and Figueroa's pistol jammed. Miranda is credited with causing most of the injuries. Despite the fact that an estimated 240 house members were on the floor that day, none was killed; five members were wounded. A bullet from the attack may still be found in the podium used by Republicans to speak on the floor of the house. The nationalists were arrested immediately and sentenced to death. President Eisenhower commuted their death sentences, and they were sentenced instead to imprisonment for life. After this attack, Albizu Campos was sent back to prison too. In an attempt at national reconciliation, Governor Muñoz Marín had pardoned Albizu Campos in 1953, but he revoked that pardon after the events of 1954. Albizu Campos remained in prison until 1964, when Muñoz Marín pardoned him for the last time.

None of these events served to resolve the issue of status. Since 1952, four referenda have been held to determine what the island's status should be: in 1967, 1991,[5] 1993, and 1998.[6] Each time the result has favored maintaining the status quo rather than independence or statehood. Interestingly, in the 1998 referendum less than 47 percent of Puerto Ricans supported statehood and over 50 percent chose 'none of the above', which suggests a general frustration with the choices offered. Independence has not had strong support in these referenda – which is not surprising, given the political repression and violence which have surrounded the independence movement and the economic uncertainty which accompanies the prospect of independence for the island. We will see below that Puerto Ricans in the United States have always been more supportive of independence than Puerto Ricans on the island, and that working to free political prisoners fighting for Puerto Rican independence will become an important part of Puerto Rican politics within the United States.

The Puerto Rican Economy: Operation Bootstrap and the Great Migration

For the first four decades of the twentieth century, Puerto Rico was an agrarian economy, with sugar as its primary export. The crash of sugar prices during the Great Depression decimated the Puerto Rican economy, leading to widespread misery and malnutrition. During the New Deal, the US government had begun developing plans to diversify and industrialize the Puerto Rican economy, so that it would no longer be so dependent on the sugar revenue. That plan accelerated during the Second World War. The US government built factories in Puerto Rico to provide goods for US domestic consumers and for the US military in the event of a possible German naval blockade of the Atlantic. After the war, the United States moved from state-driven industrialization to a system using tax and economic incentives to encourage private industry to invest on the island. In 1947 the Puerto Rican legislature approved the Industrial Incentives Act, which provided tax breaks, low-cost labor, and land to US businesses to encourage them to move manufacturing to the island. US government officials referred to this act as 'Operation Bootstrap'. The idea behind the plan was that Puerto Rico would help itself, pulling itself up by its metaphorical bootstraps in order to become industrialized. But they still received assistance from the United States in order to accomplish this. Until the 1970s the US government sent nearly $600 million annually to Puerto Rico in order to support the program.[7] The industrialization process was also helped by Puerto Rican access to US markets: these became the destination of choice for Puerto Rican exports. As a result, from 1958 to 1977, Puerto Rico experienced dramatic economic growth, averaging over 9 percent a year. Factory employment doubled during the same period and the number of factories grew by about 20 percent.[8] The industrialization also coincided with a dramatic decline in the agrarian sector. In 1950, 40 percent of the labor force worked on farms; by the late 1980s, that number had fallen to 3 percent.[9] Thus, in a very short period of time, the Puerto Rican economy was transformed from an agrarian-based system to an industrialized one.

This transformation led to significant social dislocations within Puerto Rican society, in particular to the mass migration of Puerto Ricans to the United States. Puerto Rico's dramatic rates of economic growth did little to affect employment levels on the island. In fact, total employment in Puerto Rico actually decreased, from 603,000 jobs in 1951 to 543,000 in 1960; employment did not return to the level it had in 1951 until 1963. The growth in industrial jobs was not able to keep up with the population growth, or to compensate for job losses in the agricultural sector or in the home needlework industry.[10] Some scholars argue that what made the Puerto Rican economic model sustainable was the provision of federal transfer money, particularly in the form of food assistance, to Puerto Rico. This assistance made it possible for the Puerto Rican population to survive despite the lack of available employment. In 1950, transfer payments from the federal and Puerto Rican governments constituted about 12 percent of personal income; by 1980, that proportion had risen to 30 percent.[11] This injection of funds served to increase Puerto Rican per capita income and had an important impact on the maintenance of consumer demand on the island.

Another important factor in the maintenance of this industrialization program in the face of high unemployment was the free movement of Puerto Ricans to the United States. Since the United States takeover of Puerto Rico, the US government has often used the Puerto Rican population as a source of low-cost labor. Starting in 1898, Puerto Rican workers began to be sent by the US government to different locations, to be used as contract laborers. The first group was sent to Hawaii. Later groups of Puerto Rican workers were sent to the Dominican Republic and to Cuba. The most common destination, however, was the US mainland. In 1917, the United States' Bureau on Insular Affairs issued a memorandum outlining plans for addressing the 'overpopulation' of Puerto Rico. One proposal was 'to bring to the US from 50,000 to 100,000 laboring men to be used on farms as agricultural laborers, for which they are best fitted, or as right-of-way laborers on the railroads or similar work requiring manual labor'.[12] Various US government agencies followed through with these plans, using Puerto Ricans, as they used Mexicans, as contract laborers in US agriculture, particularly in places like Arizona, New Mexico, and Ohio.

Because Puerto Ricans are US citizens, they require no immigration documentation or visas in order to migrate to the United States. In response to the economic dislocation which took place in the 1950s, large numbers of Puerto Ricans began leaving the island and settling in the United States. This large movement of people is known as the 'Great Migration'. Even though Puerto Ricans had been settling in the United States since the turn of the twentieth century, this process accelerated rapidly in the post-war period. An estimated 470,000 Puerto Ricans left Puerto Rico during the decade of the 1950s – a number which represented 21 percent of the island population. Most of these migrants settled in New York City. By 1964, Puerto Ricans made up over 9 percent of the city's population. As is clear from Table 4.1, the bulk of this migration flow occurred from the 1940s to the 1960s. Since then, Puerto Rican migration has continued, but at much lower rates.

There were a number of factors that drove this migration process. First, the industrialization program being carried out on the island had significantly increased unemployment, making it necessary for Puerto Ricans to seek their livelihoods elsewhere. Second, improved medical care during the twentieth century had lowered the Puerto Rican mortality rate and had increased population growth, creating more economic pressures. Third, air travel became much less expensive after the Second World War, putting the cost of a ticket to the United States within the reach of ordinary families. Some scholars argue that the Puerto Rican government facilitated this air travel by asking the Federal Aviation Administration (FAA) to approve low rates for transportation between Puerto Rico and the United States.[13] After centuries of immigration by boat, the Puerto Rican migration became the first great airborne migration in US history. Fourth, many Puerto Ricans had served in the US

Table 4.1 Migration from Puerto Rico to the United States, 1900–2000

Decade	Number of migrants
1900–1910	2,000
1911–1920	11,000
1921–1930	42,000
1931–1940	18,000
1941–1950	151,000
1951–1960	470,000
1961–1970	214,000
1971–1980	65,817
1981–1990	116,571
1991–2000	96,327

Source: E. Acosta-Belén and C.E. Santiago, *Puerto Ricans in the United States: A Contemporary Portrait* (Boulder, CO: Lynne Rienner, 2006), p. 81.

armed forces during the Second World War and therefore had earned college tuition benefits under the GI Bill. Many of them traveled to the United States in order to attend college. Finally, US companies began to see Puerto Rico as a source of cheap labor and recruited heavily on the island. US government officials participated in this recruitment as well. For example, New York Mayor Robert F. Wagner Jr began a campaign to recruit laborers to the city to work in its factories. In 1953 he stated publicly that he and all New Yorkers would welcome any Puerto Rican who was willing to work.

Puerto Rican migration is somewhat unique because of its circular pattern. Many Puerto Ricans participate in life both on the mainland and on the island. When economic conditions are good on the mainland, they move there. When there is an economic downturn, many return to the island. This type of migration is facilitated by the island's geographic proximity to the mainland. Other factors include the availability of inexpensive transportation and the Puerto Ricans' status as US citizens, both of which lower the barriers for re-entry on the mainland.

Puerto Rican Political Life in the United States

Puerto Ricans began settling in the United States during the independence movement of the nineteenth century, and in 1895 they created a Puerto Rican Section of the Cuban Revolutionary Committee. Puerto

Rican and Cuban activists formed other organizations, published news-letters, and raised money to support the cause of independence. They were joined by small numbers of tobacco workers, skilled laborers, and their families, who joined these groups and settled in Manhattan and Brooklyn.[14] Economically, Puerto Ricans were initially concentrated in the cigar trade – a high-skilled type of work which brought high pay and good working conditions. In 1919 the cigar-makers engaged in a strike which, although successful, marked the end of their craft, because shortly afterwards the producers began mechanizing their industry. In the 1920s, Puerto Ricans in the United States were concentrated in cigar-making, factory work, and laundry. It is estimated that 25 percent of Puerto Rican women worked outside the home during this period as cigar-makers, domestics, typists, and operators in the needle trades.[15]

After 1898, new Puerto Rican organizations arose in these communi-ties: organizations which, much like the *mutualistas* in Mexican American communities, helped community members to deal with the problems of daily life by assisting with housing and employment, by providing food for needy families, and by organizing recreational activities such as baseball. Often these organizations were formed in response to the fact that Puerto Rican migrants were not welcomed with open arms. They arrived in the United States at the height of racial segregation, at a time when Puerto Ricans on the island were depicted in newspaper cartoons as 'aboriginals' or 'negroes' incapable of governing them-selves. Puerto Ricans found their legal residency questioned by many, and there were reports of Puerto Ricans being refused the right to vote and the right of access to public services.[16] Many reported seeing signs in restaurants which read 'No dogs or Puerto Ricans allowed'. There were also numerous incidents of violence against Puerto Ricans. In the summer of 1926, fifty people were injured during a week of violence directed at Puerto Ricans in Harlem. The altercations were initiated by Jewish gangs hired by merchants who were concerned about the expan-sion of Puerto Rican-owned *bodegas* (markets) in the area. In response, the Puerto Rican Brotherhood called for a mass meeting which resulted in the formation of two organizations designed to provide protection for the community.

Many Puerto Rican organizations, like the *Liga Puertorriqueña* founded in 1922, were explicitly apolitical. Between 1922 and 1930, thirty 'civic' organizations were created in the Puerto Rican community.[17] What made this rich organizational life possible was funding from key sec-tors of the community. In Manhattan, the cigar-makers, because of their economic resources, were able to support these institutional structures. In Brooklyn, the *Boliteros* (or 'numbers runners') became quite successful during the 1920s and were able to contribute significant amounts of money to Puerto Rican associations. In 1913, the Spanish-language newspaper *La Prensa* was founded as a weekly; it became a daily in 1918. By 1927 there were a number of periodicals serving the community, including *El Gráfico*, *Metropolis*, and *El Machete Criolla*.[18]

Also in 1918, the Puerto Rican community in Brooklyn began establishing political clubs. Soon they had clubs active in a number of assembly districts. These clubs provided social services and functioned as brokers between the Puerto Rican community and the local Democratic Party. Such clubs did not flourish in the Manhattan *barrios* because the Manhattan Democratic Party was controlled by Tammany Hall, which frowned upon non-white participation in city politics. Politics in Brooklyn, on the other hand, was a little more open and allowed Puerto Ricans to exercise some influence in party politics. But that influence was mediated by two non-Puerto Rican party bosses: Jimmy Kelly and George McCure. They did not allow Puerto Ricans themselves to assume leadership positions and ensured that any contact with the party went through them, a fact which kept Puerto Ricans distant from party politics. The main political issues of concern to the community during this period were the political status of Puerto Rico; the US policies towards Latin America; the Spanish civil war; and New York City politics.

In terms of formal political participation, prior to the Second World War, Puerto Rican engagement in New York City's electoral arena was limited. Sánchez-Korrol argues that having to subject themselves to registration and an English literacy test discouraged many Puerto Ricans from engaging in electoral politics. In addition, many felt they had little to gain from their participation, as one Puerto Rican activist from the period remarked:

> Many Puerto Ricans did not exercise their right to vote. In addition, it was not an easy matter to vote at that time. The officials submitted the aspirant to an interrogation with the purpose of frightening them and making them abandon their original political persuasions. This only served to keep Puerto Ricans away from the polls. But they [Puerto Ricans] also believed that they had nothing to look for in American politics.[19]

Yet some Puerto Ricans did exercise the right to vote. It is estimated that over 7,000 Puerto Rican voters participated in the 1918 New York gubernatorial election, and in 1926 there were over 5,000 Puerto Ricans reported to be registered to vote in the city of New York.[20] In 1937, the first Puerto Rican elected official in the United States, Oscar García Rivera, was elected to the New York State Assembly with the support of the Republican Party and American Labor Party. He would serve one term.[21] Starting in the 1930s, Italian party boss Vito Marcantonio began reaching out to Puerto Rican voters. He expressed his support for Puerto Rican independence, criticized the US' treatment of the island, and pushed for aid to the poor in Harlem. In 1936 Marcantonio traveled to Puerto Rico to defend nationalist leader Albizu Campos and helped to organize a march in August of that year in support of Puerto Rican independence that attracted about 10,000 protesters.[22] These efforts resulted in strong electoral support from Puerto Rican voters in his runs for Congress. Marcantonio was elected as the US representative for East Harlem in 1934. He lost the seat in the 1936 election, but won it back in 1938 and held that office until 1951. In the 1940 election, over 30,000 voters were registered in Latino (mostly Puerto Rican) districts in New York and over 80 percent supported Franklin D. Roosevelt for the presidency and Marcantonio for Congress.[23]

Marcantonio was a member of the American Labor Party, the only political party credited with a large-scale mobilization of the Puerto Rican vote. Even though, as we saw above, there was an ongoing, informal relationship between the Puerto Rican community and the Democratic Party, that party did not embrace the community until the 1960s. In fact, neither of the two major political parties focused much energy on organizing the Puerto Rican vote.

The 1930s and 1940s marked the height of Puerto Rican engagement in New York electoral politics. That engagement was driven largely by the outreach to the community which had been undertaken by politicians such as Marcantonio and New York City Mayor Fiorello La Guardia. During this period there was a strong relationship between New York City politics and politics on the island, with island politicians visiting and speaking before the mainland community and New York organizers spending time on the island in support of candidates and causes. As the post-war period began, a number of factors combined to decrease Puerto Rican engagement in the electoral sphere. In 1948, Puerto Rico's Department of Labor set up its first Migration Office in New York City. The head of that office was appointed by the governor of Puerto Rico, and the funds came from the island government. The office was meant to help Puerto Rican migrants to adjust to life in the United States and, in particular, to help them to secure jobs and access to social services. In order to ease tensions in the New York area, the office also tried to settle Puerto Rican migrants in other parts of the United States. As such, the Migration Office took on roles which community politicians and political leaders often assume. The office often spoke for the community, and city leaders would contact the Migration Office to discuss problems facing the Puerto Rican community in New York City. This delayed the development of a New York-based Puerto Rican leadership structure; the implication was that the community could look to island officials in the Migration Office rather than to politicians in local or state government to solve their problems.

Other factors combined to decrease Puerto Rican presence in New York City politics during the 1950s. Organizational life diminished as funding for the organizations dried up. The large-scale mechanization of the cigar industry lowered the number of cigar-makers left in the community and limited their ability to provide financial assistance to Puerto Rican community groups. Similarly, staring in the 1930s, the income generated by the *boliteros* began to decrease, which rendered them, too, unable to provide the financial backing they had offered in the past. In addition, from the 1930s the Puerto Rican Democratic Clubs gave signs of wanting to distance themselves from what was considered an illicit activity, and so they began to depend solely on membership dues and other sorts of fund-raising rather than on funding from the *boliteros*.[24] On the political side, in light of growing civil rights struggles in the south, the Democratic Party was becoming more clearly a party of whites only, which in the north east meant that it was a party of white ethnics. Puerto Ricans, being seen as non-white, were defined as 'a threat to the city's white population'.[25] Besides, the Democratic Party may have seen the community's politics as being too far to the left. The Puerto Ricans' strong support of Marcantonio, an outspoken leftist, and of Puerto Rican independence, became less acceptable after the Truman assassination attempt and after the 1954 nationalist attack on Congress. Thus 'the backdrop of Cold War tensions and McCarthyism may have added to the Democrats' reticence to embrace the city's Puerto Rican electorate'.[26] This happened despite the fact that most Puerto Ricans in the early twentieth century identified with the Democratic Party.[27]

The 1950s saw another shift in Puerto Rican politics in New York: a move toward more of a focus on the US Puerto Rican experience. In 1958, what had been the 'Hispanic Day' parade in New York City became the Puerto Rican Day parade, an event designed to showcase Puerto Rican life and culture in the United States. This new sense of group identity, which was rooted in Puerto Rican experiences on the US mainland, continued to grow during the 1960s. Its development was facilitated by the establishment of a new set of Puerto Rican organizations. Lyndon B. Johnson's 'war on poverty' programs provided funding to these new groups, which slowly began to challenge the role the Migration Office played in the lives of Puerto Ricans in New York. These organizations included the Puerto Rican Day Parade Committee; the Congress of Puerto Rican Hometowns; and an educational advocacy organization called Aspira. They organized in order to address the problems of poverty, inadequate housing, nutrition, education, and health care faced by the Puerto Rican community. They were quite successful. For example, in the mid-1960s Aspira protested against a proposed change to the college admission standards for the City University of New York (CUNY). Aspira activists picketed in front of New York Governor Nelson Rockefeller's home; they were dressed as 'mothers', 'fathers', and 'children' and they carried caskets and signs asserting that Rockefeller had 'killed the future of high school Puerto Rican youth'.[28] Rockefeller reacted, meeting with Aspira and other Puerto Rican groups. The outcome was that all the students affected were granted admission to CUNY the following fall.

By the end of the 1960s, the war in Vietnam and the end of the Johnson Administration also signaled the end of the 'war on poverty'. Many of the Puerto Rican organizations which had flourished at the beginning of the decade found themselves struggling to find funding from state or local government. Some of these leaders turned to the electoral arena in order to influence the budgetary priorities at city and state levels. One such leader was Herman Badillo, a political moderate who entered politics through the reforming arm of the Democratic Party. He became Bronx president in 1965 and went on to be, in 1970, the first Puerto Rican elected to US Congress. One of his first acts upon being elected was to fly to Puerto Rico to consult with key island officials. In an interview during his trip, Badillo stressed that he considered the island to be a part of his constituency.[29] Similarly, Ramón Velez was very active in anti-poverty programs in the Bronx. Once the funds dried up, he ran for a number of political offices and served as a New York City councilman. Other Puerto Rican political leaders during this period included Carlos Rios, a district leader in East Harlem, and Gilberto Gerena Valentín, an avowed socialist who became head of the Puerto Rican Council of Hometowns in 1963.[30] In 1965 Valentín was the head of the newly formed National Association of Puerto Rican Civil Rights and went on to serve in the New York municipal government until 1971.

Yet others, becoming increasingly frustrated with the slow pace of change in their communities and being influenced by the black power movement,[31] turned to more violent tactics in order to achieve their political goals. By the 1960s, the Puerto Rican community in the United States had changed. There was now a larger proportion of individuals born in the United States who had never lived on the island. For example, in 1950 only one fourth of the community was born in the US; by 1970 the US-born constituted almost half of the Puerto Ricans in the United States. This demographic situation led to a shift towards US-based issues in the community's political organizing. It also meant that the community was quite young. Although Puerto Ricans made up only 7.9 percent of New York City's population in 1960, they accounted for '11 percent of all youth aged 15 through 19, 11 percent of those 10–14 years old, 12 percent of those 5–9, and 14 percent of all children under 5'.[32] Given these demographic changes, it is not surprising that the youths born in the US formed the backbone of the community's political movement and were highly focused on issues concerning children and the young.

The Puerto Rican Movement

As we saw in the Chicano Movement, there was no one group that constituted 'the Puerto Rican Movement', but rather a collection of different organizations. The most successful of these organizations was called the Young Lords, which originated as a youth gang in Chicago's Lincoln Park neighborhood. While in prison, one of the gang's founding members, José 'Cha Cha' Jiménez, met Fred Hampton and other Black Panther Party members. They discussed the exploitation and oppression of Latinos, African Americans, and poor people in the United States. When he was released from prison in 1968, 'Cha Cha' took back to the gang what he had learned and transformed the Young Lords into an organization committed to human rights and the liberation of Puerto Rico.

Soon afterwards, the Young Lords were restructured into ministries, in an attempt to build better organization and a Puerto Rican equivalent of the Black Panthers. The group became known as the Young Lords Organization (YLO). They did not have an official uniform, but all wore purple berets. In July 1969, the New York regional chapter was founded. It soon became independent from the national headquarters in Chicago, changing its name to the Young Lords Party. Branches were also organized in Philadelphia, PA, Bridgeport, CT, Newark, NJ, Boston, MA, and Puerto Rico. The Young Lords set up community programs:

free breakfast for children, community testing for tuberculosis and lead poisoning, free clothing drives, cultural events, and Puerto Rican history classes. In Chicago they also set up a free dental clinic and a free community day-care center. The Young Lords worked to improve conditions for incarcerated Puerto Ricans and for the rights of Vietnam War veterans. They coordinated a great deal with the Black Panther Party, and their membership was not made up exclusively of Puerto Ricans; chapters often included African American members and Latinos of other national-origin backgrounds. The group's overarching goal was self-determination for Puerto Ricans in the United States and on the island.

Unlike in the Chicano movement organizations, women's rights were a key concern for the Young Lords from the beginning, largely because the founding members often included women. In Chicago, a sub-group of the Young Lords led a group of women called 'Mothers and Others'. The group centered around women's rights and worked to educate the male members and the community at large about the issues facing Puerto Rican women. In New York, one of the first steps undertaken by the new organization was establishing a thirteen-point program delineating what the Young Lords stood for. Point #10 included a sentence stating that 'Machismo must be revolutionary and not oppressive'. The female members protested that machismo can never be revolutionary because it is always oppressive. The men agreed, and the platform was revised; point #10 was deleted and a new point #5 was added which said: 'We want equality for women. Down with machismo and male chauvinism.' This was the only change made to the original document. The female members demanded the organization provide child care, so that women could attend the meetings; and they made the point that every issue of the newspaper should contain articles about women's issues as well as articles written by women.[33]

The Young Lords quickly became famous for taking dramatic actions. Like the Black Panthers, the Young Lords based their strategy on using social service provision as a means of offering political education. For example, many of the chapters would play the Puerto Rican national anthem while serving children breakfast, as a way of encouraging cultural maintenance. In Chicago, the Young Lords, along with some members of Students for a Democratic Society (SDS), occupied the McCormick Theological Seminary. They demanded that the seminary provide funds for low-income housing in the community, a children's center, a cultural center for Latin Americans, and legal assistance. They occupied the seminary for seven days. As a result, the Lincoln

Park neighborhood received $600,000 for low-income housing. The seminary also agreed to open its facilities for community use. The Chicago Lords also established a free breakfast program for children and proposed starting a day-care center. They approached the head of the Methodist Church, asking him to provide space for housing the center. He was receptive, but the congregation was not; so the Young Lords occupied the church. In the end, they were able to establish their day-care center. Their final major project was the creation of a free health clinic for the community, which provided preventive care, prenatal care, eye exams, and other important health services for the individuals living in the area.

The New York chapter of the Young Lords engaged in similar activities as the groups in Chicago and elsewhere, but this one was able to garner the highest media attention and national recognition. Part of the reason was that this group of organizers was very adept at using the media; it published its own newspaper (*Palante*, meaning '*Forward*') and produced a local weekly radio show, also called 'Palante'. In order to decide what their first major action should be, the group canvassed the residents of Spanish Harlem. Much to their surprise, the issue that was mostly on people's minds was that of trash, specifically the fact that the city sanitation department picked up the *barrio* trash only sporadically. In the summer of 1969, the Young Lords spent a number of days sweeping up the trash into piles, so that the sanitation department could collect it more easily. When the city still did not pick up the trash, the activists moved the piles into the middle of one of Manhattan's major avenues and lit the piles on fire, making their point quite dramatically and garnering a great deal of media attention in the process.

The New York Young Lords then turned to establishing children's breakfast and free clothing programs. As the programs grew, the organization needed more space. Just as in Chicago, one of the neighborhood churches happened not to be used during the week, and this made it an ideal location to house these programs. When the Young Lords approached the pastor, a Cuban refugee, to see if they could use the church basement for their programs, he refused. The Young Lords then attended the church one Sunday to address the congregation directly. When they began to speak, a signal was given to the police, who were stationed throughout the church. Chaos quickly ensued, with the police beating and arresting Young Lord members. The next day's headlines read: 'Young Puerto Ricans ask Church for Food Programs for Children. Thirteen arrested'.[34] Three weeks later, the Young Lords occupied the church, renamed it the 'People's Church' and set up 'serve the people' programs, which included free breakfast and clothing programs, a liberation school, free health services, and community dinners. After eleven days the police moved in, arresting 106 Young Lords and their supporters. The People's Church drew national media attention and brought a national focus on Puerto Rican issues for the first time.

Health issues were also a priority for the Young Lords in New York. They went door-to-door collecting urine samples from *barrio* children, and from these samples they documented high levels of lead poisoning in the community. Similarly, they went door-to-door to conduct tuberculosis testing, finding very high levels here too. They tried to convince the city health department to bring their x-ray truck into the neighborhood for tuberculosis testing; the city refused. So the Young Lords 'liberated' the truck and brought it to the *barrio*. The driver and the technician agreed to stay and test people, hundreds of whom were tested as a result.[35] Finally, the South Bronx was home to Lincoln Hospital, a facility which had been condemned (or found unfit for human habitation) by the City of New York twenty-five years earlier but had yet to be replaced. This was the only medical facility serving this largely Puerto Rican community. To protest against the conditions there, in July 1970 the Young Lords occupied the hospital for one day; they staged a similar takeover a year later. They demanded that a new hospital be built and that preventive health care programs be established for the community. In 1976 the city responded by building a new Lincoln Hospital. The Young Lords of New York were also active in prison issues. During the riot at Attica state prison, its leaders were asked to mediate the conflict. The mediation and the subsequent negotiations resulted in improved conditions for prisoners throughout the New York State Prison system.

Over time, however, it proved difficult to maintain this level of activity and activism. The Young Lords' heyday was from 1969 to 1972. Like other radical organizations of the time, the Lords were subject to surveillance and infiltration by the FBI's COINTELPRO, which increased infighting and paranoia within the group. The group also experienced difficulty when it tried to expand to the island of Puerto Rico itself. Puerto Ricans on the island did not embrace the organization and many in the US leadership thought it more important for the Young Lords to focus on issues on the mainland. This tension between focus on the island or focus on the US was one of the key factors which undid the Young Lords' organization. Many of the group's activists went on to careers in the media, or continued community-level activism. In the early 1970s, some of the

New York Young Lords formed a new organization, the Puerto Rican Revolutionary Workers Organization (PRRWO).

Like the Chicano Movement, the movements of Puerto Ricans also included a number of student groups. The Puerto Rican Student Union (PRSU), or *La Unión*, as it was often called, was the most important Puerto Rican student group at the time. Most powerful in New York City, *La Unión* established chapters on campuses throughout the north east. It also established a community office in the South Bronx (later the office moved to East Harlem), to emphasize the fact that Puerto Rican college students needed to maintain their ties to the community (a sentiment quite similar to that of MEChA). In 1970, the PRSU, in cooperation with the Young Lords, organized the first national conference of Puerto Rican students. Within higher education, the group advocated the establishment of Puerto Rican Studies programs, the use of culturally sensitive curricula, and admissions and retention services for Puerto Rican and Latino students.[36] The PRSU was critical in the founding of the Center for Puerto Rican Studies in CUNY, the first program of its kind in the nation. It also helped to organize the 'Free Puerto Rico!' movement together with the Young Lords. In 1971, the two groups mobilized 1,000 students to attend a conference at Columbia University. The purpose was to set up 'Free Puerto Rico Now!' committees in high schools and colleges across the country. After the conference, organizers put together a mass demonstration in which 10,000 people marched from *El Barrio* to the United Nations to demand Puerto Rican independence, freedom for Puerto Rican political prisoners, and an end to police brutality. Even though the PRSU worked closely with the Lords, they were a separate organization. In the early 1970s, however, they chose to merge completely with the Lords' successor organization, the PRRWO.[37]

At the same time when this more radical political activity was occurring within the community, other Puerto Rican leaders were using more mainstream methods to achieve the community's goals. Politicians like Herman Badillo ran for local office and were successful. One of the factors explaining their success was the existence of this more radical arm within community politics. The existence of groups like the Young Lords drew public attention to Puerto Rican issues; it also made it more politically expedient for the city and state leadership to satisfy the demands of the more mainstream politicians. In this way, Puerto Rican politics in the 1960s and early 1970s contained two prongs – one moderate and one radical – and both helped each other. For example, leaders like Badillo were able to negotiate with city police so as to ensure that the Young Lords would not have to serve time in jail for occupying the People's Church. On the other hand, the Young Lords increased media scrutiny on city leaders and brought into attention the many problems that needed to be solved. This helped the mainstream political leadership to make their case and to prompt the city government to address these problems. It is unlikely that either group would have been equally successful on its own, without the other.

There were a number of other leftist Puerto Rican organizations active during this period, including the MPI–PSP (Movement for Independence, Puerto Rican Socialist Party), *El Comité* (which became the MINP), and the MLN (Movement for National Liberation). Like the Young Lords, these groups proposed broad-based programs designed to improve the status of the community. Although there was some coordination among these different groups, there was also a great deal of infighting. The one issue that managed to unite all of them was working to free the nationalist prisoners from the attack on the US capitol. In the end they were successful; President Jimmy Carter granted them all a pardon in 1979. These leftist organizations also included one paramilitary group, the *Fuerzas Armadas de Liberación Nacional* (FALN; Armed Forces of National Liberation). Made up of activists and former Chicago Young Lords, from 1974 to about 1980 this group engaged in armed actions against the US government and military, actions which included an estimated 120 bombings in Chicago and New York. Its members were eventually captured in a series of arrests in the 1980s. Sixteen were sentenced to terms in jail ranging from 35 to 105 years, despite the fact that none was connected directly to any bombing or to any injury to a person. Once the nationalist prisoners were released in 1979, Puerto Rican activists focused their attention on securing the release of the FALN prisoners. They were successful in 1999, when President Bill Clinton granted all sixteen a presidential pardon; they had served more than nineteen years in prison at the time of their pardons.

This activism on the part of Puerto Ricans had a number of effects. Most broadly, it made Americans more aware of the issues facing Puerto Ricans in the United States, and it forced elected officials to take those concerns into consideration. The Democratic Party, which was the dominant political actor in most of the cities with large Puerto Rican populations, finally included Puerto Ricans in its leadership structure; this led to many Puerto Ricans being elected to public office at the local level and being appointed to government positions as well. The use of both insider and outsider tactics on the part of political activists thus produced very tangible results. At the national level, Puerto Ricans were included

Figure 4.2 *Jennifer López and Husband Marc Anthony at the 2006 Puerto Rican Day Parade in New York City.*

Source: Henry Lamb/BEI, Rex Features

under civil rights legislation, including the Voting Rights Act, and were recognized as a group which had experienced historical discrimination in the United States. In 1972, Puerto Rican activists formed the Puerto Rican Legal Defense and Education Fund (PRLDF), which continues to use the legal system in order to ensure full political and social rights for Puerto Ricans in the United States. In New York City, the movement led to a new expression of Puerto Rican cultural identity – one that had its roots in the community's experiences in the United States as well as in Puerto Rico. The new identity, for which the term 'Nuyorican' was coined, was meant to reflect this bicultural experience and is celebrated through community arts and cultural events, for instance the Puerto Rican Day parade.

In addition to these broad changes, the Puerto Rican movement also had very tangible successes. It led to the establishment of Puerto Rican Studies programs across the north eastern United States. These programs have become centers for rigorous academic research focusing on the Puerto Rican experience. At the local level, many movement organizations continue to exist, albeit with different names. These organizations continue to work to improve access to services and the quality of life for Puerto Rican communities in the United States. At the international level, movement organizations were successful in keeping the status of Puerto Rico, and the question of colonialism more generally, on the agenda of the United Nations. Although the island was not made independent, it was not annexed to the United States either – which many thought likely to happen.

Puerto Rican Politics Today

Although the Puerto Rican middle class has grown substantially in the United States since the 1980s, poverty and a lack of socioeconomic mobility are still important concerns facing Puerto Rican communities in the United States. In addition to growing class differentiation, the mainland Puerto Rican community has changed with regard to its geographic dispersion. Until the 1970s, the majority of Puerto Ricans in the United States lived in New York City. This situation has changed dramatically, and there are now ten states which contain a Puerto Rican population greater than 45,000. As can be seen from Table 4.2, in each of these states Puerto Ricans make up a very different percentage of the total Latino population. In states like California and Texas they are likely to have political influence only in coalition with Mexican Americans. In Massachusetts and Pennsylvania, in contrast, the issues facing the Latino community will probably be driven by Puerto Rican concerns. Thus dispersion involves differences in settlement experiences and also in political power and coalition-building across localities.

The final change which has occurred in Puerto Rican politics since the 1950s is the expansion of traditional officeholding. As was mentioned above, the Puerto Rican movement paved the way for Puerto Ricans to run for political office on a major party ticket. Puerto Rican Maurice

Table 4.2 The Puerto Rican Population by Selected States, 1990 and 2000

State	1990		2000	
	Puerto Rican population	Percentage of whole Latino population	Puerto Rican population	Percentage of whole Latino population
California	126,417	1.6%	140,570	1.3%
Connecticut	146,842	69.0%	194,443	61.0%
Florida	247,010	16.0%	482,027	18.0%
Illinois	146,059	16.5%	157,851	10.3%
Massachusetts	151,193	53.0%	199,207	46.5%
New Jersey	320,133	43.0%	366,788	33.0%
New York	1,086,601	49.0%	1,050,293	37.0%
Ohio	45,853	33.0%	66,269	31.0%
Pennsylvania	148,988	64.0%	228,557	58.0%
Texas	42,981	<1.0%	69,504	1.0%
Total US	2,727,754	12.2%	3,406,178	9.6%

Source: US Department of the Census, 1990 and 2000; summary files compiled by the author

Ferre served in the Florida state house in the 1960s and was mayor of Miami from 1973 to 1985. Fernando Ferrer was a Bronx Borough president for fourteen years and ran failed bids for mayor of New York in 1997 and 2001. In 1994, Carmen Arroyo became the first Puerto Rican woman to hold a New York state assembly seat. Bonnie García, a member of the California State Assembly, is the only Republican Puerto Rican woman currently serving in the California State legislature. There were three Puerto Rican representatives serving in the 110th US Congress: Luis Gutiérrez (D–IL), Nydia Velázquez (D–NY) and José Serrano (D–NY). Puerto Rican representatives also currently serve in the Connecticut, Massachusetts, and Florida state legislatures.

Conclusion

Puerto Rican migration to the United States has been strongly affected by the status of Puerto Ricans as US citizens and by the United States' designation of Puerto Rico as a US territory after the Spanish–American War. The status of the island has always been a key concern in Puerto Rican politics, and, given that it remains unresolved, this concern will continue. The largest wave of Puerto Rican migrants arrived in the

United States at the height of racial segregation. Because of its mixed race background, the Puerto Rican community had difficulty fitting into the US' black/white racial binary. The racialization of its members limited their integration into the major political parties and limited their economic opportunities in the United States. Yet through their organizing and activism, the Puerto Ricans were able to define a new identity for themselves – one that included the community's experiences in the United States. Through this organizing they were also able to improve the quality of life in Puerto Rican communities and to get Puerto Rican issues included into US political discourse. By so doing, they increased their opportunities to hold political office and their political influence. They were also able to alter some of the structural constraints surrounding Puerto Rican socioeconomic mobility and adaptation in the United States. The one main constraint that remains, however, is the unresolved status of the island of Puerto Rico.

GUIDE TO FURTHER READINGS

Briggs, Laura. 2002. *Reproducing Empire: Race, Sex, Science, and US Imperialism in Puerto Rico.* Berkeley: University of California Press.

Jennings, James and Monte Rivera, eds. 1984. *Puerto Rican Politics in Urban America.* Westport, CT: Greenwood Press.

Sánchez, Korrol, Virginia. 1994. *From Colonia to Community: The History of Puerto Ricans in New York City*: Berkeley: University of California Press.

Sánchez, José Ramón. 2007. *Boricua Power: A Political History of Puerto Ricans in the United States.* New York: New York University Press.

Torres, Andrés and José E. Velázquez, eds. 1998. *The Puerto Rican Movement: Voices from the Diaspora.* Philadelphia: Temple University Press.

CHAPTER FIVE

Cuban Americans: Occupation, Revolution, and Exile Politics

Objectives

- Understand the political and economic relationship Cuba had with the United States
- Understand the effect of the Cuban Revolution on that relationship
- Understand how the United States' geopolitical concerns affected the treatment and benefits received by Cuban refugees in the United States
- Understand how the exile experience and US government support facilitated Cuban political incorporation

Introduction

Cuba is located ninety miles off of Key West, Florida. This proximity has resulted in an intimate relationship between Cuba and the United States since the nineteenth century. That relationship was the foundation of the US' response to the Cuban Revolution in 1959 and of its approach to Cuban migration since that time. No country in Latin America, and no Latin American immigrants, experience the same treatment as Cuba and the Cubans. The unique legal standing that Cuban-origin migrants have when they arrive in the United States, and its relationship to the US' concerns about the cold war, has had a profound impact on the social, economic, and political status of Cubans and Cuban Americans in the United States.

In the mid-nineteenth century, Cuba and Puerto Rico constituted the last of Spain's holdings in Latin America. In the 1860s a strong movement for independence began in Cuba, starting with the 'Grito de Yara' in 1868. That event began what is called the Ten Years' War, in which Cuban *independencistas* fought the Spanish. Neither side was successful in defeating the other, so the Spanish Crown offered Cuba a limited autonomy in order to put a stop to the violence. The independence movement did not end, however. Many of the pro-independence forces left the country in order to gather financial support from abroad. The vast majority, including journalist and poet José Martí, one of the principal leaders of the movement, settled in the United States. Martí published writings, gave speeches, and worked towards increasing American awareness of the situation in Cuba. In New York City, in 1892, he formed *el Partido Revolucionario Cubano* (the Cuban Revolutionary Party). Initially the party had chapters only in New York and Philadelphia, but it quickly spread to Tampa, Florida and Key West. Fighting between the insurgents and the Spanish began anew in 1895. On 24 February 1895, Martí returned to Cuba to participate in the armed struggle; he was killed on 19 May.

Martí was successful in his efforts and attracted the attention of William Randolph Hearst, publisher of, among other newspapers, the *New York Journal*. Hearst began publishing stories about the plight of the Cuban people under Spanish rule. These stories became all the more powerful when, in response to a growing insurgency on the island, Spanish general Valeriano Weyler y Nicolau instituted a policy of *reconcentración* (reconcentration) to control Cuban insurgents. Seeking to starve out the rebels operating in the countryside, he herded the rural population into garrisoned towns and placed the entire island under martial law in February 1896. The result was widespread misery and starvation, much of which was photographed and documented for the American audience by Hearst's newspapers. It is estimated that at least 30 percent of those housed in the camps perished from lack of proper food, poor sanitary conditions, and lack of access to medicine.

Yet the United States had had interests in Cuba long before Hearst began publishing his stories. During the Ten Years War, American sugar interests bought up large tracts of land in Cuba. Noting the growing American economic interests in Cuba, in 1869 the US government offered to buy Cuba from Spain for $100 million; Spain refused. Despite this, Cuba's economy continued to become more closely linked with that of the United States. On the one hand, the Cuban tobacco industry was partially transplanted to the North American south. On the other, due to a sharp drop in sugar prices that took place from early 1884, the old Cuban 'sugar nobility', unable to mechanize the trade and to cut costs, began to disintegrate and lose its dominant role in the island's economy and society. This facilitated US penetration of the Cuban economy. Sugar estates and mining interests passed from Spanish and Cuban to US hands, and it was US capital, machinery, and technicians that helped to save the sugar mills by making them competitive with European beet sugar. In 1894 nearly 90 percent of Cuba's exports went to the United States, which in turn provided Cuba with 38 percent of its imports. That same year Spain took only 6 percent of Cuba's exports, providing it with 35 percent of its imports. By 1895 the United States had more than $50 million invested in Cuba, and US annual trade with Cuba was worth nearly $100 million. These economic interests were an important factor in moving the United States towards military intervention in Cuba.

There were also political and strategic reasons for the United States to maintain an interest in Cuba. In 1896, both the US Senate and the House of Representatives overwhelmingly passed resolutions calling for the recognition of the Cuban insurgency and of Cuban independence. Also, in the 1890s US military strategists were recommending the development of US naval power, combining the establishment of naval bases in the Caribbean with the construction of a fleet of armor-plated, steam-driven battleships. This strategy was endorsed by Theodore Roosevelt when he was secretary of the navy. The first major test of this new naval strategy would be in the Spanish–American War.

Thus by 1897 there was a whole variety of American interests, economic and political, favoring US intervention in Cuba. Newly inaugurated President William McKinley was anxious to become involved; that interest only grew when the *New York Journal* published a copy of a letter from Spanish Foreign Minister Enrique Dupuy de Lôme criticizing the American president. Events moved swiftly after the explosion aboard the *USS Maine* in Havana harbor in February 1898. On 9 March, Congress passed a law allocating $50 million to build up American military strength. On 17 March, Vermont Senator Redfield Proctor, who had traveled to Cuba at his own expense in February, urged his Senate colleagues and the US business community that the situation in Cuba was so dire that US military intervention was the only answer. On 28 March, the US Naval Court of Inquiry found that a mine had blown up the *Maine*.[1] On 4 April, the *New York Journal* printed an issue dedicated to the war in Cuba and in which the publishers called for the immediate entry of the United States into war with Spain; they printed one million copies. On 19 April, the US Congress, by a vote of 311 to 6 in the House and of 42 to 35 in the Senate, adopted the Joint Resolution for war with Spain. The resolution included the Teller Amendment, named after Senator Henry Moore Teller (R–Colorado), which stated that the United States had no intention of exercising jurisdiction or control over Cuba and that the United States would leave the island as soon as the war was over. President McKinley signed the resolution on 20 April and both countries formally recognized their being at war on 25 April 1898.

American forces immediately were in contact with Cuban rebels, who supplied the United States with military maps, intelligence, and a core of rebel officers to coordinate US efforts on the island. The rebels also fought alongside the US in a number of squirmishes with the Spanish. Despite having almost 200,000 troops on the island, the Spanish were quickly defeated. Representatives of Spain and of the United States signed a peace treaty in Paris on 10 December 1898. The treaty established the independence of Cuba; ceded Puerto Rico and Guam to the United States; and allowed the United States to purchase the Philippines Islands from Spain for $20 million. The war had cost the United States $250 million and 3,000 lives; 90 percent of these victims had perished from infectious diseases such as yellow fever.

In January 1899, the United States installed a provisional military government in Cuba and began a debate as to what should happen to the country. Although many Americans still supported Cuban independence, there was growing sentiment that the United States should annex Cuba. By September 1899, Cubans on the island were taking seriously the threat of annexation. In an interview with the *Chicago Chronicle*, Cuban General Carlos García warned that Cubans would not surrender their independence and that, if the United States attempted to annex the island, it would meet with armed resistance. In November, General Máximo Gómez was quoted in the *New York Times* as saying: 'The honorable Cuban should place before himself the ideal of the republic, remembering that every day on which the sun sets until the establishment of the republic is an injury to the Cubans.'[2] In November and December of that year, Cubans staged a series of protests and rallies calling for a speedy end to the US occupation.

The first municipal elections held in Cuba after the war, which took place in June 1900, also demonstrated Cuban opposition to annexation. The Cuban National Party and the Republican Party, both strongly against annexation, won almost all of the races. The Democratic Union Party, which openly favored annexation, did not win control of any city. These electoral defeats led the American military governor, General Leonard Wood, to call for an election to choose delegates to a Cuban Constitutional Convention. The draft of the Constitution of the Republic of Cuba was published in January 1901. The new constitution was modeled after the US Constitution. Shortly afterwards, the US House and Senate passed the Platt Amendment, which stipulated that Cuba had only a limited right to conduct its own foreign and debt policy. It also gave the US an open door to intervene in Cuban affairs. Under the amendment, Cuba also agreed to sell or lease to the US 'lands necessary for coaling or naval stations at certain specified points to be agreed upon'.

Textbox 5.1 The Platt Amendment, 1901

The United States occupied Cuba for five years after 1898. In 1901 Secretary of War Elihu Root drafted a set of articles (later known as the Platt Amendment) as guidelines for future United States-Cuban relations. Despite considerable Cuban resistance, they became a part of the 1902 Cuban Constitution. In subsequent years the United States used the amendment several times to send troops to maintain or place friendly governments in power and to protect investments. The amendment was abrogated in 1934.

Whereas the Congress of the United States of America, by an Act approved March 2, 1901, provided as follows:

Provided further, That in fulfillment of the declaration contained in the joint resolution approved April twentieth, eighteen hundred and ninety-eight, entitled 'For the recognition of the independence of the people of Cuba, demanding that the Government of Spain relinquish its authority and government in the island of Cuba, and withdraw its land and naval forces from Cuba and Cuban waters, and directing the President of the United States to use the land and naval forces of the United States to carry these resolutions into effect,' the President is hereby authorized to 'leave the government and control of the island of Cuba to its people' so soon as a government shall have been established in said island under a constitution which, either as a part thereof or in an ordinance appended thereto, shall define the future relations of the United States with Cuba, substantially as follows:

'I.-That the government of Cuba shall never enter into any treaty or other compact with any foreign power or powers which will impair or tend to impair the independence of Cuba, nor in any manner authorize or permit any foreign power or powers to obtain by colonization or for military or naval purposes or otherwise, lodgement in or control over any portion of said island.'

'II. That said government shall not assume or contract any public debt, to pay the interest upon which, and to make reasonable sinking fund provision for the ultimate discharge of which, the ordinary revenues of the island, after defraying the current expenses of government shall be inadequate.'

'III. That the government of Cuba consents that the United States may exercise the right to intervene for the preservation of Cuban independence, the maintenance of a government adequate for the protection of life, property, and individual liberty, and for discharging the obligations with respect to Cuba imposed by the treaty of Paris on the United States, now to be assumed and undertaken by the government of Cuba.'

'IV. That all Acts of the United States in Cuba during its military occupancy thereof are ratified and validated, and all lawful rights acquired thereunder shall be maintained and protected.'

'V. That the government of Cuba will execute, and as far as necessary extend, the plans already devised or other plans to be mutually agreed upon, for the sanitation of the cities of the island, to the end that a recurrence of epidemic and infectious diseases may be prevented, thereby assuring protection to the people and commerce of Cuba, as well as to the commerce of the southern ports of the United States and the people residing therein.'

'VI. That the Isle of Pines shall be omitted from the proposed constitutional boundaries of Cuba, the title thereto being left to future adjustment by treaty.'

'VII. That to enable the United States to maintain the independence of Cuba, and to protect the people thereof, as well as for its own defense, the government of Cuba will sell or lease to the United States lands necessary for coaling or naval stations at certain specified points to be agreed upon with the President of the United States.'

'VIII. That by way of further assurance the government of Cuba will embody the foregoing provisions in a permanent treaty with the United States.'

Source: 'The Platt Amendment', in *Treaties and Other International Agreements of the United States of America, 1776–1949*, Vol. 8, ed. C.I. Bevans (Washington, DC: United States Government Printing Office, 1971), pp. 1116–17.

The passing of the amendment provoked massive protests and denouncements of it in Cuba. On 27 February, the Cuban constitutional convention passed five declarations which clearly expressed their opposition to the terms laid out for Cuban governance by the Platt Amendment. These were:

1 The Government of Cuba will not make a treaty or agreement with any foreign power which may compromise or limit the independence of Cuba, or which may permit or authorize any power to obtain by means of colonization or for military or naval purposes, or in any other manner, any foothold or authority, or right over any portion of Cuba.

2 The Government will not permit its territory to be used as a base of operations for war against the United States or against any foreign nation.

3 The Government of Cuba accepts in its entirety the Treaty of Paris, in which are affirmed the rights of Cuba to the extent of the obligations which are explicitly indicated, and especially those which the international law imposes for the protection of life and property, substituting itself for the United States in the pledge, which they assumed in that sense according to Articles 12 and 102 of the Treaty of Paris.

4 Cuba recognizes as legally valid all acts of the Military Government during the period of occupation, also the rights arising out of them,

in conformity with the joint resolution and the Foraker amendment and the existing laws of the country.

5 The Governments of the United States and Cuba ought to regulate their commercial relations by means of a treaty based on reciprocity, and with tendencies toward free trade in natural and manufactured products, mutually assuring ample special advantages in their respective markets.[3]

In the face of increasing Cuban opposition, General Wood wrote to the US Secretary of War Elihu Root. He asked: 'Can you indicate our [the US] action in case the Cuban Convention should refuse to accept the Platt Amendment?' Root responded: 'The Platt Amendment is, of course, final and the members of the Convention who may be responsible for refusing to establish relations on that basis will injure only themselves and their country. If the Convention takes such a course it will have failed to perform the duty for which it was elected and the duty must be performed by others.'[4] Despite this threat, in April 1901 the Cuban Constitutional Convention rejected the motion to accept the Platt Amendment by a vote of 24 to 2. A second vote, held six days later, rejected the amendment again, 18 to 10. In May, after long discussions with President McKinley and Secretary Root, the Cubans accepted the amendment by a vote of 15 to 14. The document approved by the convention included not only the exact words of the Platt Amendment, but Article I of the Treaty of Paris, as well as long extracts from Root's various explanations of the purposes of the amendment, including the assurance that 'the Platt law has for its object the guaranteeing of the independence of Cuba, and does not mean interference with its government or the exercise of a protectorate or of sovereignty. . .'.

Secretary Root immediately rejected the actions of the Cuban Constitutional Convention and insisted that Cubans could not expect the American army to withdraw until the Platt Amendment was adopted verbatim, with no changes or additions. The convention delegates acceded to this request in June, accepting the amendment verbatim by a vote of 16 to 11. After the passing of the amendment, Orville H. Platt, one of the amendment's authors, argued in the *Independent* that the amendment was necessary because 'Cubans are incapable of stable self-government' and 'in many respects . . . they are like children'.

Thus began Cuba's existence as an independent nation. The United States was intimately intertwined in the country's economics and politics and routinely exercised its power to influence both. On the economic side, in 1903 the two countries signed a reciprocity treaty which gave preference to Cuban sugar in the US market, reduced duties on American imports, and encouraged US investment in the island, thus tying the Cuban economy even more tightly to the US market. This agreement was renegotiated in 1934. The Cuban *peso* was also pegged to the US dollar, which meant that Cubans had no say about their monetary policy; the latter was set by the US Federal Reserve. By 1913 US investments in Cuba were estimated at $220 million, which constituted 17.7 percent of the total US investment in Latin America. By 1928, the United States controlled about three quarters of the Cuban sugar crop and was responsible for the move to large-scale plantations for sugar production.

On the political side, by 1906 the new Cuban government was in crisis: an armed rebellion attempting to take down the regime of President Estrada Palma was just beginning. President Theodore Roosevelt was quoted as saying, in response to this crisis: 'I am so angry with that infernal little Cuban republic that I would like to wipe its people off the face of the earth. All we have wanted from them is that they would behave themselves and be prosperous and happy so that we would not have to interfere. And now, lo and behold, they have started an utterly unjustifiable and pointless revolution and may get things into such a snarl that we have no alternative save to intervene . . .'.[5] Despite the president's frustration, the United States government intervened, taking control of the island until new elections were held and a new government installed in 1909. This intervention laid the groundwork for US–Cuba relations throughout the first half of the twentieth century. The United States' military forces took control of the Cuban government on two other occasions. In 1912 the United States entered Cuba to quell a black revolt; and in 1917 it forced Cuba to hold a special election. The US military remained in Cuba until 1922, to 'advise' the new president. In 1933 the United States government played an integral part in compelling dictator Gerardo Machado to leave office. Then the US appointed his successor. As part of Franklin Delano Roosevelt's 'good neighbor' policy, the Platt Amendment was rescinded in 1934, but the United States continued playing an important role in Cuban politics behind the scenes.

After Machado left office, a group of army soldiers led by Sergeant Fulgencio Batista took over the government. The 1930s saw a succession of puppet presidents who ran Cuba, with Batista remaining the controlling figure behind the scenes. In 1940 he took over the presidency directly, in an election widely considered fraudulent. Under his presidency Cuba passed a new constitution in 1940. Considered one of the most progressive constitutions of the time, it provided for land reform, public education, and a minimum wage. Unfortunately most of its provisions were never implemented. After a series of corrupt governments during the 1940s, Batista returned to power in a *coup* in 1952. One of his first acts was to suspend the 1940 constitution and to halt all elections.

The United States strongly supported Batista's dictatorship. In 1958 the United States provided Batista's government with $1,000,000 in military aid. All of Batista's arms, planes, tanks, ships, and military supplies came from the United States, and his army was trained by a joint mission of the three branches of the US armed forces. Batista's government largely supported US economic interests, which, by the late 1950s, were substantial. American companies controlled 90 percent of Cuban mines, 80 percent of public utilities, 50 percent of railways, 40 percent of the sugar production and 25 percent of bank deposits. Yet this high level of investment did not generate significant employment. In 1957 American firms employed only about 1 percent of the Cuban population.

Cubans were increasingly opposed to the Batista government, which was highly repressive. The opposition included a growing guerrilla movement led by Fidel Castro, Che Guevara, and Camilo Cienfuegos which attacked Cuban government outposts in the Sierra Maestra. The guerrilla movement obtained positive news coverage in the United States, including a May 1957 interview with Castro which was aired by CBS. By 1958 Batista was beginning to lose American support. In December, millionaire William Pawley offered him the use of his home in Florida in case Batista agreed to go into exile; Batista refused. But after additional pressure from the CIA Batista decided to flee the country after all on 1 January 1959. Guevara and Cienfuegos led the rebels into Havana; Castro did not arrive in Havana until 7 January, the very day when the US government officially recognized the new Cuban government.

At this point the United States was not terribly concerned about what would happen in Cuba. As historian Terence Cannon writes: 'The US did not send in the marines for one basic reason: it did not fear the Revolution. It was inconceivable to the US policy makers that a revolution in Cuba could turn out badly for them. After all, US companies owned the country' (1981: 94). Their concern began to increase, however, as the new Cuban government started to round up former police and army officers from the Batista regime and to execute them after publicly held trials. By March, almost 500 individuals had been executed in this fashion.

The new Cuban government also nationalized the telephone system

Figure 5.1 *Fidel Castro with Vice-President Richard Nixon, April 1959.*
Source: Bettmann/Corbis

and passed an agrarian reform bill, both of which raised US government concerns. In April 1959, Castro made an 'unofficial' visit to the United States (he was invited by a group of journalists) in order to talk about the revolution in Cuba. President Eisenhower, who was feeling increasingly uneasy about the regime, snubbed Castro by saying that he was busy playing golf. Instead, the Cuban leader met with US Vice-President Richard Nixon on 19 April 1959.

The meeting lasted three hours and occurred right after Castro made an appearance on NBC's 'Meet the Press' program. In a confidential memo which he wrote in order to brief Eisenhower and other cabinet officials on the meeting, Nixon said he felt that Castro's goal was 'to win support for his policies from American public opinion'. He went on to say that Castro's 'primary concern seemed to be to convince me that he was sincere, that he was not a communist and that his policies had the support of the great majority of the Cuban people'. Nixon's evaluation of Castro was prophetic. He told Eisenhower that Castro

> has the indefinable qualities which make him a leader of men. Whatever we may think of him he is going to be a great factor in the development of Cuba and very

possibly in Latin American affairs generally. He seems to be sincere, he is either incredibly naïve about Communism or under Communist discipline – my guess is the former . . . But because he has the power to lead to which I have referred we have no choice but at least to try to orient him in the right direction.[6]

Given the tone of this memo, it is not surprising that on 2 May the United States signed a four-point agreement with Cuba, consenting to provide technical cooperation so as to help Cuba in carrying out its agrarian reform. On 17 May Cuba enacted its Agrarian Reform Law, distributing all farmlands of over 1,000 acres in size to Cuban peasants and workers. The law prohibited foreign ownership of Cuban land. This was a major change: at that point in time, 75 percent of Cuban land was in foreign hands. The government agreed to purchase foreign-owned land using 20-year government bonds set at a 4.5 percent interest rate. The price the Cuban government would pay was to be based on the land's valuation as given in the Cuban tax rolls. Many of these value assessments had not been updated in thirty or forty years – which had been a boon to foreign owners: they paid much lower taxes than the land was actually worth. But when it was announced that these same valuations were to be used to provide compensation, the landowners cried foul.

Since many of those landowners were US-based companies, the agrarian reform law quickly led to increased opposition to the Cuban regime in the United States. In mid-June, the US government officially protested against the compensation levels which the Cuban government planned to provide for US-owned land. Landowners from other countries were also unhappy with the plan. Over the course of the year, the Cuban government successfully negotiated compensation agreements with landowners from Britain, Canada, France, Italy, Mexico, Spain, and Sweden. US landowners were the only group to refuse negotiation. In January 1960, Cuba expropriated 70,000 acres of land held by US sugar companies which had refused to sell the land at no matter what price. This expropriation included 35,000 acres held by the United Fruit Company, which at that time owned 235,000 acres of land in Cuba.

This expropriation soured US–Cuba relations quite significantly. The United Fruit Company had many high-level supporters in the Eisenhower Administration and began to push for US intervention in Cuba. The calls for intervention only increased in June 1960 when, after US oil companies refused to refine some crude oil which Cuba had purchased from the Soviet Union, Cuba expropriated its oil refineries, all of which were US-owned. In August the Cuban government took the final step of expropriating all the remaining US-owned companies and land in Cuba.

Thus there was only a brief window, in early 1959, when US–Cuba relations may have moved in a more positive direction. In his memo to Eisenhower, Nixon states on multiple occasions that he doubts whether his arguments have made any impression on Castro. It seems that, with the four-point plan, the United States was attempting to 'orient' the Castro government. But the terms of the agrarian reform law caused the US government to doubt its own ability to influence Castro himself. At that point we see the US government moving towards taking more drastic action to remove Castro from power. The subsequent expropriations most probably only solidified the Eisenhower Administration's sense that they could not control what was happening within the Castro regime.

In September 1960, Fidel Castro prepared to give a speech at the United Nations (UN). The US government required his movements to be restricted to the island of Manhattan; he was to remain as close as possible to the UN headquarters. The same limitations were placed on the Soviet leader Nikita Khrushchev, on the Hungarian leader Janos Kadar, and on the Albanian leader Mehmet Shehu. This was the first time when such restrictions were imposed on persons of rank visiting the General Assembly. In retaliation, Cuba announced that US Ambassador Philip Bonsal would be restricted to the Vedado district of Havana during the period when Castro was restricted to Manhattan.

In the course of that visit to the United States, the Castro delegation received less than favorable treatment from New York's Shelburne Hotel. The hotel refused to allow all the members of Castro's multiracial delegation to stay there. In response, the Castro group moved to the Hotel Theresa in Harlem. There Castro had a meeting with the black civil rights leader Malcolm X, with the author Langston Hughes, and, later, with the Soviet Premier Nikita Khrushchev, along with the leaders of Egypt, Syria, and India. Castro's meeting with Krushchev solidified Eisenhower's perception of him as a communist who therefore must be removed from power.

There was another group interested in removing Castro from power: the Cuban exile community. Responding to the political upheaval in Cuba, Cubans had begun fleeing the country as early as 1958. By 1960 the number of exiles had grown significantly. These exiles quickly learned that they had a common and powerful ally: the United States government. The Eisenhower Administration's desire to isolate the Castro regime rested heavily on the shoulders of the community in exile. The Cuban exiles served two purposes. On the one hand, their presence in the United States and their desire to flee their own homeland provided strong support for the Administration's depiction of the regime as repressive and anti-democratic. On the other hand, the Administration knew that any plan to overthrow the regime would require explicit support of the community in exile, most directly in the form of organizing a 'government in exile' which the United States could quickly recognize after any sort of military intervention on the island. This meant that, as early as 1960, the US government was providing material and personnel to support the development of nascent Cuban exile organizations in the United States. After the Administration decided, in March 1960, to invade Cuba, the CIA (which was planning the invasion) established a number of recruiting offices in south Florida, and Cuban exile volunteers were sent to training camps in Nicaragua, Guatemala, and other parts of the Caribbean to prepare for the invasion.

But the community of Cubans in exile included at least fifty disparate political factions of varied ideological stripes, all claiming to speak for the 'community'. In order to develop a reasonable alternative to the Castro regime, the United States needed these disparate forces to unite into one cohesive group which could form a reasonably legitimate and representative provisional government. That fairly simple goal, however, would prove to be elusive and led the US government to provide significant economic resources to fund the operations of a number of exile organizations before and after the Bay of Pigs invasion.

The CIA's first attempt to organize the exiled community into a coherent political group led to the creation of the *Frente Revolucionario Democrático* (FRD; the Revolutionary Democratic Front). This was the group designed to invade Cuba and establish the new government. But the group was not able to muster much support in the Cuban community at large. So Kennedy decided to use another group of exiles for the invasion, and he developed another provisional government, the *Consejo Revolucionario Cubano* (CRC; the Cuban Revolutionary Council). The Administration was more involved in the organization of this group, to which it even gave a final approval of its manifesto.

In April 1961, the United States went forward with the Bay of Pigs invasion. About 1,500 Cuban exiles, armed, trained, and supplied by the US government, using two ships donated by the United Fruit Company for use in the invasion, landed at the Bay of Pigs in south western Cuba. The plan had been for US fighter planes to take out Castro's air force before the landing, so as to diminish the regime's ability to repel the invasion. These airstrikes were unsuccessful and left most of the Cuban air force intact. The plan had also called for US air cover for the exiles during the invasion itself. President Kennedy, uncomfortable with a plan he did not create, decided to scale back the air cover; but this left the invading troops vulnerable. In addition, the spontaneous Cuban uprising against Castro, which the planners had depended upon, failed to materialize. Without any support on the island and without air cover, the invading force was stranded near the landing zone and was soon captured by the Castro government. In the end, sixty-eight of the exiles died and the remaining ones were captured. The Castro regime ended up ransoming them back to the United States for $48 million in food, medicines, and tractors. The regime remained firmly in place.

Despite the failure of the Bay of Pigs invasion, the Kennedy Administration continued to fund the CRC; it is estimated that they received between $100,000 and $200,000 monthly in order to continue their activities. The Department of Defense also created a program to enlist Cubans into the US military in order to train them in case they were needed for another military operation. As a follow-up to the Bay of Pigs, the Kennedy Administration organized 'Operation Mongoose', a program designed to incite open revolt in Cuba. Cuban exiles were very involved in the execution of this plan, particularly in gathering intelligence, conducting small-scale raids, and engaging in economic sabotage on the island. The Kennedy Administration cancelled this program, however, after the Cuban missile crisis. One of the commitments the United States made towards the Soviet Union during that crisis was not to invade Cuba. This made it impossible for the United States government to work overtly towards overthrowing the regime. But US plots against the regime continued; they simply became covert. The United States still used Cuban exiles to carry out its plans. Now it simply based these plans in other countries, for instance Costa Rica and Nicaragua. One of the central tenets in many of these plans was the elimination of Fidel Castro. It is estimated that the CIA attempted to kill Castro 638 times. Methods included the use of an exploding cigar, a fungus-infected scuba-diving suit, and mafia-style shooting. Castro is reported to have said, in regard to the numerous attempts on his life: 'If surviving assassination attempts were an Olympic event, I would win the gold medal.'

By 1963 the Castro regime had consolidated power, and the basic parameters of the US–Cuba relationship for the next forty-five years had been established. Currently the United States maintains an economic embargo against Cuba, forbidding US companies to trade with it and barring all US exports there except for food, medicines, and humanitarian aid. The United States also bans travel to Cuba. Cuba remains the only country in the world to which US citizens cannot travel freely.[7] The United States does not have formal diplomatic relations with Cuba; both countries maintain interest sections within their respective Swiss embassies.

Cuban Exiles in the United States

The post-1959 Cuban migrants to Florida were not all that different from the Cubans who had settled in Florida during the nineteenth century. Those earlier community members saw themselves as fighting for Cuban independence while at the same time quite successfully integrating themselves into the US economy and politics. The post-revolutionary exiles continued this tradition, working to change the regime on the island while establishing successful political and economic institutions in the United States. This meant that their politics, while starting with a strong focus on the situation in Cuba, evolved towards encompassing and even privileging issues of importance to the community in the United States. That being said, as María Cristina García points out, the Castro regime still looms large in community politics today: 'In a community of largely first-generation immigrants for whom the memory of the revolution is an open wound, Cuba plays a tremendous role in public debate and consciousness' (1997: 121). More than fifty years after the revolution, a pro-Castro Cuban or Cuban American candidate, even if they are running for school board, has little to no chance of winning public office in Miami.

This anti-Castro bent within the Cuban community in the United States has led many observers to describe Cubans as politically monolithic: all speaking with one opinion and one voice on political issues. Yet it is important to remember that, from the beginning, the Cuban community in exile in the United States was made up of individuals representing a variety of political ideologies and perspectives. In the early 1960s there were three main political leanings in this community regarding the future of Cuba: (1) the right wing (that is, former associates of Batista) wanted a conservative, authoritarian government – like that of Batista; (2) the moderates wanted a return to the Democratic process as guaranteed under the 1940 Constitution; and (3) the left wing (former rebels who had fought with Castro) wanted social, economic, and political change, but not necessarily socialism. These ideologically disparate exiles found themselves living side by side in Miami and being united against a common enemy: Fidel Castro. The common enemy gave the political exiles a common ground; and this is something which makes political migrants – as opposed to economic migrants – unique. First, the bulk of Cuban migrants arrived at the same time and had similar experiences. Second, their common story of oppression and loss of homeland, and the common enemy they could blame for that suffering, gave them as a community a strong sense of identity, unity, and shared purpose.

During the first few years after arrival to the US, the community of Cuban exiles was focused on survival and on returning to the homeland. On the other hand, even though the US government supported the exiles, local residents of Miami were not happy about this large influx of foreigners into their midst. Cubans who arrived in the first wave experienced significant discrimination, and it was common to find signs posted in apartment buildings that read: 'No Pets, No Kids, No Cubans.'[8] Local politicians pressured the US government to relocate these new arrivals, so the government created a program that provided Cuban migrants with financial assistance if they immediately relocated away from Miami. The federal government paid for their transportation, helped them to find housing and employment in the new locations, and provided financial support until each migrant secured employment. More than 300,000 individuals were resettled out of Miami under this program.

Yet in spite of the discrimination and of the resettlement programs, the vast majority of Cubans remained in the Miami area. As time went on, they began to place an emphasis on preserving *cubanidad* in exile so that they (and their children) would be ready to return to Cuba when the Castro regime fell. The result was a re-creation of Cuban social institutions in exile. For example, Belén had been a very prestigious Jesuit boys' school in Havana (and one which Fidel Castro attended). The majority of the school's academic board, including the principal, ended up fleeing to Miami, and so they created a new 'Belén' school in the United States, with most of the same teachers, curriculum, and materials. In fact, the first bilingual education programs in the United States were begun by Cubans in Florida, since they believed it was very important for their children to know Spanish so as to be able to return to Cuba with their parents when the time came. This strong imperative for cultural maintenance was another unique characteristic of Cuban exiles. At least over the first decade of their residence in the United States, these immigrants were certain that their return home was imminent. Even though they were integrating themselves into the US economy quite successfully, it was also very important to them to maintain their *cubanidad*. As a result, the Miami community, in exile, constructed a new sense of what it meant to be 'Cuban'. It developed Spanish-language media, particularly talk radio, and Cuban-oriented schools to deliver its message. Historically, it emphasized nineteenth-century Cuban heroes like José Martí, since Cubans of different ideological beliefs could agree on them. The result was a new understanding of what life in Cuba was like, and a very specific understanding of what 'good' (read anti-Castro) Cubans should think politically. This new identity would serve as the foundation for future political organization and activity among Cuban Americans.

Cuban Exiles and Government Support

With the consolidation of the Castro regime in the early 1960s, Cuban exile politics began to move on two tracks. On the one hand, exile political organizations continued to engage in paramilitary activities to overthrow the Castro government and worked to develop the support of the US government for their foreign policy goals. On the other, exile leaders needed to address the serious economic and settlement issues facing their community. Both tracks benefited from Cuba's perceived strategic importance to the United States. Because of this importance, exile organizations were given a great deal of access to the US president to discuss Cuba policy. The CRC reportedly met with Kennedy himself at least four times before the Bay of Pigs invasion, and continued to have access to him afterwards. The CRC dissolved in 1964, but other groups took its place and received significant financial and political support from the US government. For example, the *Movimiento de Recuperación Revolucionario* (MRR) is reported to have received between $3 million and $6 million to train and maintain a paramilitary force of about 200 men in Central America.

This high-level political access is important in terms of the material support it resulted in; but it is also important because it means that Cuban exile leaders could discuss other community-level issues during these high-level meetings. As we saw in Chapter 3, Mexican American political organizations worked for years to try to get a White House conference on Mexican American concerns, and without success. Cuban exiles, because of the historical relationship the United States had with Cuba and because of the United States' concerns about the cold war, were able to have even higher-level access, which included one-on-one meetings with the president, and these enabled them to bring attention to their economic and settlement concerns in a more informal fashion. No other Latino national-origin group has had this level of access to top US government decision-makers across multiple presidential Administrations.

This access, and the symbolic importance of Cuba, also resulted in significant material benefits to the Cuban exile community in the United States. It is estimated that this community received at least $4 billion in direct aid from the US government between 1960 and 1996 – apart from the CIA-sourced funding to Cuban paramilitary organizations discussed above. The US government provided this aid because it served its political interests, both at home and abroad. Internationally, the aid encouraged Cuban migration to the United States, which discredited the Castro regime. Domestically, it offset resentment and political opposition from local leaders in Miami Dade by helping them to pay the costs of Cuban settlement. No other immigrant group in the United States has received this level of direct economic assistance from the US government.

Between 1959 and 1962, 215,323 Cubans migrated to the United States.[9] The first program created to provide aid to these Cuban migrants was the Cuban Refugee Program, which was established by the Kennedy Administration in January 1961. The program provided direct relief, resettlement assistance, and employment assistance to all Cuban migrants. Direct relief included cash payments, food distribution, and access to health services. On the educational side, the federal government provided funding to assist local public schools with the cost of educating their new Cuban students. The government also provided adult refugees with training and educational opportunities, including English-language classes and re-training or licensing programs for professionals. During its tenure, the program provided aid to an estimated 700,000 Cubans and it cost the US government about $1 billion.[10]

The support provided to Cuban exiles under the Refugee Program, and to the Cuban migration in general, was especially controversial in the African American community in Miami. The Cuban migration occurred in the midst of the civil rights movement. African Americans in Florida had been working since the 1950s to improve their political and economic opportunities and to end segregation in the state. Although, as is mentioned above, the Cuban immigrants did experience significant discrimination in Miami, they were not segregated, unlike African Americans in the city; Cuban children were allowed to attend white-only public schools. In addition, the job assistance provided by the Refugee Program tended to situate Cuban immigrants into job sectors that had traditionally been staffed by African Americans, limiting the latter's economic opportunities. Finally, African American leaders complained that native blacks and other immigrants did not have access to the kinds of financial assistance the US government was providing for the Cuban exiles. This animosity between Cubans and African Americans would remain, and it erupted into race riots in Miami in 1980, 1982, and 1989. Thus the members of the Cuban community benefited not only from this direct government assistance, but also from the fact that they arrived in the United States after the start of the civil rights movement, and were therefore not subject to segregation and exclusion in the same ways as Mexican Americans or Puerto Ricans had been.

The Cuban Refugee Program was followed by funding provided by the US government for the Camarioca boatlift and airlift, which took place from 1965 to 1973. In September 1965, Castro announced that those Cubans with relatives in the United States could leave Cuba if their relatives asked for them.[11] This announcement created an immediate refugee crisis. Initially, relatives in Miami took boats to pick up their relatives. When this proved dangerous, the United States negotiated with the Castro government to arrange for a safer means of travel. The United States agreed to pay for the costs of flights from Varadero (a city east of Havana) to Miami. The flights would carry 3,000 to 4,000 people per month and began in December 1965. The total cost is estimated to have been $100/120 million per year. Officials in Florida were outraged. To that point, after the initial wave, Cuban migration had averaged about 35,000 per year. This made their absorption into US society fairly easy. The boatlift/airlift would lead to much larger-scale migration. From 1965 to 1973, 260,561 Cubans were brought to the United States through this program; it was the largest airborne refugee operation in US history.

The airlift more than doubled the Cuban population in the United States and led to the codification of Cubans' migratory status as refugees, which meant that they received preferential treatment under US immigration policy. In November 1966, the US government passed the Cuban Refugee Adjustment Act. Under this act, any individual who was a native Cuban or a citizen of Cuba and had been admitted into the United States after 1 January 1959 was eligible for permanent residence after just one year. Most other immigrants had to reside in the United States for a more extended period in order to receive permanent residence, and they were not guaranteed that their applications would be approved. Under this act, Cubans received not only an expeditious route to permanent residence, but also a blanket guarantee that their petitions would be granted. People fleeing from other countries, even from communist countries during the cold war, had to prove that they were being persecuted; Cubans did not. These were benefits unique to Cuban migrants, and they were the result of the historical relationship between the US and Cuba and of the symbolic importance of Cuban migration during the cold war. Thus, even though on arrival to Miami Cuban migrants faced significant discrimination and the trauma of finding themselves in the United States with little to nothing in terms of material resources, they also received significant financial support from the US government and preferential treatment in terms of US immigration policy. These factors facilitated their economic and political integration into the United States.

Cuban Exile Politics

During the 1960s, the Cuban exile community was concerned mainly with survival in a new country. Whatever politics they did engage in tended to be focused on the home country, and their political organizations often were paramilitary groups working to overthrow the Castro regime. By the 1970s, however, this focus began to change. After spending more than a decade in their new country, many Cubans came to accept that they would be staying indefinitely in the United States. As a result, they started to naturalize at much higher rates. This change in orientation led to changes in the kinds of policies advocated by their community. Some new organizations were created which argued for a more diplomatic approach towards Cuba. Some Cubans showed willingness to visit the island, softening what had been very hard line positions against such a move. In the face of these changes, the paramilitary sector became increasingly desperate, and this in turn led to increasing violence in Miami. For example, from 1973 to 1976 there were 100 bombings and at least ten assassinations in the Miami area alone.[12] Cuban hardliners would threaten, beat, and sometimes kill any Cuban who spoke out in favor of the normalization of relations with Cuba, or who complained about the violence propagated by their groups. Some of these hardliners were arrested, but many cases remain unsolved to this very day. This violence prompted many Cuban Americans to re-evaluate the tactics they had been using and led to a movement towards using incorporation into US politics as the preferred way to effect change in Cuba.

The other aspect of life which changed in the Cuban exile community in the 1970s was the increased success of Cuban-owned businesses. As of 1997, there were almost 90,000 Cuban-owned businesses in Florida. These businesses served two important purposes. On the one hand, their owners were able to employ new Cuban migrants as soon as they arrived, helping to facilitate their settlement in the United States. On the other hand, the public policy needs which arose from their business interests – for example regarding zoning policy, tax policies, or other economic development issues – served as another catalyst for Cuban integration into US politics. These business owners quickly learned that, if they wanted to influence this decision-making at the local, county, or state level, they needed to get allies elected to political office.

This feeling only increased after the Mariel boatlift. In April 1980, Castro announced that anyone wanting to leave Cuba could do so from the port of Mariel. Cuban exiles used whatever vessels they could find to travel to Cuba and retrieve their relatives. Similarly, Cubans from the island rented any available boat, to make the trip to Florida. From April to October 1980, 124,776 Cubans arrived in the United States – forming the third wave of Cuban migration. This influx of new immigrants put a tremendous amount of strain on social services in the Miami area. The US government constructed tent cities to house migrants while they were processed; those with sponsors stayed only for a few days, those without, for more than a year. Initially, Americans were sympathetic to the Cubans' plight. But, as word spread that the Castro government had used the exodus to rid the country of criminals and of the mentally ill, the tide of US public opinion quickly shifted.

The Carter Administration, sensitive to these concerns during an election year, determined that the Mariel Cubans did not satisfy the definition of 'refugee' under the 1980 Refugee Act. They were called instead 'entrants' and given limited government assistance. The states where the migrants settled were also given 100 percent reimbursement for the cost of all education, social services, and health care they pro-vided to the migrants. But even so the Mariel migrants remained deeply unpopular, even within the Cuban exile community. Earlier waves of migrants were concerned that the new arrivals would not be able to adapt to American society and would hurt the community's reputation. Despite this ambivalence among Cubans, the community raised money and provided services to assist with the resettlement of the *marielitos*. It worked towards regularizing their migration status and addressing the status of the many migrants who remained in a legal limbo (and in jail) years after their arrival to the United States. This experience made it even more clear to the Cuban community that they needed to have a greater say in government at all levels in order to influence the policies affecting their communities.

Cubans, the Political Parties, and Bloc Voting

To accomplish this, initially these Cubans turned to the Democratic Party. As late as 1979, 49 percent of Florida's Cubans were registered as Democrats, compared to only 39 percent for the Republican Party.[13] Historically, Cubans in Florida had been strongly Democratic, and the post-1959 immigrants followed this trend initially. Yet Miami, like many cities in the south, was controlled by the Democratic Party. Party registration in the city was so overwhelmingly Democratic that Republican candidates had little or no chance of winning. Most elections were one-party contests, with competition within one party rather than between them. This meant that whatever candidate the party chose to support most often won. Yet, when Cubans were forced to compete for the party nomination, Democratic Party voters did not support Cuban candidates. The Republicans, on the other hand, facing almost certain defeat, were happy to let Cuban candidates onto the ballot.

What happened then was a surprise to many in Miami: the Cuban candidates won. This was due to two key factors: (1) the geographic concentration of the Cuban community; and (2) strong Cuban bloc voting. In terms of geography, even though many Cubans were resettled to other parts of the United States, a significant number of them ended up returning to Miami. According to the 2000 census, 67 percent of all Cubans in the United States lived in Florida, and 52 percent of all Cubans in the United States lived in just one county – Miami Dade.[14] As we saw in Chapter 2, residential segregation plays an important role in ensuring that minority groups can achieve representation within a majoritarian system, because it helps them to surpass the 50 percent threshold. The second factor driving Cuban political representation, which also helped in relation to the majoritarian problem, was their bloc voting. Because of the development of *cubanidad* discussed above, when Cuban candidates ran for office, other Cuban exiles voted for them overwhelmingly. Cubans have the highest voting rates of any Latino national-origin group; in fact they vote at rates higher than those of the US population generally. High turnout combined with bloc voting led to electoral success. A good example is Ileana Ros-Lehtinen's initial run for US Congress in 1989. Her Democratic opponent, when told by Republicans that the seat should go to a Cuban, declared that it should remain 'an American seat', a statement which Ros-Lehtinen called 'racist'. Miami Spanish-language media rallied to her cause, going so far as to say that a vote for the Democrat was a vote for Fidel Castro. In response, an incredible

90 percent of Cuban voters supported Ros-Lehtinen. This overwhelming support, combined with high voter turnout in Little Havana, gave her the margin of victory, despite the fact that 96 percent of blacks and 88 percent of whites voted against her.[15]

This combination – geographic concentration, high voter turnout, and bloc voting – has led to significant levels of Cuban political representation at all levels of government. The first Cuban to win statewide office was Ileana Ros-Lehtinen, who was elected to the Florida state house in 1982. She was elected to the Florida State Senate in 1986, and she became the first Cuban American member of Congress in 1989. In 1985 Xavier Suarez became the first Cuban-born mayor of the city of Miami. In the 110th Congress, there were four Cuban American members of the US House of Representatives: Republicans Ileana Ros-Lehtinen, Lincoln Díaz-Balart, his brother Mario Díaz-Balart (all from Florida), and Democrat Albio Sires, representing New Jersey. There are two Cuban American US Senators: Republican Mel Martínez of Florida and Democrat Bob Menéndez of New Jersey. There also have been a number of high-ranking Cubans in the Bush Administration, including Secretary of Commerce Carlos Gutiérrez; Emilio González, former director of the US Citizenship and Immigration Service (formerly the INS); and Mel Martínez, former secretary of Housing and Urban Development (HUD). At the state level, Bob Martínez was governor of Florida. The speaker of the Florida House is Cuban, as are thirteen of the state's representatives. At the local level, Cubans currently serve as mayors of Miami and of Miami Dade County, and hold positions in Miami city government, local school boards, and local planning commissions.

The importance of Florida in the national presidential campaign also ensures continued Cuban American political influence. It is estimated that four out of five Cubans supported George W. Bush in the 2000 presidential race, in an election which was decided on the basis of a few hundred votes. Over time, the Cuban American community has developed a sophisticated ethnic political machine. Pollsters, consultants, and media experts work together to help in turning out the vote; this contributes to explaining why Cuban American voter turnout is so high. This fact, combined with their bloc voting, increases their ability to achieve electoral results. Cuban Americans in Miami were also seen as instrumental in putting an end to the vote recount in Florida after the 2000 presidenital election, by organizing the protests that took place outside of each vote-counting station. Cuban Americans were especially supportive of Bush's campaign on account of Elián González and of their feeling that the

Clinton Administration should have allowed the boy to remain in the United States rather than returning him to his father in Cuba. The fact that presidential elections in Florida are expected to be close for the foreseeable future means that presidential candidates from both parties, as well as presidents considering their chances of re-election, will attempt to court and maintain the support of the Cuban vote.

Other Forms of Political Influence

In addition to electoral power, the Cuban American community has been highly successful in lobbying US Administrations regarding US–Cuba policy. This process began when Cuban exiles were granted unique access to high levels of the Kennedy Administration. They retained some access with the subsequent Administrations, but there was a general feeling among exiles that the US government was not as serious about getting rid of Castro as they would have liked. All this changed with the election of Ronald Reagan in 1980. Reagan's strong anti-communist rhetoric resonated deeply with the Cuban community. In addition, Reagan was the first presidential candidate to court the Cuban vote. He was successful; over 80 percent of Cuban voters supported him. In order to capitalize on his election, a group of Cuban American business leaders set up a new political organization in 1981 which was designed to help Reagan to craft a more 'realistic' Cuban policy. It was called the Cuban American National Foundation (CANF) and was run by a Bay of Pigs veteran named Jorge Más Canosa.[16] Although the group was headquartered in Florida, they purposely established an office in Washington, DC and started a political action committee (called the Free Cuba PAC), so that they could influence the Administration and fund supportive congressmen. Since its creation, the Free Cuba PAC has taken in $1.7 million in donations and, by the year 2000, had donated $1.3 million to candidates, party committees, and leadership PACs. CANF is non-partisan. It will fund anyone who supports its policies; 56 percent of its contributions went to Democrats, the remainder to Republicans.[17] CANF also has a lobbying arm called the Cuban American Foundation (CAF), which spends over $100,000 annually on lobbying various elected officials. CANF itself is a membership organization, with a membership estimated at over 50,000.

Over time, CANF grew so as to become the most influential Cuban American political organization in the United States. Its members were successful at convincing the US government to establish and fund Radio Martí, a US radio station which broadcasts news and information to

Cuba. They also are credited with ensuring the passing of the Torricelli Bill, which promoted the Cuban embargo to US Law (until then it had been based on an executive order); and with the passing of the Helms-Burton Law, which expanded the embargo so as to prevent foreign companies doing business in the US from doing business with Cuba. Under the George W. Bush Administration, CANF and the Cuban American lobby are largely credited with President Bush's tightening of the embargo: they seem to be behind the increased restrictions on travel to Cuba and behind the increased prosecutions of those who violate the Helms-Burton Law. The perception of CANF as an important and electorally influential political constituency and its ability to provide financial support to members of Congress give it significant political access and influence. This kind of formal political lobbying and cultivation of political connections is another way in which the Cuban American community is able to exercise its political clout.

Cuban Political Ideology and Opinion

But what are the issues of greatest importance to the Cuban American community? Although it is true that anti-Castro feeling remains high there, there is growing diversity of opinion among Cubans regarding the best ways to deal with the problem. According to a 2007 poll conducted by the Cuban Research Institute, just over half of Cubans and Cuban Americans say now that they support establishing a national dialogue among Cuban exiles, Cuban dissidents, and representatives of the Cuban government – compared to only about 22 percent who supported that position in 1991. About half of the Cuban-origin respondents in that poll also said that they supported medicines and food sales to Cuba and the allowance of unrestricted travel – positions which were supported by fewer than 30 percent of respondents in 1991. Cubans and Cuban Americans clearly care deeply about what happens in Cuba and oppose the regime there, but their attitudes are not as black and white as the media or some Cuban American organizations (like CANF) portray them.

Cubans' strong affiliation with the Republican Party, combined with their strong anti-communism, has led many to define the community as conservative. Yet public opinion polls have consistently shown Cubans to hold many traditionally 'liberal' values. Cubans and Cuban Americans are the only Latino national-origin group to report being pro-choice. They also tend to support government services, including the provision of welfare, health care, and social security programs. The Cuban American members of Congress often vote with the Democratic Latino members on these kinds of social issues, and in support of immigrant rights. Cubans are quite conservative in terms of their attitudes towards homosexuality (they are one of the most anti-gay Latino groups) and in their foreign policy attitudes. But Cuban political ideology does not run neatly towards smaller government, fewer social programs, and opposition to abortion, as one would expect from strong Republican partisans. Their party identification can be explained more readily by the unique context they experienced upon arrival, their being shut out of the Democratic Party, and the loyalty the Republican Party fostered in them when it gave them the opportunity to hold political office. This, combined with the perception that Republicans are more anti-communist than Democrats, goes a long way towards explaining Cuban and Cuban American partisanship in Florida. It is important to note that the other area with a large Cuban population – Union City, New Jersey – is also politically represented by Cubans, but those two congressional representatives (Sires and Menéndez) are Democrats. This supports the proposition that partisanship among these exiles is more a product of context and history than of political ideology.

The Limits of Cuban Political Influence

The popular perception is that Cubans are the most politically powerful Latino national-origin group. Much of the evidence points in that direction. They turn out and vote at very high rates, and vote in a cohesive bloc, which strongly benefits their candidates of choice. In proportion to their population, they have the highest number of elected representatives of any Latino national-origin group. The presidential candidates from both parties, and sitting presidents, travel to Miami often in order to court them and construct policies meant to address their needs. Yet what are the policies that Cubans really have influence on? It is generally understood that the Cuban and Cuban American lobby has had an impact on US–Cuba relations. But at no point since 1959 has the Cuban lobby fundamentally *disagreed* with what the US government was already interested in doing in Cuba. Cuban exiles often wanted the United States' position to be stronger; but opposition to the Castro regime has been the goal on both sides. So, does the Cuban lobby have power? Or does its support of standing US government policy simply give that policy legitimacy? It is difficult to know. It would be interesting to see the effect the Cuban lobby might have in the face of an American Administration interested in normalizing US–Cuba relations. So far, no US president has expressed an interest in taking that step. Until they do, it is difficult to know how much influence the Cuban American lobby actually has.

A good case in point is the *balsero* ('rafter') migration crisis in 1994 and the changes it wrought in US immigration policy. In 1990, Cubans began migrating on rafts, clandestinely, to the United States. That year, 467 *balseros* were picked up by the US Coast Guard. But in each subsequent year, the numbers increased. From January to August 1994, more than 6,200 rafters were picked up. In mid-August, in the face of a number of government demonstrations, Fidel Castro announced that his government was considering another mass exodus. Unlike previous US Administrations, the Clinton Administration quickly warned Cuba that it would not allow another boatlift like the Mariel, and that it was prepared to impose a naval blockade if Cuba attempted to launch a similar exodus.[18] This forced the Cuban government to re-evaluate its strategy. Instead, it instructed the Cuban Coast Guard not to forbid Cuban vessels from leaving Cuba of their own accord. By the end of August, 17,000 Cubans had arrived in the United States. This was in spite of the fact that the Clinton Administration, reversing three decades of US policy, announced in August 1994 that Cubans intercepted at sea would no longer be brought to the United States, but rather sent to the Guantánamo naval base in Cuba or other safe haven around the Caribbean. This announcement led (for the first time since the Cuban revolution) to bilateral negotiations with the Cuban government. As a result, an agreement was reached between the two governments. Cuba would stop the *balsero* exodus. In return, the United States would grant 20,000 visas per year to Cubans petitioning to migrate to the United States, not including the immediate relatives of Cubans already in the United States.[19] Ideally, this would deal with the backlog and prevent another mass (and dangerous) exodus in the future.

In response to the *balsero* incident, in 1995 the Clinton Administration made the first major change in US immigration policy towards Cuban migrants since the 1966 Cuban Adjustment Act. The current policy is popularly called 'wet foot, dry foot'. This designation refers to the fact that, if a Cuban migrant is intercepted at sea (and therefore has a 'wet foot'), the US government returns her to Cuba. If that same migrant is able to touch one toe on dry US land (and therefore has a 'dry foot'), she is allowed to settle in the United States. The Cuban community was furious about this change in policy, because they believed it constituted a departure from historical precedent and would lead to differential treatment among migrants. They were correct. The Elián González fiasco illuminated the problems with this new policy. He migrated to the United States with his mother and her boyfriend; his father was left in Cuba, with no notice that they were migrating. Elian's mother and boyfriend drowned en route, leaving him stranded in the ocean until the US Coast Guard found him. Had they simply returned him to Cuba immediately, his feet would have been considered 'wet', and he would have gone directly to his father. As soon as the Coast Guard admitted him to a Miami hospital for medical treatment, his feet became 'dry', and he was eligible for residence in the United States. Once this occurred, releasing him into the custody of his father, his only living parent, became fraught with political meaning and calculation. This problem led to a direct confrontation between the Miami Cuban community and the Clinton Administration, and resulted in the federal government having to remove Elián forcibly from the home of his Miami relatives, so that he could be returned to his father in Cuba.

Although the 'wet foot, dry foot' policy still constitutes a form of special treatment for Cuban migrants in relation to all other immigrants to the United States, it does represent the first change to Cuban migration policy in three decades. It also reflects the growing perception among US policy-makers that Cuban migrants are better characterized as economic migrants than as political refugees. This view is not in line with what members of the Cuban American community believe the US position should be; they see Fidel Castro as a totalitarian dictator and therefore consider all those living in Cuba to be politically persecuted. Their inability to make that perception the dominant view in Washington may reflect a limitation of their political influence at the national level, even with regard to one of their deepest concerns.

Cuban political dominance in Miami may be overstated as well. It is true that the Cuban American community has been highly successful in getting its members elected to political office. Yet the fact of the matter is that the majority of elected officials in Miami are still white, despite the fact that whites make up a minority of the total population. In addition, over the past twenty years Miami has become increasingly cosmopolitan and is the destination of choice for immigrants from all over the world, but particularly from Latin America. Given that there is no continuous inflow of Cuban migrants, Cubans represent a shrinking part of the population of Latin American origin in Miami. Only time will tell if they are able to build coalitions with these other groups in order to continue to win elections and maintain their current levels of political representation.

Political Changes in Cuba and US–Cuba Policy

On 28 February 2008, Raúl Castro, younger brother of Fidel Castro, was elected president of Cuba by the Cuban National Assembly. Raúl had assumed this position informally when his brother was taken ill in July 2006. His election in 2008 marked the first time since 1959 when a person other than Fidel Castro was officially elected president of Cuba. Around the world there was immediate speculation about what this would mean in terms of Cuban politics and of Cuba's relations with the United States. The Bush Administration quickly issued a statement making it clear that nothing would change with regard to US–Cuba relations until there was a full-fledged democratic transition in Cuba.

What this change will mean for the future of Cuba is an open question. It is possible that, without the polarizing presence of Fidel Castro, greater dialogue between the two countries will develop. On 7 May 2008, the Cuban government allowed for a historical teleconference to occur directly between President Bush and three Cuban dissidents on the island: Martha Beatriz Roque, Berta Soler, and Jorge Luis García Pérez. Roque, considered to be one of the strongest hardliners of the dissident community and among its members most supportive of US policies toward the island, asked President Bush to make it easier for Cuban Americans in the United States to visit family members on the island and to send money to their relatives there. The dissidents argued that the teleconference itself was a reflection of the political opening Raúl's leadership was making possible on the island, and that the United States should help Cubans to take advantage of this opportunity. President Bush, however, was not moved. After the call, he reiterated his position that nothing will change in US policy towards the Cuban government until Cubans are allowed to pick their own leaders in free and fair elections and the government releases all political prisoners and respects human rights 'in word and deed'.

This teleconference and the Bush Administration's response could be seen as another sign of the limitations of Cuban power over US policy towards the island. In this case, individuals who historically have been very supportive of US policy asked the president to consider changing this policy, given changes on the ground. Although it is significant that they had this level of access to the president, in the end their opinions meant little. This suggests that, even if there were a sea change of opinion in Miami and among Cuban dissidents regarding the direction US–Cuba relations should take, it is not at all clear that the US government would alter course in response. Looking at the full history of US–Cuban relations, the United States has always believed that it knew what was best for Cuba and for the Cuban people. Since 1959, that view has happened to coincide with that of Cuban exiles in the US and Cuban dissidents on the island. If these views were to diverge, there is little reason to believe that the US government would fundamentally change its Cuban policy.

Conclusion: Is there a Cuban 'Model'?

Many political analysts, when considering the lack of Latino political engagement broadly in the United States, point to the Cuban case as a 'model' for other groups of Latin American origin. But is there a Cuban model? We have seen in this chapter that there are many things about the Cuban case which cannot be replicated. The first is the high level of importance attached by the US government to what was happening in Cuba, because of the close relationship which had existed between the two countries since the nineteenth century. The second is the high level of government access and support accorded to Cuban exiles in order to change what was happening politically in Cuba. The third is the very high geographic concentration of the exiled community and its common experience of exile, which gave its members a sense of shared identity and political cohesion strong enough to lead to consistent bloc voting. And bloc voting, combined with geographical concentration, has made it possible for this minority community to win elections consistently within a majoritarian electoral system. Finally, not only have Cuban immigrants enjoyed privileged status with regard to US immigration policy for more than forty-five years, but they have also received an unprecedented amount of direct assistance from the US government – an estimated $4 billion. One can only imagine how much more successful other immigrant communities would be if they had that kind of capital investment to assist with their settlement and economic adaptation to the United States.

This being said, the Cuban story remains one of very effective economic and political adaptation in the face of significant adversity. As the community moves beyond the experience of exile and the regime continues to evolve in Cuba, it will be interesting to see how the community's politics may change, what groups it may turn to for coalition-building, and what kind of political influence it may be able to exercise – locally, nationally, and internationally.

GUIDE TO FURTHER READINGS

Franklin, Jane. 1997. *The Cuban Revolution and the United States: A Chronological History*. Melbourne, Australia: Ocean Press.

García, María Cristina. 1996. *Havana USA: Cuban Exiles and Cuban Americans in South Florida, 1959–1994*. Berkeley: University of California Press.

Masud-Piloto, Félix Roberto. 1995. *From Welcomed Exiles to Illegal Immigrants: Cuban Migration to the US, 1959–1995*. Lanham, MD: Rowman and Littlefield.

Pérez, Louis. 2003. *Cuba and the United States: Ties of Singular Intimacy*, 3rd edn. Atlanta: University of Georgia Press.

CHAPTER SIX

Central Americans: Inequality, War, and Solidarity

Objectives

- Understand the relationship Central America has had with the United States, including with its military and economic interventions in the region
- Understand the role economic inequality has played in the evolution of each country's politics
- Understand the role cold war ideology has played in the response of the Central American elites and of the United States to reformist movements in the region
- Understand how violence in the region has affected migration flows
- Understand how US foreign policy goals have influenced Central Americans' migration status in the United States
- Understand how Central Americans were able to change their migration status and to influence US foreign policy in their countries of origin

Introduction

Central America's proximity to the United States has made it a target of US foreign and economic interests. The phrase 'Central America' refers to the geographic isthmus stretching from Guatemala to Panamá. As early as the 1850s, US politicians and businessmen began involving themselves in Central American affairs, seeing the region as 'the next American frontier'.[1] Private American adventurers called *filibusteros*, or filibusters, amassed small armies and attempted to take over parts of Central America through force of arms. Often they were out for personal gain, or they were hired by US business interests to protect US property in the region. One of the most famous filibusters was William Walker, who, after attempting to take over parts of Mexico in 1853, turned his sights to Central America. One of the factions in Nicaragua's civil war hired him as a mercenary and, in 1856, he declared himself president of the Republic of Nicaragua. He then tried to conquer the remaining Central American countries, but was defeated by the combined Central American forces and executed by Honduran authorities in 1860.

The stories of the filibusters' adventures were very popular in the American press, but the filibusters' actions were in violation of US law. At the turn of the twentieth century these incursions continued, and began to include actions carried out by the US military on behalf of the US government. In 1927, undersecretary of state Robert Olds described how the United States understood its interests and role in the region:

> The Central American area constitutes a legitimate sphere of influence for the United States, if we are to have due regard for our own safety and protection . . . Our ministers accredited to the five little republics . . . have been advisors whose advice has been accepted virtually as law . . . we do control the destinies of Central America and we do so for the simple reason that the national [US] interest dictates such a course . . . There is no room for any outside influence other than ours in this region . . . Until now Central America has always understood that governments which we recognize and support stay in power, while those which we do not recognize and support fall.[2]

The United States often expressed its support or opposition to these regimes through military action. The United States military invaded Nicaragua in 1894, 1896, and 1910, and occupied the country from 1912 to 1933. US troops entered Honduras in 1903, 1907, 1911, 1912, 1919, and 1924, in most cases in response to conflictual elections. In Panamá, the United States government was instrumental in making that country separate from Colombia so as to be able to build the Panama Canal, and it was heavily involved in the country's politics in order to ensure the canal's function and defense. United States companies were also heavily invested in many Central American countries, particularly the United Fruit Company (now Chiquita Banana). United Fruit developed an integrated production plan, not only producing bananas but also building and controlling the infrastructure necessary to get them to market – for instance roads, railroads, utilities, ports, and so on. In many Central American countries, United Fruit owned the majority of the existing infrastructure; this made it a key player in the countries' internal affairs. Thus US interests were deeply intertwined in Central American politics and economics. That relationship would help to shape the economic development that occurred in the region, the kinds of political leadership that developed, and the opportunities available to everyday Central Americans. After the mid-twentieth century it would also have important effects on Central American migration patterns and on US migration policy towards those migrants.

Salvadorans and Guatemalans

Even though the United States is a home for migrants from all the countries of Central America, the two largest groups are those from El Salvador and Guatemala. Table 6.1 summarizes the population of Central American origin in the United States. In 2006, there were 3,396,340 individuals of Central American origin in the United States. Of these, 1,363,726 were from El Salvador and 896,780 from Guatemala. Together, these two groups make up almost 67 percent of Central Americans living in the United States. Although Central Americans' experiences do vary in important ways by national origin, an examination of these two groups encompasses the experiences of over two-thirds of this population.

El Salvador

El Salvador declared its independence from Spain in 1821, along with the other countries of Central America. Until 1838, the country formed part of a united Central American federation. When that union dissolved El Salvador became an independent nation. Its history in the nineteenth century was marked by frequent revolutions and ongoing attempts to form a larger Central American state. Although various agreements were reached, none was able to survive. After the mid-nineteenth century, the Salvadoran economy quickly became dependent on the exportation of coffee. The expansion of coffee production led to the government's elimination of communal landholdings in 1881 and to the subsequent concentration of land ownership into a small oligarchy called *las catorce*, 'the (group of the) fourteen families'. The country's infrastructure development centered on ensuring the smooth export of coffee. In addition, the Salvadoran government was almost entirely dependent on coffee production for revenue, which ensured that this sector had a tremendous influence on the country's politics. The government passed anti-vagrancy laws to ensure an available workforce for coffee production. For example, the 1907 Agrarian Law stated that landless laborers could be arrested for vagrancy and had to carry workbooks listing their work obligations. The law established Agrarian Law judges, who, with the assistance of the army, were appointed in each village to keep lists of all day laborers and to arrange for the capture of any workers who ran away from the estates.[3] In 1912, the state created the rural National Guard to maintain peace and control in the countryside.

Table 6.1 The Central American-Origin Population in the United States

Nationality	Population	Percent of Total
Costa Rican	111,678	3.29%
Guatemalan	896,780	26.40%
Honduran	486,026	14.31%
Nicaraguan	298,928	8.80%
Panamanian	124,138	3.66%
Salvadoran	1,363,726	40.15%
Other Central American	115,064	3.39%
Total	3,396,340	100.00%

Source: 2006 American Community Survey Public Use Microdata Set (PUMS)

The Salvadoran peasantry did not passively accept this transfer of land and power from the indigenous population to the coffee elite. Between 1870 and 1900, the peasants staged four separate revolts, but they were easily defeated by the military.[4] What had already been a difficult situation for the peasantry worsened significantly during the Great Depression. Growers halved wages for coffee workers and significantly decreased production, leaving thousands of Indian families without work.[5] As a US military attaché described the situation in 1931:

> There is practically no middle class between the very rich and the very poor . . . Roughly 90 percent of the wealth in the country is held by one-half of one percent of the population. Thirty or forty families own nearly everything in the country. They live in regal splendor [while] the rest of the country has practically nothing.[6]

The Salvadoran peasantry continually protested against this state of affairs. In 1930, 80,000 protestors gathered to celebrate May Day and to denounce deteriorating wages and working conditions for workers. The following year this growing movement of students, peasants, and workers elected liberal Arturo Araujo to the presidency. Shortly afterwards, Araujo announced that the Salvadoran Communist Party would be allowed to participate in the December 1931 municipal elections. The Salvadoran military would not allow this; they deposed Araujo and replaced him with a conservative general, Maximiliano Hernández Martínez.

The peasantry broke out in rebellion. In January 1932, bands of largely Pipil Indians from western El Salvador, armed with machetes and led by Agustín Farabundo Martí, attacked local towns. Within three days they had taken control of several towns and of a number of major supply routes.

The Martínez regime responded with brutal repression. All Indians, or anyone looking like an Indian, were targeted. It is estimated that as many as 30,000 Salvadorans were killed, including Martí: this in a country with a population of only 1.4 million. The military tied the Indians' thumbs behind their backs, lined them up, and shot them. Historian Thomas P. Anderson wrote: 'The extermination was so great that they could not be buried fast enough, and a great stench of rotting flesh permeated the air of western El Salvador.'[7] The US military was alerted during the rebellion. Two destroyers and a naval cruiser were stationed off the coast, in case they were needed by the Salvadoran military. This uprising is remembered as '*La Matanza*' ('the Massacre') and resulted in many Pipil Indians adopting western dress and the Spanish language in order to avoid being targeted by the military. This traumatic event would have far-reaching effects on the future of Salvadoran politics. Martínez stayed in power until he was deposed in 1944 by a general strike called *la huelga de brazos caidos* (the strike of still arms).

The experience of the 1931 elections and of their aftermath led the military to take direct control of the government from that point forward; no other civilian would be elected president in El Salvador until 1984. Throughout this time the army controlled the government with the complicity of *las catorce*. The presidents were chosen from the military and civilians from the coffee elite served as cabinet members.[8]

Meanwhile inequality continued to increase within the Salvadoran economy. The land concentration which had begun with the coffee production only intensified after 1950, with the introduction of cotton and sugar as new cash crops. As a result, the number of landless laborers increased from 11 percent of the labor force in 1961 to 40 percent by 1975.[9] The maintenance of this rural economic system rested on an increasing use of security forces and of repression in the countryside. In 1950, the government amended the 1907 Agrarian Law, establishing that National Guard members should be used to maintain order on private estates and that the law enforcement officials should be appointed (and therefore controlled) by the landowners themselves.[10] Unwanted tenant farmers could be summarily evicted from their homes, and local police had the right to destroy the homes of anyone they considered a criminal. Any peasant found out at night could be detained by the police without cause and the National Guard could, at any time, arrest any laborer who was seen as failing to fulfill his obligations to their landowner.[11] A 1991 Americas Watch report on the status of the Salvadoran peasantry during this period found it to be in a state of 'virtual serfdom'.

The United States also assisted with the expansion of the Salvadoran security apparatus. During the 1960s, the Alliance for Progress was meant to deepen US ties throughout Latin America. In most countries, Alliance programs included assistance with counterinsurgency and support for small-scale land reform. In El Salvador, the elite equated land reform with communism, so the US Alliance for Progress assistance was focused almost exclusively on supporting counterinsurgency and on strengthening the Salvadoran police forces.[12] This investment led to the evolution of the Salvadoran security forces towards the use of paramilitary death squads. Their precursor was the Democratic Nationalist Organization (ORDEN), created in 1968 by General José Alberto Medrano. A highly paid CIA consultant, Medrano created a rural vigilante force which kept watch on progressive peasant organizations. Fifty thousand-strong, this force was considered the 'eyes and ears' of the military in the countryside and worked with the military to eliminate the peasant leadership.[13]

The first major political challenge to the military dictatorship in El Salvador came in 1972. In that year, the Unión Nacional Opositora (UNO) Coalition was formed by three political parties: the Christian Democratic Party (CDP), the Social Democratic National Revolutionary Movement (MNR), and the leftist National Democratic Union (UDN). The UNO chose José Napoleon Duarte, mayor of San Salvador (1964–70) and founder of the CDP, as their presidential candidate. The coalition was supported by urban intellectuals, professionals, and workers. The development of industry in El Salvador during the 1960s had led to growing political strength among industrial workers. Unlike their rural counterparts, these workers were allowed to form unions and grew in power over the course of the decade. Representing these interests, Duarte ran on a platform in favor of human rights and social justice. Blatant electoral fraud on the part of the military deprived him of victory in the 1972 presidential election. Instead, the military had him arrested, tortured, and exiled, and installed one of their colonels into the presidency. The 1972 elections made clear to many in El Salvador that the army was unwilling to allow for reform to occur through electoral means.

After the 1972 elections revealed that the political system could not be used to solve the country's problems, the number of mass organizations in El Salvador began to increase. Students, workers, peasants, and church members joined together to fight the military dictatorship. Their tactics included street demonstrations and the occupation of public buildings, factories, and large estates. As these movements strengthened, the military increasingly responded with violence. For example, in 1975, students in Santa Ana occupied the local campus to protest against the government's spending of $1.5 million to host the Miss Universe pageant. When San Salvador students held a march to show their solidarity with the students from Santa Ana, the National Guard opened fire. Scores of students were wounded or killed and twenty-four disappeared.[14]

These mass organizations were joined in their opposition to the regime by some sectors within a major institution in Salvadoran society: the Catholic church. Although historically the church had helped to support the regime by encouraging parishioners to focus on the afterlife rather than on any problems in the here and now, the growth of liberation theology among many in the clergy led to a change in the role of the church in Salvadoran society. Liberation theology was a movement within the Catholic church that grew out of the changes in church policy put forth by the Second Vatican Council (1962–1965) and the conference of Latin American bishops held in Medellín, Colombia, in 1968. This new theology asserted that poverty and injustice were not God's will and that believers had the right to challenge any oppressive institutions in society. To address inequality, the bishops in Medellín called for more education, increased social awareness, and the creation of *comunidades de base* (faith communities) which encouraged parishioners to meet weekly for Bible readings with a focus on New Testament readings emphasizing social justice.[15] Followers of this theology argued that it was not radical, but rather a reversion back to the original teachings of Christ. The Salvadoran military and elite, however, saw this movement as a grave threat to their social structure and death squads (*escuadrones de la muerte*) began to target nuns and priests specifically. The White Warriors Union death squad is reported to have circulated flyers in 1977 that read: 'Be a Patriot, Kill a Priest!'[16]

Thus during the 1970s violence continued to increase in El Salvador. A number of death squads were organized by the government after 1975; these included the White Warriors Union, mentioned above, the White Hand, the Anticommunist Forces for Liberation (FALANGE), the Organization for Liberation from Communism (OLC), the Secret Anti-Communist Army (ESA), and the Maximiliano Hernández Martínez brigade, named after the general responsible for *la Matanza*. According to one US official, the death squads were made up of members of the Salvadoran Army, of the Treasury Police, of the National Guard, of the National Police, or of 'the sick young sons of affluent Salvadorans'.[17]

The squads were funded by members of the oligarchy, many of whom resided in Miami.

As the 1970s came to a close, the violence continued. General Carlos Romero was fraudulently elected president in 1977; thousands gathered to protest against his election and the police fired upon the demonstrators, leaving nearly one hundred dead.[18] One of Romero's first acts as president was to promote a law to 'defend and guarantee public order', and violence and repression increased significantly under his rule.[19] Frustrated with the Romero regime, some reformist members of the military took control of the government in 1979. The new *junta* sought the support of the 'popular organizations' and wanted to ensure that El Salvador did not follow the same road as Nicaragua, whose Sandinista rebels had just succeeded in taking control of the country's government. The *junta* declared amnesty for all political prisoners and Salvadorans in exile, dissolved ORDEN, and created a special committee to investigate the 'disappeared'.[20] The decrees were never carried out. Political prisoners remained in jail, no one was prosecuted for past crimes, and ORDEN continued to function in the countryside with impunity. El Salvador's mass organizations engaged in protests, strikes, and occupations, in an effort to end the repression. The *junta* responded even more violently than the Romero regime; the protests were repressed, and killings took place at a rate of 1,000 per month.[21] Over the next few months, most of the civilian members of the *junta* resigned and the military took complete control of the government.

This only increased the bloodshed. 1980 was a particularly violent year. Death squads targeted high-profile leaders as well as the civilian population. In January 1980, to commemorate the 48th anniversary of *la Matanza*, a coalition of mass organizations mounted an enormous demonstration in San Salvador, the largest ever held in the country. Guards and sharpshooters attacked the demonstrators, leaving many dead. There is disagreement about the number of civilians killed. Estimates range from twenty to fifty-two.[22] In February 1980, one of the few progressive civilians remaining in the government, Attorney General Mario Zamora, was assassinated during a dinner party in his home. He was shot in the face a dozen times at point-blank range.[23] In March, Archbishop Oscar Romero, head of the Catholic church in El Salvador and a vocal advocate for social justice, was assassinated while he was saying mass. His funeral procession included 30,000 mourners. The military fired into the procession, killing thirty and wounding hundreds more.[24] In November, six leading members of the Democratic Revolutionary Front, one of the last mass organizations advocating non-violent tactics, were kidnapped and murdered – an act which eliminated some of the last influential reformist Salvadoran politicians.[25] In December three US nuns and a Catholic lay worker were kidnapped, raped, and murdered. Their mutilated bodies were found buried in shallow graves. The Carter Administration protested and demanded an investigation, but no real movement was made to identify those responsible. In response, the United States temporarily froze military and economic aid to El Salvador.

In 1980 alone an estimated 8,000 civilians were murdered, yet no one was ever tried for the deaths.[26] Human rights organizations calculated that between 1979 and 1983 the death squads murdered or kidnapped 36,000 Salvadorans.[27] This violence did not occur privately. Rather, the bodies of the dead were left, often mutilated, in town sewers, roads, plazas, empty lots, garbage dumps, gutters, or shallow graves, so that they may be found easily and therefore serve as a warning for others considering opposing the regime.[28]

The assassination of such prominent leaders as Zamora, and especially Romero, and the extent of the violence served to unite the reformers and the revolutionaries in El Salvador. Many groups demanded an investigation of the individual suspected of ordering the assassinations, Roberto D'Aubuisson, but the government failed to act. In response, virtually all the opposition groups in the country – political parties, religious organizations, trade unions, and peasant groups – joined together in April 1980 to create a new Democratic Revolutionary Front (FDR).[29] They became the political arm of the revolutionary opposition.[30] In October 1980, the various guerilla armies also came together under one banner, establishing the Farabundo Martí National Liberation Front (FMLN), named after the slain leader of the 1932 *Matanza*. By 1981 the FMLN had 5,000 combatants, compared to 15,000 in the Salvadoran army, and confrontations between the two intensified.[31]

The Salvadoran civil war lasted for twelve years, from 1980 to 1992, during which an estimated 75,000 Salvadorans were killed. Hundreds of thousands were displaced internally, and over one million Salvadorans fled to other countries, including the United States.

Guatemala

Like El Salvador, Guatemala also experienced a violent and brutal civil war, although the roots of Guatemala's conflict rested largely in the aftermath of the 1954 CIA-backed overthrow of a freely elected reformist government. Also like El Salvador, Guatemala's economy was based on agriculture, although in this country foreign producers, in particular the United Fruit Company, would play a critical role in the development of the country's economics and politics.

The first major export crop in Guatemala was coffee, just as in El Salvador, and, in similar ways, its production quickly generated a small wealthy oligarchy, many of whose members retain economic and political power in the country today. Unlike in El Salvador, however, the financing, processing, and marketing of Guatemalan coffee was from the beginning in the hands of foreign investors, mostly Germans.[32] These remained in control of the Guatemalan coffee market until the Second World War, when the US government forced the Guatemalan government to confiscate the German coffee holdings and to arrest German citizens. This allowed US companies to take control of the Guatemalan coffee industry.

Yet US companies had begun their involvement in the Guatemalan economy much earlier. The United Fruit Company entered the scene in 1904. At that time, the most popular fruit consumed in the United States was the apple. United Fruit set out to change that: it aimed to cultivate a type of banana which could travel long distances and be available year-round throughout the United States. To do this, the company developed a new business model, one that included not only acquiring large amounts of cheap land and ensuring low-cost labor for production, but also developing the infrastructure – roads, railroads, ports, ships, telegraph, postal service, and utilities – which was necessary in order to carry the product to market. The company painted its ships in white in order to make them reflect the sun's heat, and named them 'the Great White Fleet'. In addition to transporting bananas, the ships became major carriers of the materials used to build the Panama Canal. They also carried passengers, mostly American tourists interested in visiting Central America, and US mail. Another aspect of the company's business strategy was that it always owned much more land than it had in cultivation at any one time. That way, if any natural disaster were to strike one area, the company could quickly put the fallow land into production and avoid potential economic losses.

United Fruit was active throughout Latin America, but was particularly influential in Guatemala. In 1904, Guatemalan dictator Estrada Cabrera granted United Fruit a ninety-nine year tax-free concession to construct and maintain the country's main rail line from Guatemala City to Puerto Barrios, which the company completed in 1906. In return for the rail line's completion, United Fruit received a contract for 170,000 acres of the country's best banana-producing land, located on Guatemala's Atlantic coast.[33] In addition to its railroad investments, United Fruit also purchased controlling shares in the country's utilities, ports, and telegraph services. The company created a new city called Bananera, where it established its headquarters. By the 1930s, United Fruit was the largest landowner, employer, and exporter in Guatemala. By 1944, it owned 42 percent of the country's land. The company owned all the country's ports and charged tariffs to Guatemalan exporters for their use. Because it played such a key role in the Guatemalan economy, the company was exempt from most taxes, import or export duties, and the government provided it with guarantees of low wages for its workers.[34] The company was also a main source of government revenue, which made it difficult for any Guatemalan government to favor policies not supported by the United Fruit Company.

On the political side, during the period immediately after independence, Guatemala was run by a series of dictators. Two of the most important are Manuel Estrada Cabrera, who ruled from 1898 to 1920, and General Jorge Ubico Castañeda, who ran the country from 1931 to 1944. Guatemala at this time was characterized by extreme inequality in terms of income and land distribution. The policies of the Ubico government only served to make that situation worse. Ubico passed harsh vagrancy laws, by which all Indians who owned little or no land were required to work for local landowners for at least one hundred days a year. The landowners made the situation even more difficult for the Indians by agreeing among themselves not to compete for the labor force by offering higher wages. Additionally, Ubico made it legal for the landowners to murder stubborn or rebellious Indians. In 1944, Ubico was faced with growing opposition, centered mainly in the country's university. The protesters, made up of a coalition of students, teachers, and professionals, held mass rallies in the capital. Guatemalan security forces, not sure how to respond, resorted to violence on the occasion of breaking up a women's protest. Many of the protesters were injured and one schoolteacher was killed. The army's actions only incensed the opposition, leading to a general strike. Ubico was forced to resign and was replaced by a military triumvirate. This group was quickly overthrown by a group of junior military officers led by Jacobo Arbenz and Francisco Araña. Their action is known as the 'October Revolution'.[35]

The young officers quickly stepped aside and allowed elections to be held, a first in Guatemala. 85 percent of the voters (only literate males) elected former professor Juan José Arévalo as the country's president. Arévalo began a series of reforms, including dramatically increasing investment in the public schools; he passed labor rights legislation, ended the country's anti-vagrancy laws, and established a state bank designed to help small business owners to have access to credit.[36] He oversaw the passing of a new progressive Guatemalan constitution in 1945. It is estimated that between 1945 and 1950 industrial wages increased up to 80 percent.[37] The military and oligarchy were not idle during this period. Twenty-two *coups* were attempted during Arévalo's time in office, but none was successful.[38]

Yet, for any substantive change in the Guatemalan economy to be achieved, land reform was a necessity. In 1945, 2.2 percent of the country's population owned 70 percent of the arable land, but only 15 percent of that land was being cultivated. That meant that only 10 percent of the country's land was available for 90 percent of the population to cultivate. Arévalo's government proposed land reform as part of its agenda, but its actual implementation was left to his successor, Jacobo Arbenz. Arbenz, still popular because of his role in the October Revolution, won the 1950 elections in a landslide. He continued Arévalo's reform agenda, legalizing unions and political parties, and passing land reform legislation. He began the construction of a public port on the Atlantic coast, the building of an east–west highway, and the expansion of public works.[39] He also passed the 1952 Agrarian Reform Law, which was meant to target uncultivated lands. The government would pay for the land in twenty-five year bonds bearing a 3 percent interest rate, and the price of the land would be based on its taxable worth as of May 1952. The law distributed 1.5 million acres to over 100,000 families. The expropriations included 1,700 acres of Arbenz's own land, which he had received from his wife.[40] All cultivated land, regardless of the size of the plantation, was exempt.

Since the law only applied to uncultivated land, it included a large portion of the property owned by United Fruit; 85 percent of United Fruit land at the time was uncultivated. As the single largest landowner in Guatemala, United Fruit possessed at that time more land than the combined holdings of 50 percent of the Guatemalan population.[41] Clearly, any attempt to reform the Guatemalan economy would lead to a direct confrontation with United Fruit. The law proposed to expropriate 387,000 acres of United Fruit's fallow land. The government offered to pay the company $1.2 million. That figure was based on United Fruit's own declaration of the land's value, which the company had used for tax purposes. Instead, United Fruit and the US State Department demanded that the Guatemalan government pay the company $16 million for the land.[42]

United Fruit sought additional help from the US government and tried to convince President Truman that the United States should overthrow the Arbenz regime. When the plan fell apart, the company hired a public relations firm to create the perception in the US popular press that the Arbenz regime was a communist front with links to the Soviet Union. In Guatemala, the land reform was strongly opposed by landowners and by the military, a situation leading to growing civil unrest. When the Eisenhower Administration took office in the United States, the United Fruit Company found the new regime much more sympathetic to its concerns. This was partly due to the fact that the company had important, high-level connections within the Eisenhower Administration. Secretary of state John Foster Dulles had been a senior partner at Sullivan and Cromwell, which was United Fruit's law firm and its principal source of advice on foreign affairs. His brother, Allen Dulles, the head of the CIA, served on United Fruit's board of directors. John Moors Cabot, the assistant secretary of state on Inter-American Affairs, was the brother of Thomas Dudley Cabot, former president of United Fruit. Ed Whitman, the company's top public relations officer, was married to Ann Whitman, President Eisenhower's private secretary.[43] These connections meant United Fruit officials had the ear of very high-level US government officials and made the Administration take the company's claims about the Arbenz regime more seriously. Those US officials with ties to United Fruit would become the key architects of the US plan to overthrow the regime.

In the face of growing US hostility, President Arbenz turned to the eastern bloc countries to purchase arms and defend the country. This action was used by the United States as proof of his regime's ties to the Soviet bloc. Starting in 1953, the CIA began to plan a covert operation designed to topple the Arbenz government. The plan, called Operation PBSUCCESS, was to have the country invaded by a small group of Guatemalan exiles, led by ousted Colonel Carlos Castillo Armas and trained and equipped by the CIA. The boats used to transport the rebel troops were provided by the United Fruit Company, and the invading force conducted the training of these troops on a United Fruit plantation in Honduras.[44] The rebels were supported by a CIA-operated radio station which, falsely, announced large troop movements and the surrender of successive areas of Guatemala, and by a few Second World War fighter planes which were used to strafe Guatemala City. The planes also dropped pamphlets claiming rebel victory and urging the Guatemalan people to surrender. Duped into thinking that a large invading force was nearing the capital, Arbenz surrendered without a fight. The rebels rolled into Guatemala City being practically unopposed.[45]

The *coup* marked the end of progressive reform in Guatemala. During and after the *coup*, nine thousand people were arrested and many were tortured. The agrarian reform was reversed, with over 1.5 million acres returned to large landowners, including United Fruit. The Castillo Armas government abolished unions and signed a mutual defense pact with the United States.[46] The main result of the *coup* was the elimination of the political center in Guatemala. Reform within the political system was now impossible. The country's governments from that point forward consisted of military dictatorships, each more repressive and brutal than the last. The country's economy remained in the hands of the wealthy oligarchy and those who paid the price were the country's indigenous majority.

About 60 percent of the Guatemalan population is of Maya origin, stemming from about twenty-three different Mayan ethnic groups. These people have been subject to officially sanctioned discrimination in Guatemala since the Spanish colonial period, but they maintain their language and many of their cultural practices. The remainder of the Guatemalan population consists of *ladinos*: individuals of Spanish origin, or with a mixture of Spanish and indigenous backgrounds. Most of the Maya population did not have access to education, electricity, running water, sanitation, or other forms of basic infrastructure. As a result, in the 1960s only 19 percent of Mayas were literate, compared to over 50 percent of the rest of the population. Infant mortality among the Maya was also very high, 134 per 1,000 live births, compared to 80 per 1,000 among *ladinos*. Not surprisingly, the life expectancy of the Maya was also low – sixteen years lower than for *ladinos*.[47] Because of the land concentration policies mentioned above, most of the Maya were landless, being forced to work on plantations focused on export agriculture. The largest part of the population had to work for less than two dollars a day, with no right to organize or to protest against their working conditions. Fifty percent of the population survived on only about half of the calories needed on a daily basis to avoid malnutrition.[48] Any attempts at unionization were repressed with extreme violence.[49]

With reform within the political process closed off after 1954, the Guatemalan opposition turned to armed revolt. The various guerrilla groups operated independently through the 1960s and 1970s, and then in 1982 the four largest groups joined to form the Guatemalan National Revolutionary Unity (URNG). Their platform included support for agrarian reform and price controls, equality between the Maya and the *ladinos*, democracy and respect for civil liberties.[50] Starting in the 1960s, the Guatemalan army organized an offensive in response and received significant assistance from the United States. The Pentagon established a counterinsurgency base in the Guatemalan highlands and brought in 1,000 US Special Forces troops to train the Guatemalan army in counterinsurgency. The campaign used aerial bombings of the countryside and burned villages suspected of supporting the guerrilla rebels.[51] With the encouragement of US army officers, the Guatemalan army and landowners also created death squads during this period, to root out the 'subversives'.[52] These squads included groups such as MANO (the National Organized Action Movement), also known as *Mano Blanca* (the White Hand) because of its logo; NOA (the New Anti-Communist Organization); CADEG (the Anti-Communist Council of Guatemala); *Ojo por Ojo* (the Eye for an Eye); *Jaguar Justiciero* (Jaguar of Justice); and ESA (the Secret Anti-Communist Army). These were the transient names of the clandestine military units whose purpose was to eliminate the alleged members, allies, or collaborators of 'subversion'.

Assuming that the indigenous population was a probable source of support for the guerrillas, the army moved into the countryside, targeting indigenous communities with brutal repression. Between 1966 and 1976 50,000 people were murdered, thousands more being subjected to arrest and torture.[53] A good example of the attitude of the Guatemalan military leadership at the time is Colonel Carlos Arana Osorio, who earned the nickname of 'Butcher of Zacapa' after the massacres of *campesinos* which took place during his 1966–8 counterinsurgency campaign. Arana, who became president in 1970, is reported to have said: 'If it is necessary to turn the country into a cemetery in order to pacify it, I will not hesitate to do so.'[54] According to Amnesty International, even after the guerrillas were crushed, the military continued to engage in killings for purposes of general intimidation.[55]

It is difficult to overstate the sheer brutality of what occurred in Guatemala during the 36-year civil war. The army worked methodically across the Maya region, attacking over 600 villages and forcibly conscripting many of the youths. These atrocities were documented by the Guatemalan Historical Clarification Commission in 1999. In its final report, the commission noted:

Particularly serious cruelty in many acts committed by agents of the State, especially members of the Army, in their operations against Mayan communities. The counterinsurgency strategy not only led to violations of basic human rights, but also to the fact that these crimes were committed with particular cruelty, with massacres representing their archetypal form. In the majority of massacres there is evidence of multiple acts of savagery, which preceded, accompanied or occurred after the deaths of the victims. Acts such as the killing of defenceless children, often by beating them against walls or throwing them alive into pits where the corpses of adults were later thrown; the amputation of limbs; the impaling of victims; the killing of persons by covering them in petrol and burning them alive; the extraction, in the presence of others, of the viscera of victims who were still alive; the confinement of people who had been mortally tortured, in agony for days; the opening of the wombs of pregnant women, and other similarly atrocious acts, were not only actions of extreme cruelty against the victims, but also morally degraded the perpetrators and those who inspired, ordered or tolerated these actions. During the armed confrontation the cultural rights of the Mayan people were also violated. The Army destroyed ceremonial centres, sacred places and cultural symbols. Language and dress, as well as other elements of cultural identification, were targets of repression.[56]

The army targeted these villages because the inhabitants were Maya, which led many in the human rights community to describe what happened in Guatemala as genocide. The Historical Clarification Commission report concluded that

the reiteration of destructive acts, directed systematically against groups of the Mayan population, within which can be mentioned the elimination of leaders and criminal acts against minors who could not possibly have been military targets, demonstrates that the only common denominator for all the victims was the fact that they belonged to a specific ethnic group and makes it evident that these acts were committed 'with intent to destroy, in whole or in part' these groups,

making it, in fact, a case of genocide. After murdering the villagers, the army employed a 'scorched earth' policy, which including destroying the buildings and crops, fouling the water supply, slaughtering all livestock, and desecrating all sacred cultural sites and symbols.[57]

The violence in Guatemala was so great that during the 1980s Mexican *campesinos* in Chiapas reported that the rivers from Guatemala contained so many corpses that it was impossible to bury them all. During this period, the smell of burning and rotting corpses was a permanent fact of life along the Mexico–Guatemala border.[58] In the end, the Historical Clarification Commission determined that over 200,000 persons were killed or disappeared during Guatemala's civil war. 83 percent of the identified victims were Maya and 17 percent were *ladino*. The commission found that the Guatemalan army and death squads committed 93 percent of the atrocities; the guerrillas were responsible for 3 percent.[59] The report also showed that US officials in Guatemala and Washington, DC were well aware of the occurrence of these atrocities, and in fact 'lent direct and indirect support to some illegal state operations'.

Those Maya who survived the massacres were forcibly moved to live in 'model villages' organized by the Guatemalan government. In these villages their activities were strictly monitored. They were allowed to speak only Spanish and were discouraged from practicing Catholicism or any sort of indigenous religious ritual.They were encouraged instead to engage in a form of evangelical Protestantism which emphasized subservience to authority. While living in the villages, the Maya were forced to assist with public works projects which often involved rebuilding the very structures the army had recently destroyed.[60] This upheaval in the countryside led to significant internal displacement – an estimated 750,000 Guatemalans had to flee their homes. Another quarter of a million is estimated to have fled the country.[61]

Salvadoran and Guatemalan Migration

By the late 1970s, then, both El Salvador and Guatemala were in the throes of civil war and were the sites of extreme violence. This situation led to both economic and political dislocations. Many fled their country of origin because of political repression, but also because the civil unrest made it impossible for them to survive in their homelands. Historically there had always been Central American migration to other countries of Central America. In particular, there continually had been a large number of Salvadoran migrant workers in Honduras. In addition, the Mayan communities of Guatemala had maintained ties with Mayan communities in Mexico, particularly in Chiapas, and had worked there as seasonal labor. As these groups found themselves displaced, they followed these established social networks to settle in those areas. Due to the scale of the new migration and refugee crisis, however, the Mexican and Honduran communities were quickly overwhelmed, and the migrants were compelled to choose less traditional destinations.

One of the most popular new destinations was the United States. Although there had been small Central American populations living in cities like San Francisco, Washington, DC, Miami, Los Angeles, Houston, and New York during much of the twentieth century, large-scale Central American migration to the United States did not begin until the 1970s. According to the 1980 census, 94,447 Salvadorans and 63,073

Guatemalans were living in the United States, and about half of these had arrived within the previous five years.[62] Many of the new arrivals settled in those areas where friends, family, or other network members were living. In California, most Central Americans had migrated to San Francisco during the 1940s and 1950s; but some went to southern California as part of the *bracero* program, in which they participated by convincing program officials that they were Mexican.[63] During the 1970s, this small community mushroomed, and Los Angeles became the settlement area of choice for the vast majority of Salvadoran and Guatemalan immigrants to the United States.[64]

Some Central American migrants arrived to the United States on student or tourist visas and simply remained after these permits expired. The vast majority entered the United States illegally, by crossing the US–Mexico border. Starting in the late 1970s, the US border patrol began reporting the detention of growing numbers of OTMs (other than Mexicans). These Central American migrants posed a legal dilemma for the Reagan Administration. Although not every migrant had experienced violence directly, it was the growing violence and instability in their countries that had pushed them to migrate. So were they to be considered economic migrants or political refugees? The Reagan Administration, for largely political reasons, insisted that they were economic migrants.

When Reagan won the presidency in 1980, he did so on a strongly anti-communist platform. The leftist Sandinista revolution had just occurred in Nicaragua, and Reagan made it a key focus of his Administration's foreign policy to keep communism from spreading in Central America. Reagan argued: 'The national security of all Americans is at stake in Central America. If we cannot defend ourselves here, we cannot expect to prevail elsewhere.'[65] The Administration dramatically increased its military and economic assistance to the region. This assistance consisted of three main parts: (1) counterinsurgency training for the region's police and military; (2) increased aid for the armed forces; and (3) military and civic action programs coordinated with US economic aid.[66] The aid to El Salvador increased initially under President Jimmy Carter, and this expansion accelerated under Reagan. Throughout the 1980s, El Salvador was one of the top five recipients of US military aid. In total, the United States provided $6 billion in economic and military aid to El Salvador during its twelve-year civil war.[67] Given the country's estimated population of about 2.5 million people in 1980, this sum is the equivalent of $2,400 for each Salvadoran individual. US economic and military aid to Guatemala was not at the same level, with direct military aid there during the 1980s totaling only $30 million. Most of the aid to Guatemala was in the form of training military personnel, which was conducted in Guatemala, in the US' School of the Americas located in Panamá, or on bases in the United States. Some of the most notorious human rights abusers – including Generals Castillo Armas and Ríos Montt in Guatemala and General Humberto Romero in El Salvador – received US counterinsurgency training.[68] Over one third of the graduates of the School of the Americas came from Central America. Under Reagan, enrollment in the school, and in particular the number of Salvadoran officers receiving training there, increased dramatically.[69]

Thus the Reagan Administration had important political reasons to deny the violence and repression that characterized the Salvadoran and Guatemalan regimes. After the high-profile murders of Archbishop Romero and the US nuns, the US Congress began demanding that the Administration show improvements in the Salvadoran human rights situation before approving aid. Because of this, the Reagan Administration spent much of the 1980s downplaying the atrocities carried out by these regimes, and also implying that the victims were not so 'innocent'. For example, when discussing the four US churchwomen who had been raped and murdered in El Salvador, UN ambassador Jeane Kirkpatrick claimed that the women may have run a roadblock, and that, in any case, 'The nuns were not just nuns' – they were also 'political activists on behalf of the Frente' [the Democratic Revolutionary Front].[70] Any political violence acknowledged by the Administration was presented as the product of the left.[71] As one US diplomat who served during the Reagan Administration put it: 'Unless they [Administration officials] see a guy like D'Aubuisson running a machete through somebody, they're inclined to ignore it . . . There is absolutely zero conception of what these people are really like, how evil they really are.'[72]

Given the Reagan Administration's unwillingness to acknowledge the repression occurring in El Salvador and Guatemala, it is not surprising that it also refused to define Salvadoran and Guatemalan migrants as political refugees eligible for asylum. To do so would have undermined its support of these regimes and would have required the US to provide assistance and benefits to the hundreds of thousands of migrants who arrived in the United States from these two countries during the 1980s. Instead, Salvadoran and Guatemalan migrants spent much of the decade in a political limbo, many being forcibly deported to their country of origin (and subsequently tortured and killed). To support its arguments against refugee status, the Reagan Administration pointed out that Central American migrants most often traveled through Mexico, a country which did not persecute the refugees and allowed them to settle. Since the migrants continued on to the United States, the logic ran, they clearly were traveling further north for economic opportunities, rather than simply to escape political persecution and violence.

As a result of this policy, fewer than 5 percent of the Central American petitions for asylum were approved, and, unlike in the Cuban case, the government provided no assistance to facilitate their settlement in the United States.[73] In 1981, the United Nations High Commissioner for Refugees (UNHCR) criticized US policy, arguing that the United States was not living up to its international responsibilities. As a signatory to the UN Protocol on refugees, the United States had agreed not to force the return of refugees. According to the UNHCR, 'the United States had failed to grant asylum to any significant number of Salvadorans and was engaged in a "systematic practice" of deporting Salvadorans to their country regardless of the merits of their claims of asylum'.[74] The UNHCR urged the United States at least to grant the refugees temporary status, thus allowing them to avoid deportation. US immigration law did include such a category, called Extended Voluntary Departure (EVD). The application of this status is under State Department discretion, and is implemented when an Administration determines that conditions in the home country make it unsafe to send migrants home. The Reagan Administration refused to acknowledge that those conditions existed in Central America, and also balked at the prospect of granting this status to Salvadoran and Guatemalan migrants given the sheer scope of the migration – already estimated by 1983 to have reached over half a million.[75] The Administration worried that granting EVD to the refugees already on US territory would only encourage more migration. Thus, from 1983 to 1990, only 2.6 percent of Salvadoran asylum applicants were successful, and only 1.8 percent of those from Guatemala.[76]

The Central American Peace and Solidarity Movement

Yet these Central American migrants, despite their uncertain legal status in the United States, did not accept their situation quietly. Over the course of the 1980s, these refugees, along with actors still in Central America and progressive groups within the United States, would build a transnational social movement, which became known as the Central

American Peace and Solidarity Movement (CAPSM) and would challenge Reagan's foreign policy towards the region, pushing the Administration to provide some regularization of their migration status.

Within the Salvadoran community, the movement began with exiles organizing themselves so as to call attention to the situation at home. The first such effort occurred in San Francisco in 1975, when a group called *El Comité de Salvadoreños Progresistas* (the Committee of Progressive Salvadorans) was formed in response to the July 1975 government massacre of protesting students from the National University in San Salvador. The group organized the first march in the United States ever to denounce human rights violations on the part of the Salvadoran government.[77] Within a year, the group had established connections with student organizations in El Salvador, which sent them news, updates, and bulletins on a regular basis. The *Salvadoreños Progresistas* used this information to publish a newspaper called *El Pulgarcito* (Tom Thumb), which they used to inform Salvadorans and Americans about the situation in El Salvador. By 1978, the group had grown large enough to occupy the Salvadoran consulate in order to protest and to draw attention to the growing number of disappearances in El Salvador.[78]

The most successful and influential of the CAPSM groups was the Committee in Solidarity with the People of El Salvador (CISPES), founded in 1980. From its inception, CISPES included members of the Salvadoran exile community and in-country activists with links to the popular movement in El Salvador. Just prior to its founding, a few key activists had met with the newly formed Democratic Revolutionary Front and agreed to help to initiate a US-based solidarity effort.[79] The hope was that the US solidarity groups would help in fomenting US popular opposition to the US military aid and intervention in support of the Salvadoran regime. CISPES' strategy for creating this opposition was to bring attention to the situation on the ground in El Salvador. To do so, they relied on a network of in-country activists and grassroots organizations which coordinated visits of American journalists, human rights workers, and church workers to the region and provided the visitors with first-hand accounts and other evidence of their claims of human rights abuses. Similarly, CISPES coordinated the travel of Salvadoran witnesses to the United States, so that these could speak directly to American audiences about their experiences with death squad activity and government repression.[80] This direct contact with the victims of government abuses helped to raise the profile of the situation in El Salvador among the general US population.

These visits, both in Central America and in the United States, received coverage in the US mainstream media, which resulted in increasing pressure on the Reagan Administration to change US policy towards the region. At the start of the 1980s, few Americans were aware of what was happening in Central America. By the end of the same decade, thanks largely to this political strategy, the situation had transformed significantly. Changing US foreign policy in Central America had become one of the main political goals of US progressives and was part of US political discourse. This being said, the movement was not successful in stopping US funding to El Salvador and Guatemala. The movement did succeed in cutting off funding to the *Contra* rebels in Nicaragua, which occurred in 1982, with the unanimous passing of the Boland Amendment in Congress. It was this refusal of funding by the US Congress that led to the Iran *Contra* affair. The Reagan Administration, unwilling to stop its *Contra* support, covertly sold arms to Iran in order to raise the funds needed. This became one of the biggest political scandals of the decade, and ten Administration officials were found guilty for their participation in the subterfuge. Later in the decade, Congress resumed funding to the *Contras*.

But, what the movement did achieve was the creation of a narrative about what was happening in Central America which was very different from the one espoused by the Reagan Administration. The movement managed to make Central American funding highly controversial and pushed Congress to require the Administration to prove that these regimes were making progress on human rights. American presidents have the greatest amount of power in foreign policy, and during the cold war the tendency was to defer to the commander-in-chief on issues seen as being related to national security. In the case of Central America, CAPSM activities ensured at least that Reagan was not given a blank check and that the atrocities committed in the region were brought to the attention of US lawmakers and of the American public.

In addition to focusing on foreign policy issues, CAPSM worked towards having a positive impact on the political status of Central American refugees in the United States. An important nationwide US-based CAPSM organization which focused on these issues was the Salvadoran Humanitarian Aid, Relief, and Education Foundation (SHARE), created in 1981. SHARE worked directly with the mainstream US religious community, to provide assistance and support for the growing refugee population in the United States.[81] The organization 'served as an ecumenical clearinghouse of information and coordination, linking US parishes with Salvadoran parishes and communities, especially those devastated or displaced by the war.'[82] SHARE's goal was to help to repopulate and restore the war zones. To do so, groups of US activists would travel to El Salvador and act as human shields, literally walking with their Salvadoran counterparts to help them to begin the rebuilding process.[83]

Many of the parishes affiliated with SHARE were also instrumental in the creation of the sanctuary movement, in which Salvadoran exiles also played a key role. Initially, Salvadoran migrants were taken in by their kinship networks and assisted to integrate into life in the United States. But, given the scope of the migration, the activists quickly realized that they needed additional assistance in addressing their compatriots' needs. As a result, a number of the immigrant-based organizations which had been striving to stop the war in El Salvador created special branches to deal exclusively with the refugee crisis. One such group was the Central American Refugee Center (CARECEN), now called the Central American Resource Center, with offices in Los Angeles and Washington, DC. CARECEN was founded in 1983 by a group of Central American refugees in order to help their compatriots to achieve legal status in the United States. CARECEN provided free legal aid to refugees, engaged in community education, and coordinated with the other CAPSM groups to lobby the US Congress to address the migration status issues facing Central American migrants. Today CARECEN continues to lobby Congress on behalf of refugees and to provide legal and educational services to the community.

These organizations would end up building a multinational movement which involved thousands of individuals across nations and religions in providing sanctuary to Central American refugees. These participants engaged in civil disobedience – by transporting, harboring and assisting refugees – in order to protest against the inhumanity of US foreign policy.[84] The sanctuary movement began officially in 1982, when a church in Tucson, Arizona and five churches in Berkeley, California agreed to make a public declaration that they would provide sanctuary to Central American refugees. In an open letter to the US Attorney General, they stated:

> We take this action because be believe the current policy and practice of the US government with regard to Central American refugees is illegal and immoral. We believe our government is in violation of the 1980 Refugee Act and international law by continuing to arrest, detain, and forcibly return refugees to terror, persecution, and murder in El Salvador and Guatemala.[85]

Modeling themselves after the underground railroad, sanctuary activists facilitated the transportation of migrants from Central America, provided them with housing and financial assistance, and facilitated their establishment in the United States or their settlement in Canada, which had a more liberal refugee policy. At its height, the movement included over 400 churches, temples, and synagogues in the United States, who coordinated with religious and activist organizations in Central America, Mexico, the United States, and Canada in order to accomplish their work.[86]

The Reagan Administration was strongly opposed to the movement's work, and the Justice Department emphasized that anyone participating in the latter would be prosecuted to the full extent of the law. A number of sanctuary workers were arrested and tried. The most high-profile prosecution was that of sixteen activists in Tucson, Arizona, who were charged with seventy-one counts of conspiracy and harboring illegal aliens. In 1984 and 1985, the FBI used four informants to infiltrate the church and to record meetings and conversations over a 10-month period. The FBI codenamed the effort 'Operation Sojourner'. On the basis of the FBI's findings, the US government brought charges against sixteen sanctuary movement activists. Eight of them were found guilty and were given suspended sentences of three to five years' probation. The Justice Department claimed victory, yet from a public relations standpoint the prosecutions largely backfired. The trial was covered by national news agencies and by international networks such as the BBC. Dozens of magazines and newspapers reported the stories, and much of the coverage was highly sympathetic to the refugees' plight and supportive of the sanctuary movement's work. One editorial cartoon even showed the Border Patrol arresting Jesus Christ and his apostles.[87]

Many people credit this publicity with invigorating and expanding the sanctuary movement. By 1987 the movement comprised 450 sanctuaries, spread over two states and twenty-eight cities which had pronounced themselves officially sanctuaries for refugees. Some 430 distinct religious bodies, located in thirty-nine states, had joined the movement, along with over 70,000 active participants.[88] Although the sanctuary movement did not provide direct assistance to the vast majority of Central American refugees, it did raise public awareness about the migration status of these individuals and pushed the US public and the US Congress to consider the moral implications of US foreign policy towards the region and of US policies towards the migrants. The result was to secure some regularization of the migration status of these Salvadorans and Guatemalans.

Salvadorans, Guatemalans, and US Immigration Policy

Most Central American migrants entered the United States illegally, without documentation. Central American activists and their allies continually objected to this state of affairs. In response to the 1985 arrest of the Tucson sanctuary workers, a group of eighty churches and refugee assistance groups sued the American government, arguing that the government was discriminating against Salvadoran and Guatemalan asylum applicants.[89] The case, *American Baptist Churches in the USA, et al., v. Edwin Meese III and Alan Nelson*, combined two plaintiffs' suits. The first group was made up of sanctuary workers who sought an injunction against government interference in their sanctuary work, which they argued was protected by the First Amendment. The second group was a set of refugee assistance organizations which wanted an injunction against deportations of Salvadorans and Guatemalans and a declaratory judgment that they would be granted temporary status until the situations in their home countries improved sufficiently for them to return home.[90] The US government moved that the suit be dismissed, but the court disagreed and the suit was allowed to move forward; it became known as the ABC lawsuit. The plaintiffs reached a settlement with the US government in 1991. The settlement required that (1) Salvadorans and Guatemalans still in the United States, whether they had applied for political asylum previously or not, would be given a new adjudication process, which was to be examined by a newly trained set of asylum officers; (2) petitioners would be provided with work authorization while they waited for their cases to be resolved; and (3) asylum officers would not be allowed to consider past denials of asylum in their deliberations, nor the petitioners' country of origin, nor the State Department's opinions or recommendations. Asylum officers were, however, allowed to consider human rights reports from non-governmental agencies such as Amnesty International.[91] As a result of this settlement, 150,000 asylum cases were overturned and new trials were granted to Salvadorans who had entered the United States before 19 September 1990 and to Guatemalans who had entered before 1 October 1990.[92] This settlement was a major victory for Central American immigrants and activists.

Another legal change to affect the migration status of Central Americans in the United States was the 1986 passing of the Immigration Reform and Control Act (IRCA). Intended to address the problem of undocumented migration, this law allowed for individuals who were present in the United States illegally, but who could prove they had entered the country prior to 1 January 1982, to regularize their status. As a consequence of this law, 227,642 Central Americans were able to make their presence legal, 60 percent of whom were Salvadoran and 25 percent of whom were Guatemalan.[93] Unfortunately, since most Central American refugees arrived in the United States after 1982, they did not fall under the IRCA amnesty.

In 1990 Congress engaged in another immigration reform which created a new category: Temporary Protected Status (TPS).[94] TPS was intended to apply to aliens in the United States who are temporarily unable to return safely to their home country because of ongoing armed conflict, an environmental disaster, or other extraordinary and temporary conditions. Salvadorans were the first group designated to be eligible for this status, which was scheduled to expire in 1992. Over 200,000 Salvadorans living in the United States registered for TPS.[95] As their TPS was about to expire, a new status, Deferred Enforced Departure (DED), was created, which delayed their deportation for another year. The Salvadorans' DED was extended twice more, until March 1996. Salvadorans who were part of the ABC class could then apply for asylum after their DED expired. Thus, over the course of the 1990s, Congress passed a number of laws designed to deal with the Central American migration in a piecemeal fashion. In 1996 Congress passed the Illegal Immigration Reform and Immigrant Responsibility Act (IIRIRA), which, among other things, removed many of the potential remedies which would have been available to members of the ABC class in the event that their asylum petitions were denied. Central American activists protested vehemently, and this led to the 1997 passing of the Nicaraguan and Central American Relief Act (NACARA), which gave some Nicaraguans a preferential migration status much like that of Cubans. Salvadorans and Guatemalans under the act are permitted to apply for US residency under the pre-IIRIRA terms.[96] Yet their petitions will be adjudicated on a case-by-case basis, with no guarantee of success.

The result of these legal changes was that many Central Americans were able to regularize their status and become legal permanent residents in the United States. This being said, today many Salvadoran and Guatemalan immigrants remain in a legal limbo, waiting for the final resolution of their cases. Yet at the start of the 1980s few observers would have thought that the US government would address their concerns at all. This group of political refugees, made up of non-citizens many of whom did not have legal status, was able to help to create a multinational social movement which not only restricted the US government's foreign policy activities in their home countries but also moved the US Congress to attempt to address their migration status. As political scientist Hector Perla points out, these Central American activists 'relied on symbolic politics that used personal testimonies, stories, revolutionary and religious narratives, movies, art, posters, poetry, and music to frame their plight in a viscerally tangible way for North American audiences' (2008: 10). That strategy was successful and allowed them, together with their allies, to change US policies in very important ways.

Traditional Political Engagement

Since their arrival in the United States, Central American immigrants' political activism has been focused on ending the wars in their home countries and on regularizing their status in the United States. Because it took so many years to address their legal status, it is only recently that large numbers of Central Americans began to naturalize. For example, according to the United States Citizenship and Immigration Service (USCIS), between 2004 and 2006 about 34,000 Salvadorans were naturalized. Given the large numbers of Salvadorans in the United States, this is a fairly small number. It is likely that, as their legal situation normalizes, more Central Americans will choose to naturalize, which is the first step towards engaging in US electoral politics. Given the high level of activism in the community, it seems likely that their formal participation levels will be high as well. In terms of elected officials, a growing proportion of the local ones are of Central American origin, and Central American organizations continue to lobby local and state governments on behalf of their constituents. At national level, there is one US congressperson, Hilda Solís, who is half-Nicaraguan.

Conclusion

Salvadorans and Guatemalans constitute a growing and important segment of the Latino population in the United States. Their journeys to the United States have been strongly influenced by the role the US government played in their countries' political and economic development. The key role which Central America was seen as playing in the cold war was also important and affected the ability of reformist political movements to address the extreme inequality present in both countries. As a result, both countries experienced extremely violent civil wars. These structural factors had an important impact on the immigrants' decision to leave and on the legal status they faced when they arrived in the United States.

Despite the end of the civil wars in both countries, many of the political and economic problems that drove these groups' migration subsist. Paramilitary groups continue to operate in both countries, and there continue to be important human rights violations. Economic inequality also remains a significant problem, and it has only been exacerbated under the neo-liberal economic restructuring which intensified under the Central American Free Trade Agreement with the United States. In response, as we saw in the Mexican case, Central American migrants also play an important role in the economic development of their home countries through the provision of remittances. Salvadorans are believed to send over $3 billion in remittances annually. It is estimated that over one fifth of Salvadoran families receive remittances from their relatives in the United States. This is one of the country's largest sources of hard currency. Similarly, in 2007 Guatemalan emigrants sent over $4 billion home in remittances. This is the equivalent of almost 10 percent of the country's gross domestic product. Given the current political and economic pressures, it is unlikely that Central American migration patterns to the United States will change in the near term.

But the Central American story is not solely about structural limitations. These migrants, despite their poverty and uncertain legal status, were able to help to organize a unique, transnational movement which would not only change their situation in the United States, but also influence international public sentiment towards what was occurring in their countries of origin. From this point forward, human rights would become an important consideration in evaluating US activity abroad. Central American activism helped to change the structural situation faced by new migrants, who arrived later in the 1980s, and shows that minority groups without voting rights can still influence the US political system in important ways.

Yet the movement's goals remain incomplete. Many Central Americans remain in a legal limbo, under threat of deportation. Their countries of origin continue to struggle economically and politically, which makes it difficult for them to integrate these potential returnees back into their homelands. And Central American communities in the United States continue to face poverty, lack of access to education, and discrimination. Resolving these issues will continue to be the focus of Central American social service organizations such as CARECEN for the foreseeable future.

Guide to Further Readings

Coutin, Susan Bibler. 2003. *Legalizing Moves: Salvadoran Immigrants' Struggle for US Residency*. Ann Arbor: University of Michigan Press.

García, María Cristina. 2006. *Seeking Refuge: Central American Migration to Mexico, the United States, and Canada*. Berkeley: University of California Press.

Hamilton, Nora and Norma Stoltz Chinchilla. 2001. *Seeking Community in a Global City: Guatemalans and Salvadorans in Los Angeles*. Philadelphia: Temple University Press.

Perla, Hector. 2008. '*Si Nicaragua Venció, El Salvador Vencerá*: Central American Agency in the Creation of the US–Central American Peace and Solidarity Movement', *Latin American Research Review*, 43 (2): 136–58.

CHAPTER SEVEN

Conclusion: The Context of Latino Migration and Mobilization

Objectives
- Understand what undocumented migration is, its causes, and why it is an important issue for Latinos in the United States
- Understand the structural factors that supported the 2006 immigration marches
- Understand the racialized attitudes underlying the anti-immigrant movement in the United States
- Understand the broader context framing the political engagement of all Latino national-origin groups

Introduction

We have seen that the different national-origin Latino groups discussed in this volume have engaged in a variety of political activities in order to address their social, economic, and political concerns. Mexican Americans created social service organizations, engaged in labor organizing, brought legal challenges to segregation, and fomented a mass political movement. Similarly, Puerto Ricans engaged in New York City politics, formed organizations to support community needs, and used non-traditional methods to get local, state, and national officials to pay greater attention to the status of Puerto Rico and of Puerto Ricans living in the United States. Cubans developed a shared political identity which allowed them to achieve political and economic success and to ensure the successful integration of subsequent waves of Cuban migrants. Central American refugees formed a transnational political movement which curtailed US foreign policy activity and regularized the migration status of millions of Central American migrants. We have seen that the tactics and effectiveness of each group has been affected by their time of migration, geographic location, and opportunity structures available to them within those contexts. We have also seen the important ways in which US immigration policy affects the reception and incorporation of Latino migrants to the United States. The recent wave of Latino pro-immigrant mobilization provides yet another example of this kind of political engagement in response to government policies affecting Latino migration status. Yet this mobilization should not be understood in isolation, but rather as a continuation of the kinds of collective activity and engagement we have seen throughout this volume.

The 2006 Marches and Undocumented Migration

On 25 March 2006, between 500,000 and one million immigrant supporters marched in Los Angeles to protest against HR 4437. The bill, passed by the House of Representatives in December 2005, made illegal presence in the United States a felony (currently illegal *entry* into the United States is a misdemeanor, but to remain in the country without documents is not a crime). The law would also have made it illegal for anyone to provide aid or assistance to undocumented immigrants. The sheer size of the 25 March demonstration took the media and law makers by surprise. Over the next few months, millions of immigrants and their supporters would take to the streets in cities across the United States to protest against HR 4437 and to demand a fair and humane reform to the nation's immigration laws. This constitutes the largest mass mobilization to have occurred in the United States since the civil rights movement and the Vietnam anti-war movement.

The passing of HR 4437, and the pro- and anti-immigrant political mobilization it fomented, brought the issue of undocumented migration to the forefront of US political discourse. Undocumented migration refers to the migration of individuals to the United States without legal documentation. In many cases, individuals arrive on tourist or student visas and overstay the amount of time allowed them, which makes them 'undocumented'. In other cases, individuals cross the international border between the United States and Mexico, or between the United States and Canada, without visas or other legal permission to be present in the United States. For these migrants, the act of entering the country illegally is a misdemeanor, but being in the country without permission is not a crime.

As we have seen in the previous chapters, whether or not an individual has permission to be in the United States depends on that individual's status in the eyes of US immigration authorities. For migrants from the western hemisphere, it was not possible until 1965 to be undocumented because there were no restrictions on migration to the

United States. In 1965 the United States passed the Immigration and Nationality Act. This act removed the national quota system which had been passed under the 1924 National Origins Act. The 1924 act was designed to limit migration from southern and eastern Europe and restricted the allocation of visas to countries from those areas, while encouraging northern European migration. The 1965 act awarded all eastern hemisphere countries an equal number of visas. It also placed restrictions on western hemisphere migration for the first time: it granted 120,000 visas to western hemisphere countries, to be allotted on a 'first come first serve' basis. The law also provided for an unlimited number of visas for family reunification, which allowed naturalized US citizens and permanent residents to petition for permission to bring their family members to the United States.

The 1965 act had a number of unintended consequences. First, it fundamentally changed the racial/ethnic make-up of US migration flows. After its passing, European countries did not send large numbers of migrants. Instead, immigrants already present in the United States, most of whom were Latino or Asian American, petitioned to bring their family members, dramatically changing the racial/ethnic make-up of immigrants to the United States.[1] Second, the act created the phenomenon of undocumented western hemisphere migration. Up until that point, there had been no restriction on these migration flows. The 1965 act attempted to restrict migration patterns from Mexico which, by 1965, were already well established. The result was that individuals continued to come, and they often did so without the new documentation required by the 1965 act.

In the 1980s, US politicians began to express concern about this phenomenon. This led to discussions in Congress about how to curb undocumented migration. The result was the passing of the Immigration Reform and Control Act (IRCA) in 1986. This act contained two parts. The first part made it illegal for employers knowingly to hire undocumented workers. It required employers to verify their workers' migration status. Second, it allowed for the legalization of two categories of immigrants: (1) all immigrants who could prove continuous residence in the United States since 1 January 1982; and (2) seasonal workers employed in agricultural work for at least sixty days of the year prior to May 1986. Of the 3 million immigrants who applied for legalization under IRCA, 2.7 million, or nine out of ten applicants, had their petitions approved. Of those 2.7 million immigrants, over 2 million, or seventy-five percent, were of Mexican origin.[2]

Although IRCA did curb undocumented migration to the United States for the first few years after it was passed and reduced the aggregate number of undocumented migrants present in the United States through the legalization program, in the long term it did not fundamentally change undocumented migration flows to the United States.[3] As a result, Congress and sectors of the US public continued to see undocumented migration as a problem and, in response, Congress has quadrupled the funding for the Border Patrol since 1990. These funds have gone towards hiring more Border Patrol agents and towards providing them with manned and unmanned technology for monitoring the border. The Border Patrol is currently made up of 10,000 agents, which constitute 60 percent of all federal law enforcement officials. Congress also passed two other immigration reform bills in the 1990s – the 1990 Immigration Act and the 1996 Illegal Immigration Reform and Immigrant Responsibility Act. The 1990 law increased the number of legal immigrant visas available, in the hope that this would decrease the need for immigrants to resort to illegal entry into the United States. The 1996 law was more extensive and, among other things, it doubled the size of the Border Patrol, decreased immigrants' opportunities for appeal to deportation orders, required the mandatory detention of criminal aliens, and allowed for the retroactive deportation of non-citizens previously convicted of crimes. Yet these laws seem to have had little impact on the levels of undocumented migration to the United States. Critics argue that this is because they do not address the structural causes of migration flows. Instead they focus on policing the behavior of individual migrants.

As a result, it is estimated that currently there are between 10 and 12 million undocumented immigrants living in the United States. Even though there are non-trivial numbers of undocumented Canadian, Irish, and Asian immigrants in the United States, about 55 percent of the undocumented are of Mexican origin and another 22 percent are from other countries in Latin America. Therefore the undocumented immigrant problem is often characterized as a 'Mexican' or 'Latino' problem. The presence of these undocumented migrants, and the significant demographic change which has occurred in the United States since the passing of the 1965 act, have resulted in waves of anti-immigrant backlash targeting Latino immigrants. Groups like the Minutemen, a vigilante group formed to patrol the border and guard against illegal crossings; or the Federation for American Immigration Reform (FAIR), a group which lobbies Congress to tighten restriction on all types of immigration; or Save our State (SOS), a group which sponsored a series of ballot initiatives aimed at denying public services to undocumented immigrants and their children, were formed in response to a perceived immigration crisis and work to lobby state governments and the US Congress to restrict immigration to the United States severely. A look at some of the comments of the leaders of these groups shows the degree to which little differentiation across types of immigrants, documented or undocumented, and racialized assumptions about Latinos in general are often included in their rhetoric:

> We need the National Guard to clean out all our cities and round them [immigrants] up . . . They have no problem slitting your throat and taking your money or selling drugs to your kids or raping your daughters, and they are evil people. (Chris Simcox, co-founder of the Minuteman Project and president of the Minuteman Civil Defense Corps)[4]

> Mexican men have a reputation for leering and worse at little girls, which shouldn't surprise us, since sex with children is socially acceptable in Mexico. (Brenda Walker, California anti-immigrant leader and publisher)[5]

Other commentaries by anti-immigration advocates also point to their authors' conceptualization of this fight as a 'war', with echoes of manifest destiny and the need to control conquered territories:

> My message to them [Mexicans] is, not in two weeks, not in two months, not in two years, never! We must be clear that we will not surrender America and we will not turn the United States over to the invaders from south of the border. (United States Representative Virgil Goode (R–VA))[6]

> Our enemies are bloodied and beaten. We cannot relent. Our boot is on their throat and we must have the willingness to crush their 'throat' so that we can put our enemy down for good. The sovereignty of our nation and the future of our culture and civilization is [sic] at stake. The United States is a beacon of salvation unto the rest of the world. Our freedoms, our culture is man's salvation. If we perish, man perishes. (Joseph Turner, organizer of Save Our State, now a staff member in the Federation for American Immigration Reform)[7]

Many of the comments, particularly from those involved with the Minutemen, also include calls to violence, such as this one:

> What we'll do is randomly pick one night every week where we will kill whoever crosses the border . . . step over there and you die. You get to decide whether it's your lucky night or not. I think that would be more fun. (Brian James, anti-immigrant talk radio host with KFYI–AM on the air in Phoenix in 2006, proposing his solution to the immigration problem in Arizona)

Given this kind of rhetoric, it is not surprising that, according to the FBI, from 2004 to 2006 hate crimes against Latinos increased by 25 percent, reaching the highest level ever reported since the agency began compiling data on these types of crimes. The perpetrators of those crimes rarely distinguished between documented and undocumented Latinos.

Thus US immigration policy is a very heated issue, with strong feelings on both sides. Given this larger context, the 2006 immigration marches were not so surprising. The first major march was in Los Angeles, the site of a previous wave of anti-immigrant backlash during the 1990s. In 1994, Proposition 187 was on the California ballot, an initiative that called for denying health care and social services to undocumented immigrants and their children. It was approved by over 60 percent of California voters. The months leading up to the November 1994 election were marked by heated demonstrations on both sides, which resulted in protest marches and school walkouts that constituted the largest mass protests Latinos in California had engaged in since the Chicano movement mobilization in the late 1960s. Even though the proposition passed (it was never implemented because it was found to be unconstitutional), this experience, and the mobilization surrounding it, led to increased rates of naturalization and voting among Latinos who engaged in this activity. This experience also laid the groundwork for how Latino organizations and community members understood the threat of HR 4437 and how they framed their reactions to it.

Although not all the protesters who engaged in the 2006 marches were themselves immigrants, many of them were, and many were undocumented. These are not individuals who would normally be expected to engage in the political process. Undocumented immigrants, because of their vulnerable position, generally try not to bring attention onto themselves, and certainly do not often take to the streets demanding their rights. So what happened in the spring of 2006 to change their behavior? The greatest impetus was simply the harshness of the House Bill. It was easy for these activists to see that criminalizing immigrants would do nothing to solve the United States' immigration problems and would only make life more difficult for people who often live in the shadows of our society. In this case, the offending legislation was so extreme that it was easy for people to see why they should be protesting against it.

The other factor that made this mobilization possible was the organizational structure, both in terms of advocacy organizations and of ethnic media, which now exists in Latino communities across the United States. As we saw in the previous chapters, one of the main outcomes of the social mobilizations which occurred in Latino national-origin communities during the late 1960s and early 1970s was the establishment of Latino-oriented civil rights organizations such as MALDEF, PRLDEF, the National Council of La Raza, and the Southwest Voter Registration Education Project (SVREP), together with the revitalization of long-term organizations such as LULAC. These bodies were joined by Central American social service organizations like CARECEN in putting together a response to HR 4437. Many analysts saw these protests as spontaneous, but in fact they were the product of months of meetings and planning on the part of community activists.[8] As early as February 2006, groups of community leaders were meeting to discuss the best ways to respond to the House Bill. Before the Los Angeles march was held, about 30,000 immigrant supporters had marched in Washington, DC, and an estimated quarter million had taken to the streets in Chicago. At the same time, using text messaging and MySpace, students across the country began coordinating school walkouts to protest the bill.

The tendency in the popular media was to see these actions as spontaneous, spurred by popular Spanish-language radio personalities such as 'El Piolín' and 'El Cucuy' in Los Angeles and 'El Pistolero' in Chicago. While it is true that these radio hosts played an important role in educating the community about the bill and in mobilizing people to get out and express opposition, the marches would not have been possible without the organizational and financial support of Latino civil rights and social service organizations. For example, for the Los Angeles event to happen, these groups had to take out permits to hold the march, set up a stage and provide audio equipment for the day's speakers, and work with the Los Angeles police in mapping out the march's route and required street closures; and they had to ensure that there were additional trash receptacles and portable toilets available for the marchers to use. All this required significant coordination, effort, and money. Without this organizational infrastructure in place, the community could never have responded to HR 4437 in such an immediate and dramatic way. Yes, the movement needed the people; but it also needed this infrastructure and logistical support.

The political implications of organization often get underestimated. Many of those who look at the post-civil rights United States lament the lack of any ongoing mass mobilization to address issues of social justice. But there is a great deal going on behind the scenes, as became clear with the 2006 immigration marches. The organizational development which came out of the 1970s can be seen as an important structural change that increases the Latino community's ability to lobby Congress and to inform law-makers about issues important to their constituencies. These organizations also represent an important social network, one that, as we saw in 2006, can be activated when there are issues of great importance to the community. This being said, the marches of 2006 were an exceptional circumstance and a response to an extreme piece of legislation. But the fact that they were possible shows the tremendous political potential of the Latino community and the significant structural resources that have been developed within it since the 1970s.

Only time will tell if this unprecedented level of activism on the part of pro-immigrant Latinos will have long-term effects on their engagement in other kinds of politics. Attending a march is very different from contacting an elected official or from voting. As we saw in Chapter 2, Mexicans and Puerto Ricans in particular are more likely to engage in this kind of activity than in voting. Political scientists like to distinguish between *expressive* and *instrumental* forms of civic engagement. Expressive forms constitute activity that is solely meant to express an opinion about an issue. Instrumental engagement is activity meant to address a particular policy question or to solve a particular problem. The marches clearly were expressive; the question is whether that momentum can be shifted towards focusing on more instrumental activities.

The preliminary evidence suggests that this transition may be occurring. After the marches, the participating groups began the '*Hoy Marchamos, Mañana Votamos*/Today we march, tomorrow we vote', campaign, which was meant to focus on registering Latinos to vote and on determining them to turn up for the 2008 elections. For many, the first step in this process is naturalization, and naturalization applications have increased significantly since 2006. Of course, this may be because immigrants feel insecure in the current anti-immigrant environment; or the rise may be due to USCIS significantly increasing the fees for naturalization in 2008: many people may be rushing to get their applications in before the fee increases. Again, only time will tell. But results from studies undertaken in California during the 1990s show that Latinos who naturalized and registered to vote after 1994, when an anti-immigrant proposition was on the state ballot, remain more likely to vote than Latinos who registered during less politically charged periods. The question is whether the current environment will provide the same type of political socialization at the national level.

The marches also showed other structural limitations when one considers issues of immigration reform. Since immigration law is under the jurisdiction of the federal government, any changes to current law have to be passed by Congress. The fate of the congressional immigration reform bill during the spring and summer of 2006 shows the difficulty Latinos have in significantly influencing the national debate on this issue. A bi-partisan group of congressional reformers, led by Senators Edward Kennedy and John McCain, attempted to craft a bill that would provide a path to citizenship for the estimated 12 million undocumented immigrants currently residing in the United States, while still providing enough border enforcement and security provisions to earn the support of law makers who were vehement about maintaining a hard line against undocumented migration. Even though all the members of the Congressional Hispanic Caucus were in favor of immigration reform, the bill failed to pass, largely because Republican law makers defined any path to citizenship as 'amnesty' and few in Congress were willing to say that they were in support of such a measure. With the failure of reform in Congress, localities across the nation have been implementing their own measures, some of which make it illegal for anyone to rent housing to an undocumented person, or ask local police to enforce federal immigration law. This experience shows the difficulty which Latino law makers have in influencing what happens in Congress. Even though this is an issue which affects the Latino community more than any other, the votes of Latino law makers make up only a small proportion of the 218 votes needed to pass legislation in the House of Representatives, and only three of the fifty-one votes needed for a bill to pass the Senate. The marches failed to move law makers to pass comprehensive reform. Given the extreme rhetoric used by those who are against immigration, it is difficult to see how a position of compromise can be reached. Until that happens, the vast majority of those 12 million undocumented migrants, many of whom are Latino, will remain in the United States, but they will keep to the shadows.

Latino Political Engagement in Context

With each national electoral cycle in the United States, the popular media discuss the 'Sleeping Giant' and whether Latinos will 'wake up' and flex their political muscle. Although it is true that Latinos have yet to exercise their power at the ballot box at a level commensurate with their numbers, the national-origin groups we have studied clearly have not been idle in terms of their political organizing. Time and again, we see groups engaging in union organizing, community organizing, and political protest, most often targeted at very specific issues which are key to the quality of life within each community. So it clearly is not the case that Latinos do not engage in collective political activity, but rather that that activity is often of the type that flies beneath the radar of politicians and the popular media. Within this context, the large-scale mobilization that happened in the spring of 2006 is not so surprising.

This being said, Latinos, because they are a minority group with relatively low socioeconomic status and high levels of non-citizenship, face important structural barriers in US politics. Given the majoritarian nature of the electoral system, they will need to build political coalitions in order to achieve electoral success. Those coalitions will continue to be necessary within the legislative institutions themselves, and may limit the degree to which Latino elected officials can implement their desired policy agenda. Although past organizing within the community has changed a number of structural factors – including the group members' migration status and ability to exercise the vote – the majoritarian orientation of the US political system is here to stay. This means that Latino political influence will vary significantly at the local, state, and national levels, and that Latinos will probably continue to engage in non-traditional forms of politics in order to address the pressing needs of their communities.

Notes

CHAPTER 1 INTRODUCTION: LATINOS AND US POLITICS

1 *Merriam Webster's Collegiate Dictionary*, 11th edn (Springfield, MA: Merriam-Webster Inc., 2003.)

2 Thus individuals from Haiti, for example, or Brazil, would not be included in the definition of 'Latino' used in this book.

3 For a complete overview of the prerequisite cases, see Ian Haney López, *White by Law: The Legal Construction of Race* (New York: New York University Press, 1997).

4 New Orleans did have a racial system which included quadroons and other categories of *mulatto*, but this was the exception rather than the rule.

5 George Lipsitz, *The Possessive Investment in Whiteness: How White People Profit from Identity Politics* (Philadelphia: Temple University Press, 1998).

6 See Dalton Conley, *Being Black, Living in the Red: Race, Wealth, and Social Policy in America* (Berkeley: University of California Press, 1999).

CHAPTER 2 LATINA/O PARTICIPATION: INDIVIDUAL ACTIVITY AND INSTITUTIONAL CONTEXT

1 Katherine Tate, *From Protest to Politics: The New Black Voters in American Elections* (Cambridge: Harvard University Press, 1993); F. Chris García, Angelo Falcón and Rodolfo de la Garza, 'Ethnicity and Politics: Evidence from the Latino National Political Survey', *Hispanic Journal of Behavioral Sciences*, 18 (1996): 91–103; and John A. García, 'Political Participation: Resources and Involvement among Latinos and the American Political System', in F. Chris García, ed., *Pursuing Power: Latinos and the Political System* (Notre Dame: University of Notre Dame Press, 1997), 44–71.

2 For linked fate, see Michael C. Dawson, *Behind the Mule* (Princeton: Princeton University Press, 1995); for political alienation, see Marvin E. Olsen, 'Two Categories of Political Alienation', *Social Forces*, 47 (1969): 288–99; for group identity, see Tate, 1993, and Carol Hardy-Fanta, *Latina Politics, Latino Politics: Gender, Culture and Political Participation in Boston* (Philadelphia: Temple University Press, 1993); for group conflict, see Henri Tajfel and J. Turner, 'The Social Identity Theory of Intergroup Behavior', in Stephen Worchel and William Austin, eds, *Psychology of Intergroup Relations* (Chicago: Nelson-Hall, 1986), 7–24.

3 The other US immigrant group least likely to be naturalized is that of Canadians, which leads scholars to suggest that geographic proximity may have a negative impact on immigrants' decision to naturalize.

4 Unfortunately, this survey did not allow for separate analysis of Guatemalan registration and voting levels because there were too few respondents with that national-origin background.

5 National Association of Latino Elected Officials, 'National Directory of Latino Elected Officials' (Los Angeles: NALEO Educational Fund, 2007). Totals compiled by the author.

6 They are the cities of: San Joaquín, CA, 63.5%; Maywood, CA, 59.5%; Cudahy, CA, 58.9%; Bell Gardens, CA, 56.5%; Huron City, CA, 55.9%; Huntington Park, CA, 55.9%; Bell, CA, 53.9%; Arvin, CA, 53.8%; Mendota, CA, 53.5%; King City, CA, 52.3%; Santa Ana, CA, 51.9%; Orange Cove, CA, 51.6%. From Joaquín Avila, 'Political Apartheid in California: Consequences of Excluding a Growing Noncitizen Population', in *Latino Policy and Issues Brief* (Los Angeles: UCLA Chicano Studies Research Center, 2003).

7 Granted, both systems were quite exclusionary in terms of who was accorded 'citizenship', particularly in terms of gender and class, and both systems allowed for slavery; but they did, despite their flaws, allow all their 'citizens' to have a say.

CHAPTER 3   MEXICAN AMERICANS: CONQUEST, MIGRATION, AND ADAPTATION

1 John C. Calhoun, speech on the floor of the senate, 1848, as found at http://www. teachingamericanhistory.org/library/index.asp?document=478 (downloaded 11 December 2008).

2 Library of Congress, 'A Century of Lawmaking for a New Nation: Congressional Documents and Debates, 1774–1875', pp. 929–30. Found at http://memory.loc.gov/ cgi-bin/ampage.

3 Chapter XLVII, 'An Act for the Protection of Actual Settlers and to Quiet Land Titles in this state. Approved March 26, 1856', in *Statutes of California passed at the Seventh Session of the Legislature, Begun on the Seventh Day of January, One Thousand Eight Hundred and Fifty-six, and Ended on the Twenty-first Day of April, One Thousand Eight Hundred and Fifty-six, at the City of Sacramento* (Sacramento, CA: James Allen, 1856), pp. 54–7.

4 New Mexico's population was almost evenly split between Mexicans, Anglos, and Native Americans until the early twentieth century, which made multi-racial power-sharing more the norm there than it was in other parts of the southwest. See M. Menchaca, *Recovering History, Constructing Race: The Indian, Black and White Roots of Mexican Americans* (Austin: University of Texas Press, 2001).

5 R. E. Fernández and G. González, *A Century of Chicano History: Empire, Nations, and Migration* (New York: Routledge, 2003), p. 37.

6 Ibid., p. 38.

7 Gilbert González, *Guest Workers or Colonized Labor? Mexican Labor Migration to the United States* (Boulder, CO: Paradigm, 2006), p. 2.

8 Since 1993, almost 400 women and girls have been murdered and more than 70 remain missing in Ciudad Juárez and Chihuahua, Mexico. Very few individuals have been prosecuted for these crimes.

9 I should note that these restrictions were not enforced in south Texas, where landowners would, through coercion and bribery, 'deliver' their Mexican workers'

votes to whichever political candidate they supported. See J. L. Pycior, *LBJ and Mexican Americans: The Paradox of Power* (Austin: University of Texas Press, 1997).

10 Ibid., p. 7.

11 William T. Carrigan and Clive Webb, 'The Lynching of Persons of Mexican Origin or Descent in the United States, 1848 to 1928', *Journal of Social History*, 37 (2003): 411–38.

12 Pycior, 1997, pp. 7–8.

13 *Méndez v. Westminster School District*, 64 F. Supp. 544 (D.C.CAL. 1946).

14 Vicki Ruiz, *From Out of the Shadows: Mexican American Women in Twentieth Century America* (New York: Oxford University Press, 1998), p. 89.

15 We will see, with the advent of the United Farm Workers Union, that these laws were often not enforced. That being said, these actions at least got the statutes put on the books.

16 This is a standard practice of parliamentary procedure used to run meetings (how people make motions, second them, etc.). A history of Robert's Rules may be found at http://www.robertsrules.com/history.html.

17 See Cynthia Orozco, 'Regionalism, Politics, and Gender in Southwest History: The League of United Latin American Citizens' Expansion into New Mexico from Texas, 1929–1945', *Western Historical Quarterly*, 29 (1998): 459–83.

18 Vicki Ruiz, '*Una mujer sin fronteras*: Luisa Moreno and Latina Labor Activism', *Pacific Historical Review* 73 (2004): 1–20.

19 Clare Sheridan, '"Another White Race": Mexican Americans and the Paradox of Whiteness in Jury Selection', *Law and History Review*, 21 (2003): 109–44.

20 Margaret Rose, 'Dolores Huerta: The United Farm Workers Union', in Eric Arnesen, ed., *The Human Tradition in American Labor History* (Wilmington, DE: SR Books, 2004), pp. 211–30.

21 Lisa García Bedolla, *Fluid Borders: Latino Power, Identity, and Politics in Los Angeles* (Berkeley: University of California Press, 2005).

22 A. Navarro, *Mexicano Political Experience in Occupied Aztlán* (Lanham, MD: AltaMira Press, 2004), p. 277.

23 J. D. Skrentny, *The Minority Rights Revolution* (Cambridge, MA: Harvard University Press, 2002), p. 198.

24 Julie Pycior, 'From Hope to Frustration: Mexican Americans and Lyndon Johnson in 1967', *Western Historical Quarterly*, 24 (1993): 469–94, at 477.

25 As quoted in Pycior, 1993, p. 478.

26 Ibid.

27 Peter Nabokov, *Tijerina and the Courthouse Raid* (Albuquerque: University of New Mexico Press, 1969).

28 Individuals of Mexican descent living in New Mexico often refer to themselves as Hispanos rather than Hispanics, Latinos, or Mexican Americans.

29 Matt S. Meier and Margo Gutiérrez, *Encyclopedia of the Mexican American Civil Rights Movement* (Westport, CT: Greenwood Press, 2000).

30 As quoted in G. Mariscal, *Brown-Eyed Children of the Sun: Lessons from the Chicano Movement, 1965–1975* (Albuquerque: University of New Mexico Press, 2005).

31 Juan Gómez-Quiñones, *Chicano Politics: Reality and Promise, 1940–1990* (Albuquerque: University of New Mexico Press, 1990), p. 118.

32 Carlos Muñoz, *Youth, Identity, Power: The Chicano Movement*, 2nd edn (New York: Verso, 2007), p. 64.

33 Ibid., p. 65.

34 Ibid., p. 68.

35 Dolores Delgado Bernal, 'Grassroots Leadership Reconceptualized: Chicana Oral Histories and the 1968 East Los Angeles School Blowouts', *Frontiers: A Journal of Women Studies*, 19 (1998): 113–42.

36 José Angel Gutiérrez, *The Making of a Chicano Militant: Lessons from Cristal* (Madison: University Wisconsin Press, 1998), pp. 187–8.

37 Gómez-Quiñones, 1990, p. 130.

38 Ibid., p. 132.

39 Alma M. García, *Chicana Feminist Thought: The Basic Historical Writings* (New York: Routledge, 1997).

40 Denise A. Segura, 'Challenging the Chicano Text: Toward a More Inclusive Contemporary Causa', *Signs*, 26 (2001): 541–50.

41 Aida Hurtado, '*Sitios y Lenguas*: Chicanas Theorize Feminisms', *Hypatia*, 13 (1998): 134–61; Alma García, 1997.

42 Gisele Henriques and Raj Patel, 'NAFTA, Corn, and Mexico's Agricultural Trade Liberalization', Special Report. Interhemispheric Research Center (IRC) Americas Program, 2004. (http://americas.irc-online.org/reports/2004/0402nafta.html.)

43 Fred Krissman, '"Them" or "Us"? Assessing Responsibility for Undocumented Migration from Mexico', Working Paper, UC San Diego: Center for Comparative Immigration Studies (2001).

44 Interhemispheric Resource Center, 'Mexican Hometown Associations', *Citizen Action in the Americas*, 5 (2003).

CHAPTER 4   PUERTO RICANS: FROM COLONIZED PEOPLE TO POLITICAL ACTIVISTS

1 Nuclear DNA, or the genetic material present in a gene's nucleus, is inherited in equal proportions from one's father and mother. Mitochondrial DNA is inherited only from one's mother and does not change or blend with other materials over time. See http://www.centrelink.org/KearnsDNA.html.

2 There are seven ways in which a US-born individual may lose her citizenship: (1) by being naturalized in a foreign country, upon the person's own application, made after reaching 18 years of age; (2) by making an oath or other declaration of allegiance to a foreign country or division thereof – again, after reaching 18 years of age; (3) by serving in the armed forces of a foreign country, if those armed forces are engaged in hostilities against the US, or if the person serves as an officer; (4) by working for the government of a foreign country, if the person also obtains nationality in that country, or if, in order to work in such a position, an oath or some other declaration of allegiance is required; (5) by making a formal renunciation of US citizenship before a US consular officer or diplomat in a foreign country; (6) by making a formal written statement of renunciation during a state of war, if the US Attorney General approves the renunciation as being not contrary to US national defense; and (7) by committing an act of treason against the US, or by attempting by force or the use of arms to overthrow the government of the US. Renunciation by this means can be accomplished only after a court has found the person guilty.

3 Statehood and independence were not given as options in this plebiscite.

4 Both major US political parties do allow Puerto Rican delegates to participate in their nominating conventions, but Puerto Ricans on the island have no formal say in the general election.

5 This vote was to amend the island's constitution, and was not a referendum on the status of the island.

6 These referenda are non-binding. Although they do provide important information about Puerto Rican opinion on the subject, if Puerto Rico were to vote in favor of either statehood or independence, the US Congress is under no obligation to act so as to support that decision.

7 Brett Wallach, 'Puerto Rico: Growth, Change, Progress, Development', *Focus*, 39 (1989): 27–33.

8 Pedro A. Cabán, 'Industrial Transformation and Labour Relations in Puerto Rico: From "Operation Bootstrap" to the 1970s', *Journal of Latin American Studies*, 21 (1989): 559–91, at p. 565.

9 Wallach, 1989.

10 Cabán, 1989, p. 566.

11 James L. Dietz, *Economic History of Puerto Rico: Institutional Change and Capitalist Development* (Princeton, NJ: Princeton University Press, 1984), p. 297.

12 As quoted in José Ramón Sánchez, *Boricua Power: A Political History of Puerto Ricans in the United States* (New York: New York University Press, 2007), p. 57.

13 Felix Padilla, *Puerto Rican Chicago* (Notre Dame, IN: University of Notre Dame Press, 1987).

14 Much of this discussion of early political life in New York City is taken from Virginia Sánchez-Korrol, *From Colonia to Community: The History of Puerto Ricans in New York City* (Berkeley: University of California Press, 1994), ch. 6.

15 Ibid., p. 26.

16 Angelo Falcón, 'A History of Puerto Rican Politics in New York City: 1860s to 1945', in James Jennings and Monte Rivera, eds, *Puerto Rican Politics in Urban America* (Westport, CT: Greenwood Press, 1984), pp. 15–42, at p. 23.

17 Sánchez, 2007, p. 70.

18 Falcón in Jennings and Rivera, eds, 1984, p. 26.

19 As quoted in Sánchez-Korrol, 1994, p. 183.

20 Ibid., p. 184.

21 'Introduction', in Jennings and Rivera, eds, 1984, p. 3.

22 Falcón in Jennings and Rivera, eds, 1984, p. 32.

23 Sánchez-Korrol, 1994, p. 184.

24 Ibid., p. 177.

25 Sherrie Baver, 'Puerto Rican Politics in New York City: The Post-World War II Period', in Jennings and Rivera, eds, 1984, pp. 43–59, at p. 45.

26 Ibid.

27 Sánchez-Korrol, 1994, p. 191.

28 Sánchez, 2007, p. 197.

29 Baver, in Jennings and Rivera, eds, 1984, p. 49.

30 Ibid., p. 47.

31 The black power movement was a movement advocating violence and led by the Black Panthers; it was very influential in US leftist politics in the late 1960s.

32 Sánchez-Korrol, 1994, p. 214.

33　Iris Morales, 'iPalante, Siempre Palante! The Young Lords', in Andrés Torres and José E. Velásquez, eds, *The Puerto Rican Movement: Voices from the Diaspora* (Philadelphia: Temple University Press, 1998), pp. 210–27, at p. 218.

34　Ibid., p. 213.

35　Ibid., p. 216.

36　Torres, 'Introduction', in Torres and Velázquez, eds, 1998, p. 9.

37　Ibid.

CHAPTER 5　CUBAN AMERICANS: OCCUPATION, REVOLUTION, AND EXILE POLITICS

1　It is now suspected that the explosion of the *USS Maine* was an accident, the result of an overheated boiler. But at the time the US military and most government officials felt certain the explosion was the result of Spanish sabotage. Regardless of the facts, this explosion did set the stage for the US' declaration of war against Spain.

2　*New York Times*, 'Gomez to Write on the War', 1 November 1899, p. 5.

3　*New York Times*, 'Cubans Define Relations', 28 February 1901, p. 2.

4　Louis A. Pérez, *Cuba between Empires, 1878–1902* (Pittsburgh, PA: University of Pittsburgh Press, 1998), p. 325.

5　H. W. Brands, *T.R.: The Last Romantic* (New York: Basic Books, 1998), p. 569.

6　Jeffrey J. Safford, 'The Nixon–Castro Meeting of 19 April 1959', *Diplomatic History* 4 (1980): 425–31, at p. 431.

7　This ban remains in place despite a 1958 Supreme Court ruling to the effect that US citizens have a constitutional right to travel abroad. In *Rockwell Kent and Walter Briehl* v. *John Foster Dulles*, the court held that 'the right to travel is a part of the "liberty" of which the citizen cannot be deprived without due process of law under the Fifth Amendment': Jane Franklin, *The Cuban Revolution and the United States: A Chronological History* (Melbourne, Australia: Ocean Press. 1997), p. 17.

8　Dario Moreno, 'The Cuban Model: Political Empowerment in Miami', in F. Chris García, ed., *Pursuing Power: Latinos and the Political System* (Notre Dame: University of Notre Dame Press, 1996), pp. 208–26.

9　F. R. Masud-Piloto, *From Welcomed Exiles to Illegal Immigrants: Cuban Migration to the US, 1959–1995* (Lanham, MD: Rowman & Littlefield, 1995).

10　Ibid., p. 54.

11　During 1961, commercial flights continued between the US and Cuba, even though both countries had ended diplomatic relations. After the Cuban missile crisis in 1962 direct flights were cancelled, and were restarted only as part of the Camaroica airlift.

12　Dick Russell, 'Little Havana's Reign of Terror', *New Times*, 29 October 1976.

13　Moreno, 1996, p. 219.

14　US Census Bureau, 'The Hispanic Population: Census 2000 Brief', May 2001.

15　'Cuban Emigré Wins Election to US House', *New York Times*, 31 August 1989.

16　Jorge Más Canosa passed away in 1997. The organization is now run by his son, Jorge Más Santos.

17　For more detailed information on the Free Cuba PAC and its financial disclosures, see http://www.opensecrets.org/pacs/lookup2.php?strID=C00142117&cycle=2004 (last accessed 14 December 2008).

18 M. C. García, *Havana USA: Cuban Exiles and Cuban Americans in South Florida, 1959–1994* (Berkeley: University of California Press, 1996), p. 79.

19 Since the accord, the United States has failed to approve anything near the expected number of 20,000, mostly because immigrant interviewers have found it difficult to prove that the petitioners were subject to overt political persecution rather than simply being economic migrants.

CHAPTER 6   CENTRAL AMERICANS: INEQUALITY, WAR, AND SOLIDARITY

1 Tom Barry and Deb Preusch, *The Central America Fact Book* (New York: Grove Press, 1986), p. 3.

2 Ibid., p. 4.

3 Americas Watch, *El Salvador's Decade of Terror: Human Rights Since the Assassination of Archbishop Romero* (New Haven, CT: Yale University Press, 1991), p. 2.

4 Thomas E. Skidmore and Peter H. Smith, *Modern Latin America* (3rd edn, New York: Oxford University Press, 1992), p. 333.

5 As quoted in Barry and Preusch, 1986, p. 201.

6 As quoted in Skidmore and Smith, 1992, p. 333.

7 Quoted in Barry and Preusch, 1986, p. 200.

8 Americas Watch, 1991, p. 3.

9 Ibid., p. 4.

10 Ibid.

11 Ibid.

12 Ibid.

13 Americas Watch, 1991, p. 5; Barry and Preusch, 1986, p. 204.

14 Barry and Preusch, 1986, p. 201.

15 Skidmore and Smith, 1992, p. 334; María Cristina García, *Seeking Refuge: Central American Migration to Mexico, the United States, and Canada* (Berkeley: University of California Press, 2006), p. 21.

16 Barry and Preusch, 1986, p. 201.

17 Ibid., 205.

18 Americas Watch, 1991, p. 6.

19 Skidmore and Smith, 1992, p. 335; Americas Watch, 1991, p. 6.

20 Americas Watch, 1991, p. 7.

21 Skidmore and Smith, 1992, p. 335.

22 Americas Watch, 1991, p. 8.

23 García, 2006, p. 23.

24 Ibid.

25 Americas Watch, 1991, p. 10; Skidmore and Smith, 1992, pp. 335–6.

26 García, 2006, p. 23.

27 Anthony Lewis, 'A Bloody Joke', *New York Times*, 17 October, 1983, p. A1.

28 García, 2006, p. 22.

29 Ibid., p. 23.

30 Americas Watch, 1991, p. 9.

31 Ibid.

32 Barry and Preusch, 1986, p. 226.

33 Ibid.
34 Ibid.
35 Skidmore and Smith, 1992, p. 339.
36 Barry and Preusch, 1986, p. 227.
37 Skidmore and Smith, 1992, p. 339.
38 Ibid.
39 Ibid.
40 Ibid., p. 340.
41 Barry and Preusch, 1986, p. 228.
42 Skidmore and Smith, 1992, p. 340.
43 Barry and Preusch, 1986, p. 228.
44 Ibid.
45 Ibid., p. 341.
46 Ibid.
47 García, 2006, p. 27.
48 Barry and Preusch, 1986, p. 225.
49 García, 2006, p. 26.
50 Ibid., p. 27.
51 Barry and Preusch, 1986, p. 229.
52 Ibid.
53 García, 2006, p. 27.
54 Barry and Preusch, 1986, p. 229; García, 2006, p. 27.
55 Barry and Preusch, 1986, p. 230.
56 http://shr.aaas.org/guatemala/ceh/report/english/conc2.html (last accessed 14 December 2008).
57 The full text of the report may be seen at: http://shr.aaas.org/guatemala/ceh/report/english/toc.html (last accessed 14 December 2008).
58 García, 2006, p. 28.
59 http://shr.aaas.org/guatemala/ceh/report/english/conc2.html (last accessed 14 December 2008).
60 García, 2006, p. 29.
61 Ibid.
62 Ibid., p. 31.
63 Nora Hamilton and Norma Stoltz Chinchilla, *Seeking Community in a Global City: Guatemalans and Salvadorans in Los Angeles* (Philadelphia: Temple University Press, 2001), p. 44.
64 Ibid., p. 45.
65 Barry and Preusch, 1986, p. 83.
66 Ibid.
67 García, 2006, p. 26.
68 Barry and Preusch, 1986, p. 88.
69 Ibid., p. 89.
70 Quoted in Americas Watch, 1991, p. 120 and in García, 2006, p. 25.
71 Americas Watch, 1991.
72 As quoted in García, 2006, p. 25.
73 Ibid., p. x.
74 Ibid., p. 89.

75 Ibid., p. 90.

76 Ibid.

77 Hector Perla, '*Si Nicaragua Venció, El Salvador Vencerá*: Central American Agency in the Creation of the US–Central Amerian Peace and Solidarity Movement', *Latin American Research Review*, 43 (2) (2008): 136–58.

78 Ibid.

79 Ibid.

80 Ibid.

81 Ibid.

82 Ibid.

83 Ibid.

84 García, 2006, p. 98.

85 Quoted in ibid., p. 99.

86 García, 2006, p. 100; Perla, 2008.

87 García, 2006, p. 107.

88 Ibid.

89 Susan Bibler Coutin, *Legalizing Moves: Salvadoran Immigrants' Struggle for US Residency* (Ann Arbor: University of Michigan Press, 2003), p. 4.

90 García, 2006, p. 111.

91 Ibid.

92 Ibid., p. 112.

93 García, 2006, p. 91.

94 Coutin, 2003, p. 5.

95 García, 2006, p. 112.

96 Coutin, 2003, p. xiv.

CHAPTER 7 CONCLUSION: THE CONTEXT OF LATINO MIGRATION AND MOBILIZATION

1 Charles B. Keely, 'Effects of the Immigration Act of 1965 on Selected Population Characteristics of Immigrants to the United States', *Demography*, 8 (1971): 157–69.

2 Nancy Rytina, 'IRCA Legalization Effects: Lawful Permanent Residence and Naturalization through 2001', paper presented at the Effects of Immigrant Legalization Programs on the United States, Mary Woodward Lasker Center, NIH Main Campus, October 2002.

3 Pia M. Orrenius and Madeline Zavodny, 'Do Amnesty Programs Reduce Undocumented Migration? Evidence from IRCA', *Demography*, 40 (2003): 437–50.

4 As quoted in the Southern Poverty Law Center's Intelligence Report magazine, Summer 2005.

5 From VDARE.com, article titled 'Top Ten Reasons Why the US Should not Marry Mexico', 1 January 2007.

6 Speech given at the March for America, Washington, DC, 18 June 2007.

7 Message sent to Save Our State supporters on 7 October 2006.

8 Ted Wang and Robert C. Winn, 'Groundswell Meets Groundwork: Preliminary Recommendations for Building on Immigrant Mobilizations', New York: Four Freedoms Fund, 2006.

Bibliography

Acosta-Belén, E. and C.E. Santiago. 2006. *Puerto Ricans in the United States: A Contemporary Portrait*. Boulder, CO: Lynne Rienner.

Alcoff, Linda. 2000. 'Is Latina/o Identity a Racial Identity?', in Jorge J. E. Gracia and Pablo DeGreiff, eds, *Hispanics/Latinos in the United States: Ethnicity, Race and Rights*. New York: Routledge.

Americas Watch. 1991. *El Salvador's Decade of Terror: Human Rights Since the Assassination of Archbishop Romero*. New Haven, CT: Yale University Press.

Avila, Joaquín. 2003. 'Political Apartheid in California: Consequences of Excluding a Growing Noncitizen Population', in *Latino Policy and Issues Brief*. Los Angeles: UCLA Chicano Studies Research Center.

Barry, Tom and Deb Preusch. 1986. *The Central America Fact Book*. New York: Grove Press.

Baver, Sherrie. 1984. 'Puerto Rican Politics in New York City: The Post-World War II Period', in James Jennings and Monte Rivera, eds, *Puerto Rican Politics in Urban America*. Westport, CT: Greenwood Press, pp. 43–59.

Brands, H.W. 1998. *T.R.: The Last Romantic*. New York: Basic Books.

Briggs, Laura. 2002. *Reproducing Empire: Race, Sex, Science, and US Imperialism in Puerto Rico*. Berkeley, CA: University of California Press.

Cabán, Pedro A. 1989. 'Industrial Transformation and Labour Relations in Puerto Rico: From "Operation Bootstrap" to the 1970s', *Journal of Latin American Studies*, 21: 559–91.

Cannon, Terence. 1981. *Revolutionary Cuba*. New York: Crowell.

Carrigan, William T. and Clive Webb. 2003. 'The Lynching of Persons of Mexican Origin or Descent in the United States, 1848 to 1928', *Journal of Social History*, 37: 411–38.

Conley, Dalton. 1999. *Being Black, Living in the Red: Race, Wealth, and Social Policy in America*. Berkeley: University of California Press.

Coutin, Susan Bibler. 2003. *Legalizing Moves: Salvadoran Immigrants' Struggle for US Residency*. Ann Arbor: University of Michigan Press.

Dawson, Michael C. 1995. *Behind the Mule: Race and Class in African American Politics*. Princeton: Princeton University Press.

Delgado Bernal, Dolores. 1998. 'Grassroots Leadership Reconceptualized:

Chicana Oral Histories and the 1968 East Los Angeles School Blowouts', *Frontiers: A Journal of Women Studies*, 19: 113–42.

Dietz, James L. 1984. *Economic History of Puerto Rico: Institutional Change and Capitalist Development*. Princeton, NJ: Princeton University Press.

Falcón, Angelo. 1984. 'A History of Puerto Rican Politics in New York City: 1860s to 1945', in James Jennings and Monte Rivera, eds, *Puerto Rican Politics in Urban America*. Westport, CT: Greenwood Press, pp. 15–42.

Fernández, Raúl E. and Gilbert G. González. 2003. *A Century of Chicano History: Empire, Nations, and Migration*. New York: Routledge.

Franklin, Jane. 1992. *The Cuban Revolution and the United States: A Chronological History*. New York: Talman Company.

Franklin, Jane. 1997. *The Cuban Revolution and the United States: A Chronological History*. Melbourne, Australia: Ocean Press.

García, Alma M. 1997. *Chicana Feminist Thought: The Basic Historical Writings*. New York: Routledge.

García, F. Chris, Angelo Falcón and Rodolfo de la Garza. 1996. 'Ethnicity and Politics: Evidence from the Latino National Political Survey', *Hispanic Journal of Behavioral Sciences*, 18: 91–103.

García, John A. 1997. 'Political Participation: Resources and Involvement among Latinos and the American Political System', in F. Chris García, ed., *Pursuing Power: Latinos and the Political System*. Notre Dame: University of Notre Dame Press, 44–71.

García, María Cristina. 1996. *Havana USA: Cuban Exiles and Cuban Americans in South Florida, 1959–1994*. Berkeley: University of California Press.

García, María Cristina. 2006. *Seeking Refuge: Central American Migration to Mexico, the United States, and Canada*. Berkeley: University of California Press.

García Bedolla, Lisa. 2005. *Fluid Borders: Latino Power, Identity, and Politics in Los Angeles*. Berkeley: University of California Press.

Gómez-Quiñones, Juan. 1990. *Chicano Politics: Reality and Promise, 1940–1990*. Albuquerque: University of New Mexico Press.

González, Gilbert. 2006. *Guest Workers or Colonized Labor? Mexican Labor Migration to the United States*. Boulder, CO: Paradigm.

González, Gilbert G. and Raúl A. Fernández. 2003. *A Century of Chicano History: Empire, Nations, and Migration*. New York: Routledge.

Gutiérrez, José Angel. 1998. *The Making of a Chicano Militant: Lessons from Cristal*. Madison: University Wisconsin Press.

Hamilton, Nora and Norma Stoltz Chinchilla. 2001. *Seeking Community in a Global City: Guatemalans and Salvadorans in Los Angeles*. Philadelphia: Temple University Press.

Haney López, Ian. 1997. *White by Law: The Legal Construction of Race*. New York: New York University Press.

Hardy-Fanta, Carol. 1993. *Latina Politics, Latino Politics: Gender, Culture and Political Participation in Boston*. Philadelphia: Temple University Press.

Henriques, Gisele and Raj Patel. 2004. 'NAFTA, Corn, and Mexico's Agricultural Trade Liberalization', Special Report. Interhemispheric Research Center (IRC) Americas Program. http://americas.irc-online.org/reports/2004/0402nafta.html (accessed 14 December 2008).

Hurtado, Aida. 1998. '*Sitios y Lenguas*: Chicanas Theorize Feminisms', *Hypatia*, 13: 134–61.

Interhemispheric Resource Center. 2003. 'Mexican Hometown Associations', *Citizen Action in the Americas*, no. 5.

Jennings, James and Monte Rivera, eds. 1984. *Puerto Rican Politics in Urban America*. Westport, CT: Greenwood Press.

Keely, Charles B. 1971. 'Effects of the Immigration Act of 1965 on Selected Population Characteristics of Immigrants to the United States', *Demography*, 8: 157–69.

Krissman, Fred. 2001. '"Them" or "Us"? Assessing Responsibility for Undocumented Migration from Mexico', Working Paper, UC San Diego: Center for Comparative Immigration Studies.

Lewis, Anthony. 1983. 'A Bloody Joke', *New York Times*, 17 October, p. A1.

Lipsitz, George. 1998. *The Possessive Investment in Whiteness: How White People Profit from Identity Politics*. Philadelphia: Temple University Press.

Mariscal, George. 2005. *Brown-Eyed Children of the Sun: Lessons from the Chicano Movement, 1965–1975*. Albuquerque: University of New Mexico Press.

Masud-Piloto, Felix Roberto. 1995. *From Welcomed Exiles to Illegal Immigrants: Cuban Migration to the US, 1959–1995*. Lanham, MD: Rowman and Littlefield.

Meier, Matt S. and Margo Gutiérrez. 2000. *Encyclopedia of the Mexican American Civil Rights Movement*. Westport, CT: Greenwood Press.

Menchaca, Martha. 2001. *Recovering History, Constructing Race: The Indian, Black and White Roots of Mexican Americans*. Austin: University of Texas Press.

Morales, Iris. 1998. '¡Palante, Siempre Palante! The Young Lords', in Andrés Torres and José E. Velásquez, eds, *The Puerto Rican Movement: Voices from the Diaspora*. Philadelphia: Temple University Press.

Moreno, Dario. 1996. 'The Cuban Model: Political Empowerment in Miami', in F. Chris García, ed., *Pursuing Power: Latinos and the Political System*. Notre Dame, IN: University of Notre Dame Press.

Muñoz, Carlos. 2007. *Youth, Identity, Power: The Chicano Movement*, 2nd edn. New York: Verso.

Nabokov, Peter. 1969. *Tijerina and the Courthouse Raid*. Albuquerque: University of New Mexico Press.

Navarro, Armando. 2004. *Mexicano Political Experience in Occupied Aztlán*. Lanham, MD: AltaMira Press.

Olsen, Marvin E. 1969. 'Two Categories of Political Alienation', *Social Forces*, 47: 288–99.

Omi, Michael and Howard Winant. 1994. *Racial Formation in the United States from the 1960s to the 1990s*. New York: Routledge.

Orozco, Cynthia. 1998. 'Regionalism, Politics, and Gender in Southwest History: The League of United Latin American Citizens' Expansion into New Mexico from Texas, 1929–1945', *Western Historical Quarterly*, 29: 459–83.

Orrenius, Pia M. and Madeline Zavodny. 2003. 'Do Amnesty Programs Reduce Undocumented Migration? Evidence from IRCA', *Demography*, 40: 437–50.

Padilla, Felix. 1987. *Puerto Rican Chicago*. Notre Dame, IN: University of Notre Dame Press.

Pérez, Louis. 1998. *Cuba between Empires, 1878–1902*. Pittsburgh, PA: University of Pittsburgh Press.

Pérez, Louis. 2003. *Cuba and the United States: Ties of Singular Intimacy*, 3rd edn. Atlanta, GA: University of Georgia Press.

Perla, Hector. 2008. *Si Nicaragua Venció, El Salvador Vencerá*: Central American Agency in the Creation of the US–Central Amerian Peace and Solidarity Movement', *Latin American Research Review*, 43 (2): 136–58.

Pycior, Julie Leininger. 1993. 'From Hope to Frustration: Mexican Americans and Lyndon Johnson in 1967', *Western Historical Quarterly*, 24: 469–94.

Pycior, Julie Leininger. 1997. *LBJ and Mexican Americans: The Paradox of Power*. Austin: University of Texas Press.

Rose, Margaret. 2004. 'Dolores Huerta: The United Farm Workers Union', in Eric Arnesen, ed., *The Human Tradition in American Labor History*. Wilmington, DE: SR Books.

Ruiz, Vicki. 1998. *From Out of the Shadows: Mexican American Women in Twentieth Century America*. New York: Oxford University Press.

Ruiz, Vicki. 2004. '*Una Mujer Sin Fronteras*: Luisa Moreno and Latina Labor Activism', *Pacific Historical Review*, 73: 1–20.

Ruiz de Burton, María Amparo. 1997. *The Squatter and the Don*, 2nd edn. Houston, TX: Arte Público Press.

Russell, Dick. 1976. 'Little Havana's Reign of Terror', *New Times*, 20 October.

Rytina, Nancy. 2002. 'IRCA Legalization Effects: Lawful Permanent Residence and Naturalization through 2001', paper presented at the Effects of Immigrant Legalization Programs on the United States, Mary Woodward Lasker Center, NIH Main Campus, October.

Safford, Jeffrey J. 1980. 'The Nixon–Castro Meeting of 19 April 1959', *Diplomatic History*, 4: 425–31.

Sánchez, José Ramón. 2007. *Boricua Power: A Political History of Puerto Ricans in the United States*. New York: New York University Press.

Sánchez-Korrol, Virginia. 1994. *From Colonia to Community: The History of Puerto Ricans in New York City*. Berkeley: University of California Press.

Segura, Denise A. 2001. 'Challenging the Chicano Text: Toward a More Inclusive Contemporary Causa', *Signs*, 26: 541–50.

Sheridan, Clare. 2003. "Another White Race": Mexican Americans and the Paradox of Whiteness in Jury Selection', *Law and History Review*, 21: 109–44.

Skidmore, Thomas E. and Peter H. Smith. 1992. *Modern Latin America*, 3rd edn. New York: Oxford University Press.

Skrentny, John David. 2002. *The Minority Rights Revolution*. Cambridge, MA: Harvard University Press.

Tajfel, Henri and J. Turner. 1986. 'The Social Identity Theory of Intergroup Behavior', in Stephen Worchel and William Austin, eds, *Psychology of Intergroup Relations*. Chicago: Nelson-Hall, pp. 7–24.

Tate, Katherine. 1993. *From Protest to Politics: The New Black Voters in American Elections*. Cambridge, MA: Harvard University Press.

Torres, Andres and José E. Velásquez, eds. 1998. *The Puerto Rican Movement: Voices from the Diaspora*. Philadelphia: Temple University Press.

US Census Bureau. 2001. 'The Hispanic Population: Census 2000 Brief', May.

Wallach, Brett. 1989. 'Puerto Rico: Growth, Change, Progress, Development', *Focus*, 39: 27–33.

Wang, Ted and Robert C. Winn. 2006. 'Groundswell Meets Groundwork: Preliminary Recommendations for Building on Immigrant Mobilizations', New York: Four Freedoms Fund.

Young, Iris Marion. 2000. 'Structure, Difference and Hispanic/Latino Claims of Justice', in Jorge J. E. Gracia and Pablo De Greiff, eds, *Hispanics/Latinos in the United States: Ethnicity, Race, and Rights*. New York: Routledge, pp. 147–65.

Index

Note: page references followed by t *or* illus *indicate material only included in tables or illustrations*

ABC lawsuit 174
accountability 31–2, 34
Adams, John 10
Adams, John Quincy 11
Adams–Onis Treaty (1819) 94
AFL-CIO 64, 69
African Americans: political participation 8, 18, 19t, 20t, 23, 24, 32, 72, 73; race and racial discrimination 4, 8, 9, 44, 56, 57, 68; relations with Cubans 136–7; relations with Puerto Ricans 109, 110
Africans 7, 8
age: Latino demography 15, 16t, 17t; Mexicans 92; political participation 26
agency/structure 1–3, 9–10, 12, 13; *see also* structure
AGIF *see* American GI Forum
Agricultural Workers Organizing Committee (AWOC) 69
Alabama, Mexicans 91t
Alaska natives 23
Albizu Campos, Pedro 97, 98, 99, 100, 106
Alcoff, Linda 4–5
La Alianza 75–7
Alliance for Progress 155

Alvarez v. *Lemon Grove School District* 61
American Baptist Churches in the USA, et al., v. *Edwin Meese III and Alan Nelson* 174
American Civil Liberties Union 62
American Federation of Labor (AFL) 64, 69
American GI Forum (AGIF) 67–8, 70, 71, 72, 73, 74, 77, 84
American Jewish Congress 62
American Labor Party 106
Americanization 60, 62
Americas Watch 154
Amnesty International 164, 174
Anderson, Thomas P. 154
Anderson Bill (1947) 63
Anthony, Marc 115illus
anti-Communism 67, 162, 167; Cubans 143, 144
Anti-Communist Council of Guatemala (CADEG) 164
Anticommunist Forces for Liberation (FALANGE) 156
Apodaca, Jerry 88
Araña, Francisco 160
Arana Osorio, Carlos 164
Araujo, Arturo 153
Arbenz, Jacobo 160, 161, 162, 163
Arévalo, Juan José 161

Arizona 36, 39; Central Americans
    172, 173; Latino political
    participation 24; Mexican
    political activism 65, 80, 82;
    Mexican political participation
    42, 71, 88; Mexicans in 56, 60,
    63, 90, 183; Puerto Ricans 102;
    racial discrimination 56, 60,
    63
Arkansas, Mexicans 91t
Arroyo, Carmen 117
Asian Americans 7; political
    participation 19, 20t, 23, 32;
    racial discrimination 56
Asian Indians, race 6
Aspira 108
Attica state prison 112
authenticity 31

Baca, Joe 88
Badillo, Herman 108, 113
Balsara case 6
balsero ('rafter') migration crisis
    (1994) 145
Batista, Fulgencio 126–7, 133
Becerra, Xavier 88
Belén school 134
Black Panther Party 109, 110
black power movement 109
bloc voting 31, 140–2, 144, 148
Boland Amendment (1982)
    171
Boliteros 105, 107
Bolívia 7
Bonsal, Philip 130
Border Patrol 51, 167, 173, 182
Boricua 3, 93
Bracero Program 52, 53, 167
Brooke, John R. 96
Brown v. *Board of Education* (1954)
    61, 62–3
Bureau on Insular Affairs 102
Bush, George W. 14, 88

Bush administration, Cuba and
    Cubans 141, 143, 147
Bustamente, Cruz 88

Cabot, John Moors 162
Cabot, Thomas Dudley 162
Cabral, Anna Escobedo 88
CADEG 164
Calhoun, John C. 39–40, 41
California 36, 38, 39; Central
    Americans 167, 172; Latinos
    22, 24, 66–7, 184, 186; Mexican
    citizenship status 42, 45; Mexican
    deportations 52; Mexican
    political activism 64–5, 66–7,
    68–9, 79, 80–2; Mexican political
    participation 42, 70–2, 73, 86,
    88; Mexicans in 56, 57–60, 61–3,
    90; political representation 33–4;
    Puerto Ricans 116, 117; race and
    racial discrimination 6, 56, 60,
    61–3, 70; voting rights 25
Camarioca boatlift and airlift
    (1965–1973) 137–8
Canada, Canadians 173, 180,
    189n3
CANF 142–3
Cannon, Terence 127
CAPSM 2, 169–74, 175–6, 177, 179
CARECEN 172, 177, 186
Caribbean 7, 8, 93
Carta Autonómica (The Autonomy
    Charter) 94–5
Carter administration: Cubans
    139; El Salvador 158, 167; Puerto
    Ricans 114
Castillo Armas, Carlos 162, 163, 168
Castro, Fidel 127–9, 130, 132, 133,
    134, 137, 139, 140, 142, 145, 146
Castro, Raúl (brother of Fidel) 147
Castro, Raúl (governor of Arizona)
    88
Castro, Sal 81

Catholic Church: El Salvador 156;
Guatemala 166; Mexico 37, 46
las catorce ('the [group of the]
fourteen families') 152, 154
CBS 127
Central America 7, 150–1, 176;
relations with US 150–1, 154,
167–8, 176, 179; *see also* Central
Americans; Costa Rica; El
Salvador; Guatemala;
Nicaragua
Central American Free Trade
Agreement 177
Central American Peace and
Solidarity Movement (CAPSM) 2,
169–74, 175–6, 177, 179
Central American Refugee Center
(CARECEN) 172, 177, 186
Central Americans 7; demographics
15, 17; migration 2, 151,
152, 153t, 166–9, 173, 174–7,
179; political activism and
participation 169–74, 175–6,
179; *see also* Guatemalans;
Nicaraguans; Salvadorans
Chambers, Claude 61
Chamizal Treaty (1967) 74
Chávez, César 69, 74
Chicago Chronicle 122
Chicana feminism 85
Chicano, use of term 3, 75
Chicano Coordinating Council on
Higher Education (CCHE) 81
Chicano identity 78
Chicano Moratorium (1970) 82
Chicano Movement 67, 70, 75–85;
end and legacy of 85–7
Chicano Youth Liberation
Conferences (1969 and 1970) 80,
81
Chinese 5, 7
Christian Democratic Party (CDP),
El Salvador 155

CIA: Cuba 127, 131, 132, 136; El
Salvador 155; Guatemala 158, 162
Cienfuegos, Camilo 127
Cisneros, Henry 88
citizenship: Latinos 24, 187;
Mexicans 40, 41–6; Puerto Ricans
96–7, 103, 117; and race 5, 9; and
voting 24–5
citizenship law (1790) 5, 6, 40
City University of New York (CUNY)
108; Center for Puerto Rican
Studies 113
civil rights: Cubans 130, 136–7;
Guatemala 164; Latino 66–7,
86–7, 185; Mexicans 71, 73, 78,
81, 86, 88; Puerto Ricans 107,
115; voting 23
class: Mexicans 41, 42, 46, 92; and
political participation 12–13, 18;
Puerto Ricans 116
Clinton administration: Cubans
142, 145–6; Mexicans 88; Puerto
Ricans 114
coalition building: Cubans 147, 149;
Latinos 22, 28, 32, 188; Mexicans
72, 87; Puerto Ricans 116
COINTELPRO (Counter Intelligence)
program 85, 112
cold war 12, 107, 135, 171, 176
Collazo, Oscar 98
Colombia 7
colonialism: Puerto Ricans 116; *see
also* Spanish colonialism
Colorado 39; Mexican political
activism 65, 77–80, 81, 82;
Mexican political participation
71, 77–8, 80, 87; Mexicans in 56,
90
Columbia University 113
El Comité 114
El Comité de Salvadoreños Progresistas
(The Committee of Progressive
Salvadorans) 170

el Comité de Vecinos de Lemon Grove (the Committee of Lemon Grove Neighbors) 61
Comité Revolucionario de Puerto Rico (The Puerto Rican Revolutionary Committee) 94
Committee in Solidarity with the People of El Salvador (CISPES) 170
Community Service Organization (CSO) 68–9, 70, 71, 72
community-based organizations 26, 184–6, 187; Cubans 134; Mexicans 63–4, 85, 87, 90; Puerto Ricans 104–5, 108, 109–13, 115–16
El Congreso de Pueblos de Habla Española (the Congress of Spanish-Speaking Peoples) 66–7, 80
Congress of Puerto Rican Hometowns 108
Congressional Hispanic Caucus 187
Connally, John 73
Connecticut, Puerto Ricans 117t
Consejo Revolucionario Cubano (CRC, Cuban Revolutionary Council) 131, 132, 135
Corona, Bert 66
Costa Rica 132
Costa Ricans 153t
CRC 131, 132, 135
criminal justice system *see* legal rights and protection
Crusade for Justice 77–80, 83
Cruzado, Juan Martínez 93
CSO 68–9, 70, 71, 72
Cuba 102; Bay of Pigs invasion 131–2; colonialism 119–22; constitution (1902) 122–5; constitution (1940) 127; economy 120–1, 125–6, 127, 129, 132; independence movement 119–20,

121, 122–6, 133; recent political changes 147–8; relations with US 11, 95, 119–33, 142–3, 144–5, 147–8; Revolution (1959) 119, 127–33; *see also* Castro, Fidel; Cubans
Cuban American Foundation (CAF) 142
Cuban American National Foundation (CANF) 142–3
Cuban Refugee Adjustment Act (1966) 137–8, 145
Cuban Refugee Program 136–7
Cuban Research Institute 143
Cuban Revolutionary Committee 103
Cuban Revolutionary Council (CRC) 131, 132, 135
Cubans: demographics 15, 17; identity 134–5, 148, 179; limited applicability of Cuban 'model' 148–9; limits of political influence 144–8; migration 119–20, 130–1, 133–4, 136, 137–8, 139, 141–2, 145–6; political activism 26, 27t, 103–4, 131–2, 142–3, 179; political ideology 143–4; political interests of exiles 111, 133–47, 149; political participation 20, 21, 139–42, 144, 146, 148; US economic and military support for exiles 130–2, 134, 135–8, 148
El Cucuy 185
Cuellar, Henry 88
cultural identity: Cubans 134–5; Mexicans 86, 87; Puerto Ricans 107–8, 115–16
cultural nationalism, Chicano 84, 85

D'Aubuisson, Roberto 158, 168
Del Monte plant 72

Democratic Nationalist
Organization (ORDEN), El
Salvador 155, 157
Democratic Revolutionary Front
(FDR), El Salvador 157–8, 168,
170
Democrats 32; Cubans 140, 142,
144; Latinos 14; Mexicans 56–7,
70–1, 77–8, 81, 82, 84; Puerto
Ricans 105, 106, 107, 108, 114
descriptive representation 30–1,
35
Díaz, Porfirio 46–7
Díaz-Balart, Lincoln 141
Díaz-Balart, Mario 141
Dole, Bob 14
Domínguez, Manuel 42
Dominican Republic 11, 102
Duarte, José Napoleon 155
Dulles, Allen 162
Dulles, John Foster 162
Dupuy de Lôme, Enrique 121

Echaveste, María 88
economic interests of US 10–12;
Cuba and Cubans 120–1, 125–6,
127, 129, 132, 138–9; Mexico and
Mexicans 46–7, 51, 52–4, 80, 89;
Puerto Rico 93, 94–5, 100–3
education: Central Americans 177;
Cubans 134, 136; Latinos 15,
16t, 17t, 66, 185; Mexicans 60–3,
69–70, 71, 78, 79, 80–2, 85, 86, 87,
89, 92; and political participation
18, 26; Puerto Ricans 108, 113,
116; racial discrimination and
segregation 9, 60–3
Education and Workforce
Committee 27–8
EEOC 73, 74
Eisenhower administration: Cuba
128–30; Guatemala 162; Puerto
Ricans 99

El Salvador 152–8, 166, 176–7;
economy 152–3, 154, 176, 177;
independence from Spain 152;
'La Matanza (the Massacre)' (1923)
154, 156, 157; relations with US
154, 155, 157, 167–8, 170–1, 176;
la huelga de brazos caidos (the strike
of still arms) (1944) 154; *see also*
Salvadorans
Equal Employment and
Opportunity Commission (EEOC)
73, 74
equal opportunities *see* social
equality/inequality
ESA 156, 164
Estado Libre Asociado status 98
Estrada Cabrera, Manuel 159, 160
ethnic media 184, 185
ethnicity, Latinos and 3–10
ethnorace (Alcoff) 4–5
expressive civic engagement 186

FALANGE 156
Farabundo Martí National
Liberation Front (FMLN) 158
fascism 70
FBI 183; Central Americans 173;
Mexicans 85–6; Puerto Ricans
112
Federal Aviation Administration
(FAA) 102
Federation for American
Immigration Reform (FAIR) 182,
183
feminism 85
Ferre, Maurice 117
Ferrer, Fernando 117
FHA program 9
Fierro, Josefina 66
Figueroa Cordero, Andrés 99
filibusteros 150–1
Fisher, King 57
Flores, Irving 99

Florida: Cuban political
    participation 140–2, 146–7;
    Cubans in 120, 133–47; Latino
    political participation 24; Puerto
    Ricans 117; Salvadorans 157
Foraker Act (1900) 96
Ford, Richard 64–5
Ford Foundation 83
foreign policy 10–12; Central
    America 150–1, 154, 167–8,
    170–1, 176, 178; Cuba 11, 95,
    119–33, 142–3, 144–5, 147–8; El
    Salvador 154, 155, 157, 167–8,
    170–1, 176; Guatemala 158, 159,
    162, 163, 164, 166, 168, 171,
    176; Mexico 36–7, 38–47, 51, 74;
    Puerto Rico 95–103, 117, 122; *see
    also individual administrations*
Franco, Minerva 63
Free Cuba PAC 142
'Free Puerto Rico!' movement
    113
Frente Revolucionario Democrático (FRD,
    The Revolutionary Democratic
    Front) 131
Fuerzas Armadas de Liberación Nacional
    (FALN, Armed Forces of National
    Liberation) 114

García, Bonnie 117
García, Carlos 122
García, Hector 67, 71
García, María Cristina 133
García Pérez, Jorge Luis 147
García Rivera, Oscar 106
Gates, Henry Louis 4
gender: Mexicans 84–5, 92; Mexico
    53; Puerto Ricans 104, 110, 117;
    voting rights 25
genocide, Guatemala 165
Georgia, Mexicans 91t, 92
GI Bill 67, 69, 81, 103
GI Forum *see* American GI Forum

Gomez, Anna Nieto 85
Gómez, Máximo 122
Gonzales, Alberto 88
Gonzáles, Rodolfo 'Corky' 74,
    77–80, 82, 83–4; 'I am Joaquin'
    78, 79
González, Charlie 88
González, Elián 141–2, 146
González, Emilio 141
González, Henry B. 72, 84
Goode, Virgil 183
Gore, Al 14
El Gráfico 105
Great Depression 52, 100, 153
Greece, ancient 30
Grijalva, Raúl 88
'Grito de Lares' (The Revolt of Lares)
    (1868) 94
'Grito de Yara' 119
Guam 122
Guantánamo naval base 145
Guatemala 150, 158–66, 176–7;
    constitution (1945) 161;
    demography 163; economy
    159–60, 161–3, 176, 177; October
    Revolution (1944) 160, 161;
    relations with US 158, 159, 162,
    163, 164, 166, 168, 171, 176; *see
    also* Guatemalans
Guatemalan Historical Clarification
    commission 164–6
Guatemalan National Revolutionary
    Unity (URNG)
    164
Guatemalans 153t; migration
    152, 166–9, 174–7; political
    participation 20, 190n4
Guerra, Pablo de la 42
guerrilla movements: Cuba 127; El
    Salvador 158; Guatemala 163–4,
    166; Mexico 37
Guevara, Che 127
Gutiérrez, Carlos 141

Gutiérrez, José Angel 77, 80, 82–4
Gutiérrez, Luis 117

Haiti 11
Hampton, Fred 109
Hawaii 102
Hearst, William Randolph 120
Helms-Burton Law 143
Hernández, Pete 68
Hernandez v. *Texas* (1954) 68
Herrera, José Joaquin de 38
Hidalgo, Miguel 37
Hinojosa, Rubén 88
Hispanic, use of term 3
Hitler, Adolf 70
homosexuals 85, 144
Hondurans 153t
Honduras 151, 162, 166
household size, Latinos 15, 16t
housing: Mexicans 71, 78, 79, 86,
    92; Puerto Ricans 108; and race
    9; *see also* residence; residential
    segregation
'Hoy Marchamos, Mañana Votamos
    (Today we march, tomorrow we
    vote)' campaign 186
HR 4437 180, 184–5
Huerta, Dolores 69
Hughes, Langston 130
human rights: Guatemala 165, 177;
    El Salvador 155, 158, 168, 170,
    171, 177; Puerto Ricans 109

'I am Joaquin' 78, 79
identity: Cubans 134–5, 148, 179;
    Mexicans 86; minority groups
    and political participation 18;
    Puerto Ricans 107–8, 115–16,
    118
illegal immigration 167, 174, 180–7
Illegal Immigration Reform and
    Immigrant Responsibility Act
    (IIRIRA) (1996) 175, 182

Illinois: Mexicans 81, 90; Puerto
    Ricans 109–11, 117t; voting
    rights 25
immigrants: Central Americans 2,
    151, 152, 153t, 166–9, 173, 174–7,
    179; Cubans 119–20, 130–1,
    133-4, 136, 137–8, 139, 141–2,
    145–6; Latinos 1, 6–10, 12–13,
    180–7; Mexicans 47–63, 89–91,
    92, 181, 182, 183; Puerto Ricans
    94, 101–3, 117–18; Salvadorans
    and Guatemalans 152, 153t, 158,
    166–9, 174–7
Immigration Act (1990) 182
Immigration and Nationality Act
    (1965) 54, 181
immigration policy 10, 51–4,
    174–6, 179–80; Deferred
    Enforced Departure (DED) 175;
    deportations 52, 61, 67, 174;
    Extended Voluntary Departure
    (EVD) 169; political refugee or
    economic migrant status 2, 137,
    139, 146, 167, 168–9; Temporary
    Protected Status (TPS) 175; 'wet
    foot, dry foot' policy 145–6; *see
    also* illegal immigration
Immigration Reform and
    Control Act (IRCA) (1986) 174–5,
    181–2
income: Latinos 15, 16t, 17t; and
    political participation 18, 26
Indiana, voting rights 25
indigenous people *see* native
    Americans
industrialization: Mexico 53; Puerto
    Rico 100–1, 102
instrumental civic engagement 22,
    186
International Workers of the World
    (IWW) 64–5
Iowa, Mexicans 91, 92
Iran *Contra* affair 171

Jackson, Andrew 38
Jaguar Justiciero (Jaguar of Justice)
  164
James, Brian 183
Japan 7
Japanese American Citizens League
  62
Japanese-Mexican Labor Association
  (JMLA) 64
Jews 66, 104
Jim Crow laws *see* racial
  discrimination and
  segregation
Jiménez, José 'Cha Cha' 109
Johnson, Lyndon 67–8
Johnson administration: Mexicans
  73–5; Puerto Ricans 108
Jones Act (1917) 96–7, 99
Juárez, Benito 46

Kadar, Janos 130
Kansas: Mexicans 91; voting rights
  25
Kelly, Jimmy 105
Kennedy, Edward 187
Kennedy, John F. 71
Kennedy administration: Cuba and
  Cubans 131–2, 135, 136, 142;
  Mexicans 72–3, 75
Kent, James L. 62
Kentucky: Mexicans 91t; voting
  rights 25
Khrushchev, Nikita 130
King, Martin Luther 79, 80
Kirkpatrick, Jeane 168
Korean War 52

La Gardia, Fiorello 106
labor activism 9, 187; Guatemala
  163; Mexicans 64–5, 66, 69–70,
  71, 92
ladinos, Guatemala 163, 164,
  165

land rights 9; Cuba 129; El Salvador
  152–3, 154; Guatemala 161–2,
  163; Mexicans in US 75–7, 78, 79;
  Mexico 46–7
language: Mexicans 60, 61, 62;
  voting rights 23
Latino culture 66–7
Latinos 1–13; agency and structure
  1–3, 9–10, 12, 13; definition
  3; demographics 14–18, 22;
  ethnicity and race 3–10; limited
  applicability of Cuban 'model' to
  148–9; migration 1, 6–10, 12–13,
  180–7; political activism 26, 27t;
  179–88; political participation
  1, 9–10, 12–13, 14, 18–21, 22–7,
  28, 29–30, 32–3, 86, 184, 186,
  187–8; representation 32–3,
  35; as social group 3–4; 2006
  immigration marches 180–7,
  188; *see also* Central Americans;
  Cubans; Guatemalans; Mexicans;
  Nicaraguans; Puerto Ricans;
  Salvadorans
League of United Latin American
  Citizens (LULAC) *see* LULAC
Lebrón, Lolita 99
legal rights and protection:
  Mexicans 42, 43–4, 45, 57–60;
  Puerto Ricans 115; and race 5, 9
liberalism, Cubans 143
liberation theology 156
Liga Puertorriqueña 104
Lincoln, Abraham 57
Lincoln Hospital, NY 112
literacy tests 56, 105
lobbying: Central Americans 172,
  176; Cubans 142–3, 145; Latinos
  185
local government, Latino political
  participation 25, 32–4
Longoria, Felix 67–8
López, Henry 71

Lopez, Jennifer 115illus
'Los Angeles Thirteen' 81
Los Angeles Times 81
Louisiana, New Orleans racial
   system 189n4
LULAC 62, 63, 65–6, 68, 70, 72, 73,
   84, 86, 185

Machado, Gerardo 126
El Machete Criolla 105
Madison, James 30, 31
majoritarianism 21–2, 27, 28, 29,
   30, 35, 140, 188
MALDEF 86, 185
manifest destiny 10–11, 38, 183
MANO (National Organized Action
   Group) 164
Mano Blanca (The White Hand) 164
MAPA 70–2, 73, 74, 86
Marcantonio, Vito 106, 107
Mariel boatlift (1980) 139, 145
Marín, Rosario 88
Martí, Agustín Farabundo 153, 154,
   158
Martí, José 120, 135
Martínez, Bob 141
Martínez, Elizabeth 85
Martínez, Maximiliano Hernández
   153–4
Martínez, Mel 141
Maryland, voting rights 25
Más Canosa, Jorge 142
Más Santos, Jorge 194n15
Massachusetts, Puerto Ricans 116,
   117
Maximiliano Hernandez Martínez
   brigade 156
Maya Indians 163, 164–6
MAYO 80, 83
McCain, John 187
McCarran Walter Act (1952) 5
McCarthyism 107
McCormick, Carlos 71

McCormick, Paul 62–3
McCormick Theological Seminary
   110–11
McCure, George 105
McGovern, George 83
McKinley, William 95, 96, 121
McPherson, Henry 73–4
MEChA 81–2, 87, 113
Medrano, José Alberto 155
Méndez, Gonzalo 61–2
Mendez v. *Westminster* case 61–3
Menéndez, Bob 141, 144
mestizos 7, 42
Metropolis 105
Mexican-American border 36–7, 51,
   74, 167, 180
Mexican American Legal Defense
   and Education Fund (MALDEF)
   86, 185
Mexican American Political
   Association (MAPA) 70–2, 73, 74, 86
Mexican American Student
   Confederation 80
Mexican American Student
   Organization 80
Mexican-American War (1846-1848)
   11, 36, 39
Mexican American Youth
   Organization (MAYO) 80, 83
Mexican Hometown Associations 90
Mexicans 3, 36, 37, 116; citizenship
   40, 41–6; current politics 87–9;
   demographics 15, 17; future
   prospects for politics 89–91;
   migration and settlement 47–63,
   89–91, 92, 181, 182, 183; political
   activism 26, 27t, 63–70, 75–87,
   89–90, 91–2, 135, 179, 186;
   political participation 20–1,
   56–7, 68–9, 70–5, 86, 87–9; race
   and racial discrimination 6, 7, 8,
   46, 56–63, 92, 137; voting 23, 24,
   46, 56, 57

Mexico 7, 11, 150, 169, 173; *La Alianza* and 76; contacts with Guatemala 165, 166; economy 37, 46–7, 51, 52–4, 89–90; independence and early republic 37–41; Maquiladora Program 52–3; Porfiriato 46–7; relations with US 36–7, 38–47, 51, 74; Revolution (1910-1920) 47

Michigan: Mexicans 91; voting rights 25

Minerva Franco v. *Bastrop Independent School District* (1947) 63

Minnesota: Mexicans 91t; voting rights 25

MINP 114

Minutemen 182, 183

Miranda, Rafael Cancel 99

Missouri: Mexicans 91; voting rights 25

MLN (Movement for National Liberation) 114

modernization, Mexico 47

Monroe, James 11

Monroe doctrine 10, 11

Moreno, Luisa 66

Movimiento de Recuperación Revolucionario (MRR) 135

El Movimiento Estudiantil Chicano de Aztlán (MEChA) 81–2, 87, 113

MPI-PSP (Movement for Independence, Puerto Rican Socialist Party) 114

mulattos 6, 7, 189n4

Muñoz, Carlos 78

Muñoz, Cecilia 88

Muñoz Marín, Luis 98, 100

Murguía, Janet 88

mutualistas 63–4, 104

NAACP 62, 70

Napolitano, Grace 88

National Association for the Advancement of Colored People (NAACP) 62, 70

National Association of Latino Elected and Appointed Officials (NALEO) 86

National Association of Puerto Rican Civil Rights 108

National Council of La Raza (NCLR) 86, 185

National Democratic Union (UDN), El Salvador 155

National Farm-Worker Association (NFWA) 69

National Labor Relations Act (1935) 9, 69

National Origins Act (1924) 51, 181

native Americans 7–8; El Salvador 153–4; Guatemala 160, 163, 164–6; Mexico 40; Puerto Rico 93–4; voting 23, 32, 42

naturalization 184, 186; Central Americans 176; and race 5, 6, 40

NBC 128

NCLR 86, 185

Nebraska: Mexicans 91t; voting rights 25

Nevada 36, 39; Mexicans 91t; voting rights 25

New Anti-Communist Organization (NOA) 164

New Deal 100

New Jersey: Cubans 144; Puerto Ricans 117t

New Mexico 36, 38, 39; Latinos 22, 24; Mexican political activism 65–6, 75–7, 80, 82; Mexican political participation 42, 46, 68, 71, 88; Mexicans in 8, 56, 90; Puerto Ricans 102; race 8

New York, New York City: Cubans
120; Latino political participation
24; local government 33; Puerto
Ricans 3, 24, 79, 81, 94, 99, 102,
103, 104–9, 111–12, 113, 115–16,
117, 179
New York Journal 120, 121
New York Times 72, 122
The News Chieftain 76
Nicaragua 11, 132, 150, 151, 171;
Sandanista revolution 157, 167
Nicaraguan and Central America
Relief Act (NACARA) 175
Nicaraguans 153t, 175
Nixon, Richard 83, 128–9, 130
North American Free Trade
Agreement (NAFTA) 89
North Carolina, Mexicans 91t, 92
North Dakota, voting rights 25
Nuñez, Fabián 88
Nuyorican, use of term 3, 116

Obama, Barack 88
OEO 83
Ohio: Puerto Ricans 102, 117t;
voting rights 25
Ojo por Ojo (the Eye for an Eye)
164
Oklahoma, voting rights 25
Olds, Robert 151
Omi, Michael 4, 5
'one-drop rule' 6, 7
Operation Bootstrap 100–1
Operation Mongoose 132
Operation PBSUCCESS 162
Operation Sojourner 173
Operation Wetback 52
ORDEN 155, 157
Oregon 38; Mexicans 91; voting
rights 25
Organization for Liberation from
Communism (OLC) 156
Ortiz, Solomon 88

Palante (Forward) 111
Palma, Estrada 126
Panamá 150, 151
Panama Canal 151, 159
Panamanians 153t
paramilitary groups: Cubans
135, 136, 138; El Salvador
death squads 155, 156–8, 177;
Guatemalan death squads 164,
177; Puerto Ricans 114
el Partido Revolucionario Cubano
(the Cuban Revolutionary Party)
120
Pastor, Ed 88
Pawley, William 127
Peña, Federico 88
Pennsylvania, Puerto Ricans 116,
117t
'People's Church' initiative 111–12,
114
Perla, Hector 176
Perú 7
Philadelphia, Cubans 120
Philippines 122
Pierre v. the State of Louisiana 44
Piñero, Jesus 98
El Piolín 185
Pipil Indians 153–4
El Pistolero 185
El Plan de Santa Bárbara 81, 85
El Plan Espiritual de Aztlán 80, 81,
85
'Plan of the Barrio' 79–80
Platt Amendment 122–5, 126; text
123–4
Political Association of Spanish-
Speaking Organizations (PASSO,
PASO) 72
political parties 27, 28–30, 31–2;
Cubans and 140–2; *see also*
Democrats; Republicans
political protest 26, 187; Mexicans
74, 78, 79, 82

political system 21–30; electoral
rules 21–7, 34; implications for
Latinos 188; legislative rules 21,
27–30, 34; *see also* representation
Polk, James 11, 38
poll taxes 56, 66, 72
poor people's campaign 79–80
poverty: Central Americans 156,
177; Latinos 15, 16t; Mexicans
and Mexico 89; Puerto Ricans
108, 116; 'war on poverty'
programs 73, 74, 77–8, 83, 108
La Prensa 105
PRLDEF 115, 185
Proctor, Redfield 121
progressive movement 33
property: and voting rights 25; *see*
also land rights
Protestantism, Guatemala 166
psychological resources, and
political participation 18
public policies: Latinos 15–16,
18; political parties 29–30, 32;
representation 31, 32, 34–5
Pueblo Indians 42
Puerto Rican Day parade 107–8,
115–16
Puerto Rican Day Parade
Committee 108
Puerto Rican Legal Defense and
Educational Fund (PRLDF) 115,
185
Puerto Rican Movement 109–16
Puerto Rican Nationalist Party 97
Puerto Rican Revolutionary
Workers Organization (PRRWO)
113
Puerto Rican Student Union (PRSU)
113
Puerto Ricans 3, 6, 137, 179;
demographics 15, 17, 109;
identity 107–8, 115–16, 118;
migration 94, 101–3, 117–18;

political activism 26, 27t, 79,
81, 84, 103–16, 118, 179, 186;
political participation 20, 21, 24,
105–7, 108, 113–14, 116–17, 118;
present politics 116–17; voting
23, 24, 104, 105
Puerto Rico: ambivalent status
96–100, 116, 117, 118, 179;
colonialism 93–6, 119;
constitution (1952) 98–9;
economy 94–5, 100–3; genetics of
population 93–4; independence
movement 94–6, 97–100, 103–4,
106, 107, 109, 110, 113; Jayuya
uprising (1950) 98; Migration
Office 106–7, 108; 'Ponce
Massacre' (1937) 98; relations
with US 93–103, 117, 122; Young
Lords 109, 112; *see also* Puerto
Ricans
El Pulgarcito (Tom Thumb) 170

quadroons 189n4
Quevedo, Eduardo 66

race, Latinos and 3–10
racial bloc voting 31, 140–2, 144,
148
racial discrimination and
segregation: changes in 1948
70; Guatemala 163; Mexicans 8,
42, 46, 55–63, 65–6, 68, 78, 179;
Puerto Ricans 104, 118; voting
rights 25
racial gerrimandering 23, 24
Radio Martí 142
railroads, Mexico 47
'La raza unida' meeting 74–5
La Raza Unida Party 74, 80, 82–4
Reagan administration: Central
Americans 167–9, 170, 171, 173;
Cubans 142
Refugee Act (1980) 139

representation 25, 30–5; local and regional differences 32–4
registration 86, 105; levels and political participation 18–21; *see also* voting
Republic of San Joaquín del Río de Chuma 76, 77
Republicans 14; Cubans 140, 142, 143, 144; and immigration reform 187; Mexicans 56–7; Puerto Ricans 106
residence, voting rights 25
residential segregation 70; Cubans 140; Mexicans 56, 60, 63; and minority representation 34, 140
Revolutionary Democratic Front (FDR) 131
Reyes, Silvestre 88
Rice, Ben 63
Richardson, Bill 88
Río Arriba Courthouse raid (1967) 76–7
Ríos, Antonio 68
Rios, Carlos 108
Ríos Montt, José Efraín 168
Robert's Rules of Order 65
Rockefeller, Nelson 108
Rockwell Kent and Walter Briehl v. *John Foster Dulles* 194n6
Rodríguez, Ciro 88
Roman Catholic Church *see* Catholic Church
Rome, ancient 30
Romero, Carlos 157
Romero, Humberto 168
Romero, Oscar, archbishop 157, 158, 168
Romo, Jesus 57
Roosevelt, Franklin Delano 11, 98, 106, 126
Roosevelt, Theodore 11, 121, 126
Root, Elihu 123, 125
Roque, Martha Beatriz 147

Ros-Lehtinen, Ileana 140–1
Ross, Fred, Sr 68
Roybal, Edward 68–9, 71, 72
Roybal-Allard, Lucille 88

Sacramento Union 44
Salazar, John 88
Salazar, Ken 87
Salazar, Rubén 82
Salvadoran Communist Party 153
Salvadoran Humanitarian Aid, Relief, and Education Foundation (SHARE) 171–2
Salvadorans 153t; migration 152, 158, 166–9, 174–7; political activism 26, 27t, 169–74; political participation 20–1, 176
Sánchez, Alonso 76–7
Sánchez, Loretta 88
Sánchez, Linda 88
Sánchez Korrol, Virginia 105
sanctuary movement (Salvadorans) 172–3, 174
Save our State (SOS) 182–3
Second Vatican Council (1962-1965) 156
Second World War 52, 67, 68, 70, 100, 103, 159; letter from Youth Committee for the Defense of Mexican American Youth 58–9
Secret Anti-Communist Army (ESA) 156, 164
Serrano, José 117
Shehu, Mehmet 130
Simcox, Chris 183
Sires, Albio 141, 144
skin color 5–9; Mexicans 8, 39–40, 41–2, 43, 56, 57, 61–3; and political participation 8, 22, 35, 41–2, 43, 57; Puerto Ricans 107
slavery 7, 38, 40, 41, 93, 94
social conflicts 4

social constructions, racial
    processes as 5
Social Democratic National
    Revolutionary Movement (MNR),
    El Salvador 155
social equality/inequality: Central
    Americans 177; Latinos 10;
    Mexicans 71, 78, 79–80, 86, 89,
    92; Mexico 37; Puerto Ricans 118;
    and race 9
social group, Latinos as 3–4
social justice/injustice: El Salvador
    155, 156; Mexicans 77–80, 82
social networks 12, 85, 89, 90,
    186
social welfare: Cubans 143–4;
    Latinos 15, 184, 185; Mexicans
    63–4, 87, 89; Puerto Ricans 104,
    108, 110–12
socioeconomic status (SES) see class
Soler, Berta 147
Solís, Hilda 88, 176
Sosa, Lionel 14
South Americans 15
South Carolina, Mexicans 91t
South Dakota, voting rights 25
Southwest Voter Registration
    Education Project (SVREP) 86,
    185
Soviet Union 132, 162; see also cold
    war
Spanish–American War (1898) 95–6,
    121–2
Spanish colonialism: Cuba 119;
    Mexico 37; Puerto Rico 93–6, 119;
    and race 7
structure: and agency 1–3, 9–10,
    12, 13; Central Americans 176–7;
    immigration reform 186–7;
    Latino community resources
    184–6; Mexicans 90, 92; political
    system 23–4, 26, 35, 188; Puerto
    Ricans 118

student groups: and Latino
    immigration 185; Mexicans 78,
    80–2; Puerto Ricans 113
Students for a Democratic Society
    (SDS) 110
Suarez, Xavier 141
substantive representation 31,
    35

Tainos 93–4
Tate, Katherine 18
taxation system 44
Teller, Henry Moore 121
Teller Amendment 121
Telles, Raymond 72
Ten Years' War (1868-) 119, 120
Tennessee, Mexicans 91t
Texas 38; Latino political
    participation 24; Mexican
    political activism 65, 67–8, 79,
    80, 81, 82–3; Mexican political
    participation 24, 42, 56, 68,
    71, 72, 74, 86; Mexicans in
    55illus, 56–7, 60, 63, 90, 92;
    Puerto Ricans 116, 117t; racial
    discrimination and segregation
    8, 55illus, 56–7, 60, 63, 68
Texas Rangers 57, 65, 72
Texas revolution (1835) 38
Tijerina, Reies López 74, 75–7, 79
Torresola, Griselio 98
Torricelli, Bill 143
trade liberalization 89
transnational political activism
    89–90, 169–74, 175–6, 177
Treaty of Córdoba (1821) 37
Treaty of Guadalupe Hidalgo (1848)
    8, 36, 39–41, 44–5, 46, 76
Treaty of Paris (1898) 96, 122
Truman administration: Guatemala
    162; Puerto Rico 98, 107; racial
    discrimination 70
Turner, Joseph 183

Ubico Castañeda, Jorge 160
UCAPAWA-CIO 66
UFW 69–70, 80
UFWOC 69, 73
La Unión 113
Unión Nacional Opositora (UNO)
 Coalition 155
unions 9, 163, 187
United Cannery, Agricultural,
 Packing, and Allied Workers of
 America (UCAPAWA-CIO) 66
United Farm Workers movement
 69–70, 80, 191n15
United Farm Workers Organizing
 Committee (UFWOC) 69, 73
United Fruit Company: Central
 America 151; Cuba 129, 131;
 Guatemala 159–60, 161–2
United Mexican American Students
 (UMAS) 80
United Nations 113, 116, 130
United Nations High Commissioner
 for Refugees (UNHCR) 169
United States Constitution 30;
 Article II 41; First Amendment 174;
 Fifth Amendment 62; Fourteenth
 Amendment 44, 62, 63, 68
United States House of
 Representatives: Appropriations
 Committee 29; Puerto Rican
 attack on (1954) 99, 107, 114
United States-Mexican border 36–7,
 51, 74, 167, 180
United States-Mexican War
 (1846–1848) 11, 36, 39
United States-Spanish War (1898)
 95–6, 121–2
University of California 81
University of New Mexico 66
Univisión 14
USCIS 186
USS Maine explosion 121
Utah 36, 39; Mexicans 56

Valentín, Gilberto Gerena 108
Varela, María 85
Vasconcelos, José 7, 42
Velázquez, Nydia 117
Velez, Ramón 108
Vidaurri, Soledad 61–2
Vietnam War 78, 82, 108
vigilante justice 57, 182, 183
Villaraigosa, Antonio 88
VISTA 83
'Viva Kennedy' movement 71–2,
 77, 81
voting 18–21, 31, 34; citizenship
 and 24–5, 41–3; Cubans 140–2,
 144, 148; Latinos 22–5, 32, 184,
 186; Mexicans 8, 41–3, 56, 66, 71,
 86; Puerto Ricans 104, 105; and
 race 8
Voting Rights Act (1965) 22–4, 30,
 31, 32, 34, 86, 115

Wagner, Robert F., Jr. 103
Walker, Brenda 183
Walker, William 150
Wall Street Journal 72
Wallace, Henry A. , text of letter
 from Youth Committee for the
 Defense of Mexican American
 Youth 58–9
'war on poverty' programs 73, 74,
 77–8, 83, 108
Warren, Earl 63
Washington, voting rights 25
Weyler y Nicolau, Valeriano 120
White Hand death squad 156
White Warriors Union death squad
 156
whiteness 5–6, 39; *see also* skin
 color
Whitman, Ann 162
Whitman, Ed 162
Winant, Howard 4, 5
Winship, Blanton 97

Winter Garden Project 83
Wisconsin: Mexicans 91; voting
  rights 25
women ; Chicano movement 81,
  84–5; Mexican political activism
  65–6; political participation 22,
  35, 88, 117; Puerto Ricans 104,
  110, 117
women's rights, Puerto Ricans 110
Wood, Leonard 122, 125
World War II *see* Second World
  War
Wyoming 36, 39; voting rights 25

X, Malcolm 130
Ximenes, Vicente 74

Young, Iris 3–4
Young Lords 109–14
Young Lords Organization (Party)
  109
Youth Committee for the Defense of
  Mexican American Youth, text of
  letter to Henry A. Wallace 58–9

Zamora, Mario 157, 158
'zoot suit riots', Los Angeles 57–60